Museum Archaeology in Europe

*Proceedings of a conference held at the British Museum
15–17th October 1992*

Edited by David Gaimster

The Museum Archaeologist vol. 19
(The Society of Museum Archaeologists)

Oxbow Monograph 39

1994

Published by
Oxbow Books, Park End Place, Oxford OX1 1HN

© Oxbow Books, 1994

ISBN 0 946897 73 5

This book is available direct from
Oxbow Books, Park End Place, Oxford OX1 1HN
(Phone: 0865-241249; Fax 0865-794449)

and

The David Brown Book Company
PO Box 5605, Bloomington, IN 47407, USA
(Phone: 812-331-0266; Fax: 812-331-0277)

Printed in Great Britain by
The Short Run Press, Exeter

Foreword

Since its formation in 1976 the Society of Museum Archaeologists has maintained a cherished tradition of annual conferences at which its members, and whenever possible other archaeological colleagues, have gathered to consider topical themes relevant to their common professional interests. Through the exchange of expert knowledge, experience and ideas, and by stimulating constructive debate, the aim has been to promote good practice and understanding towards all aspects of archaeology, with which museums are integrally involved in one form or another. The general context of conference themes has naturally concentrated on archaeological practice as it relates to museums within the United Kingdom.

By contrast, the conference held in London on 15th–17th October 1992 was intended to break entirely new ground. In recognition of the start of the Single European Market the opportunity was taken to sweep away any real or imaginary barriers between ourselves and our continental colleagues, to focus on wider horizons than those surrounding our own national concerns and to try to stimulate a broader international approach to Museum Archaeology in Europe.

Whether this aim was at all successful is for the readers of this publication to judge for themselves. Those of us who were privileged to hear these papers delivered were much impressed by their excellent quality and content as a reflection of the personal experience and achievements of museum archaeologists throughtout Europe. There was also the striking realization that many apparently individual concerns were in fact common to a great variety of European countries and deserved a more co-operative approach.

The Society is most grateful to all the contributors for their enthusiastic committment both to the conference and to the speedy publication of its proceedings. The original concept was provided by David Gaimster, wno also took the major share of responsibility for its organization, for which he is to be congratulated. Thanks are also due to the British Museum for kindly providing a most fitting venue for what hopefully will prove to have been only the first of many such conferences of European museum archaeologists.

G. Mark R. Davies
Chairman, S.M.A. (U.K.)

Contents

Foreword *(Mark Davies)*.. iii

Introduction *(David Gaimster)* vii

1. Museums and archaeology: coping with the Chimaera *(Ian Longworth)*............................ 1

2. The European Community and heritage protection: boom or bust? *(Jeremy Warren)* 9

3. Archaeology and the National Museum of Antiquities, The Netherlands
   (Jan Verwers) 15

4. Archaeology in Dutch town-museums *(Jan Baart)* 19

5. A facelift for the Royal Museums of Art and History, Brussels *(Francis Van Noten)*...... 37

6. Museum rescue-archaeology in Duisburg, the Lower Rhineland *(Günter Krause)* 49

7. Archaeology and the Museum of National Antiquities, Stockholm *(Hans Lidén)*............. 77

8. Excavations in the medieval centre of Malmö and in the surrounding area:
   museum archaeology in practice *(Ingmar Billberg)*.. 85

9. A new archaeological museum on Funen as an example of current trends in
   Danish archaeology *(Henrik Thrane)* 95

10. L'acquisition des objets archéologiques par les musées en France
    (Jean-Yves Marin) 107

11. A new archaeological museum at Neuchâtel, Switzerland *(Bruce Dunning)*.................. 117

12. Museum archaeology in Poland: an outline *(Wojciech Brzeziński)* 123

13. Archaeology in the Kiev History Museum *(Ljudmila Pekars'ka)* 135

14. Archaeological museums in Croatia: past, present and future *(Branko Kirigin)* 147

15. Artefact research in the National Museums of Scotland *(Alan Saville)* 155

16. Can we expect museums to cope? Curatorship and the archaeological explosion
    (Martin Biddle) 167

List of Contributors 173

Introduction

David R. M. Gaimster

Whatever happens to the Maastricht Treaty, the official opening in 1993 of the Single European Market is a welcome reminder of the growth in cross-border contact and cooperation within the European Community – and beyond. Such networking has been underway for many years and the benefits are indisputable, particularly in the cultural heritage sector. Moreover, since the collapse of the Iron Curtain, there is now a stronger incentive than before for museums and related organizations in western Europe to liaise with their eastern counterparts. The fledgeling European Museums Network promises to cement these links in the future and promote the further and more formal exchange of information, skills and personnel.

But what of archaeology in European museums? How do organizational structures, government policies, responsibilities and approaches differ across the Continent? In this period of rapid change and development for Europe, how are museum archaeologists in different countries coping with the increasing threat to the archaeological heritage, its recording, preservation, and interpretation? How similar or diverse are current curatorial ideologies and practices in bordering countries? Have curators in Britain, for instance, anything to learn from the experience of their archaeological counterparts elsewhere in Europe? These questions, and more besides, led me to propose the theme "Museum Archaeology in Europe" for the 1992 conference of the Society of Museum Archaeologists (UK) which took place between 15th and 17th October. Essentially the meeting was conceived as a learning exercise, aiming to identify common interests, approaches and

challenges faced by archaeologists working in museums across the Continent. It was hoped that the conference, in providing much-needed background and insight, would lead in the future to more frequent exchanges and collaboration between museum archaeologists in different parts of Europe. As Mark Davies says in his foreword to this book, our ultimate goal was to "focus on broader horizons than those surrounding our own national concerns and to try to stimulate a broader international approach to museum archaeology in Europe".

In these tentative first days of European federalism there has been a growing realization that steps must be taken to promote the interests and concerns of museum archaeology not only on the national, but more importantly, the wider international stage. The other primary aim of this gathering, therefore, was to establish the need or desire for some kind of international association which would act as a forum for curatorial or archaeological issues or as a professional lobby or pressure group within the European Community. Clearly such a federation of groups or individuals would provide a far more effective and authoritative voice both on the domestic and international front. At the conclusion of the conference delegates agreed unanimously to initiate discussions within their own countries with a view to establishing a federation of European museum archaeologists. Professor Van Noten of the Royal Museums of Art and History, Brussels, subsequently confirmed the offer to host an inaugural meeting of the federation in two years time (1995).

With these general proposals in mind speakers were attracted from no less than eleven different

European countries, mostly from the European Community but also from Scandinavia and the former Eastern Block. Their lectures, all of which are reproduced in this volume, covered a wide variety of topical themes, all of great interest and relevance outside their country of origin. While there is a rich cultural diversity in the European archaeological heritage, delegates to the conference found considerable common ground in issues and problems faced in all the countries concerned. It is always salutory on these occasions to be reminded that so many concerns regarded as uniquely British, such as the "finds mountains" caused by pressure of continuous rescue excavation, are shared by colleagues throughout Europe.

In the text of his keynote address entitled "Museums and archaeology: coping with the Chimaera" Dr Ian Longworth of the British Museum sets out the agenda for these proceedings. In this wide-ranging paper he considers current trends in European museum archaeology and the many vital but often problematic intellectual and professional challenges facing the modern curator. The author highlights the various pressures caused by continuous rescue excavation, inadequate portable antiquities legislation and those caused by an increasingly commercial cultural environment. Getting "back to basics", the British Museum Keeper of Prehistoric and Romano-British Antiquities, reminds us of the primary curatorial roles of the museum archaeologist both in the field and back in the museum. The fundamental and often conflicting responsibilities of conservation, storage, research and public presentation and the dissemination of information are discussed in detail. On the subject of public presentation of the past (gallery displays, special exhibitions etc.), an area in which the museum-based archaeologist plays a primary role, Longworth warns us against the trend towards artifice and vulgarization. Instead we are reminded of the primacy of objects in museums, in other words what survives from the past, its "actuality"; in which case, he says, it is up to curators as archaeologists to interpret the evidence and decode its messages for all.

The themes and challenges invoked by Longworth are addressed to a greater or lesser extent by all the contributors to this volume. Each one provides a case-study of trends on the national or regional level. Many of them (such as Verwers, Lidén, Brzeziński, Thrane and Pekars'ka) explain the relative roles and responsibilities of national and regional archaeological museums, a subject of great interest, not only in Britain. One overriding concern which cuts across national boundaries is the growing threat to the museum archaeologist's role in coordinating local archaeological activity. The success of large-scale urban excavation programmes in Duisburg, Germany (Krause), Malmö, Sweden (Billberg) and Kiev, Ukraine (Pekars'ka) has depended essentially on the operational continuity afforded by the archaeological staff of the town museum. The projects concerned have demonstrated the central role of the local museum curator, with his expert knowledge, in the investigation, conservation, interpretation and pesentation of the regional archaeological heritage.

The growth of rescue archaeology across Europe, particularly in towns, during the past three decades, has created perhaps the greatest headache for museum archaeologists. Several contributors address the problems of storage and research caused by the growing "finds mountain" which, as Henrik Thrane puts it, has led to an enormous "gulf between input and output": in other words the unacceptable time-lag between excavation, interpretation and the public presentation of results. One solution, as various case-studies here illustrate, is for museum archaeologists to set their own research agenda for their locality, instead of simply responding on an *ad hoc* basis to individual threats. In the case of Duisburg, for instance (Krause), the town museum – despite the lack of support from the local authority – has been able to establish a long-term urban archaeology programme leading to the presentation of results in a series of major exhibitions and publications. Thrane has achieved this on the regional level in Denmark. In eastern Europe Pekars'ka (Ukraine) and Kirigin (Croatia) explain the advantages of collaboration with regional and international archaeological institutions in the formulation of research strategies for their areas which include rescue archaeology. In the case of Duisburg, however, the successes of the town museum have antagonised its political masters, the civic authorities, to the extent that they have now begun to employ contract archaeological firms to undertake rescue excavations in the town. It is clear that the emergence of contract archaeology as a real threat to the museum management of local archaeology is as much a danger now on the Continent as it has been in Britain for some time.

Alan Saville of the National Museums of Scotland explains how its Artefact Research Unit (the only such specially-designated museum department in Europe) copes with the finds mountain on a national level. Although only recently established, their record of research and publication is already impressive. Here, echoing Longworth's words, the museum is rightly seen as the "locus and focus of artefactual research" and artefacts themselves are regarded more as a "multifarious curatorial challenge rather than in any sense a burden". I, for one, would be surprised if this Scottish initiative is not widely adopted within a short time by archaeological museums on the Continent. Finally, Professor Martin Biddle of Oxford University considers the problem of the growing finds mountain from the consumer point-of-view, that of the archaeological researcher, in a paper entitled "curatorship and the archaeological explosion". His suggestions for the storage of bulk-finds from excavations in regional archaeological warehouses will stimulate much needed discussion.

Finally, in terms of content, this volume also includes news of a number of exciting museum construction projects on the Continent (papers by Van Noten and Dunning) and of some of the latest permanent exhibitions of regional and national archaeology (Baart and Ververs respectively). Again these case-studies provide an opportunity for museum archaeologists to preview the latest developments in display techniques on an international level. Readers will also find Jeremy Warren's guide to the complexities of heritage protection under the Single European Act an invaluable source of reference particularly for those dealing with the movement of portable antiquities across national boundaries. Jean-Yves Marin's explanation of archaeological acquisition policies in France will be of equal relevance to curators working outside its borders.

This first meeting of European museum archaeologists could not have taken place without the generous support of a number of sympathetic institutions. Firstly, I am most grateful to the Museums and Galleries Commission (UK) who provided funds to cover speakers' travel and accommodation costs. Thanks are also due to the British Council offices in Poland, Croatia, The Netherlands, Belgium and Germany which also assisted with speakers' airfares. Finally, the Society of Museum Archaeologists is grateful to the British Museum which generously provided such an ideal venue and a grant towards conference receptions.

On a personal note I would like to thank the following colleagues who assisted me in the organization of this event: Dr Robert Anderson, Director of the British Museum, who kindly opened the conference; my colleagues on the Council of the Society of Museum Archaeologists (UK), notably Mark Davies (Chairman), Tim Schadla-Hall (Vice-Chairman), Penny Spencer (Secretary) and Nick Merriman; Judith Simmons, British Museum Design Department, who designed the conference prospectus; and Dafydd Kidd and Cathy Haith of the Department of Medieval & Later Antiquities, British Museum, who assisted with technical translations. I am most grateful also to David Brown and Val Tomlin at Oxbow Books, Oxford, for producing this attractive volume so efficiently and so swiftly. Last, but not least, let me thank all the contributors to this book. Their participation in this project represents a bold investment in the future of European museum archaeology.

Öland (Sweden) and London,
September 1993

1. Museums and Archaeology: Coping with the Chimaera

Ian Longworth

In Britain at least, the last fifteen years or so have proved to be a testing time for museums. Shortage of money, the cult of short-termism and an increasingly hostile environment for intellectual pursuits has led in large measure to a collective loss of nerve. It has been a period, of "living in the fast lane", and of "get rich quick". Life, we were told by the media, was about the here and now, and market forces would regulate whether that life was to be short or long. Fundamental, as opposed to market values, were not necessarily prized. Not until the '90s had dawned was it realized, and then a mite too late, that to openly acknowledge for example that you were selling "crap" – to quote Gerald Ratner's memorable admission[1] – was no longer a thing of which to boast. The impact of commercialism also changed the vocabulary. The public became customers, not visitors, since they were expected to pay, and future plans having undergone an obligatory SWOT analysis became not intentions but "mission statements". In this era of commercial colonialism museums were seen as institutions that had to justify their existence financially. Not surprisingly those museums which had believed that their role lay in serving the needs of the future as much as those of the present found themselves filled with uncertainties and doubts as to how to position themselves in this new society – a society which appeared to be seeking, not only instant wealth, but immediate gratification and constant entertainment. Were museums henceforth to be part of the world of intellectual enlightenment and of education, a segment of the tourist industry maybe, or should they become a mindless extension

to the side shows of the Golden Mile? Indeed some began to ask whether museums as such were actually relevant to modern life.

Museums which saw their brief as extending over archaeology were stretched in other ways and found their problems particularly acute. The very success of rescue archaeology in the '60s and '70s, more recently enhanced by the emergence of developer funding in the '80s, had created a massive problem first of processing, then of storage. In this connection it is somewhat depressing that the real debate over what to collect, over sampling strategies, selection, retention and disposal only appeared as a by-product of the practical difficulties emerging particularly in those museums charged with coping with the fallout from large-scale urban excavation. More significantly these problems have exposed the very limited role of the museum in the overall archaeological scene, often marginalized, passive and reactive, only rarely pro-active. Instead of being central to an integrated archaeological discipline in which extraction and initial assessment formed but short-term prolegomena to the on-going survival of the database and its active use over time, museums in Britain began to find themselves treated as simple repositories. Part of the problem lay in the early developments of rescue archaeology when it was rare for active excavation units to be attached to museums, and still rarer for museums so endowed to exercise control so that the resulting product made a meaningful addition to the museum's own collections. The cry that everything must be rescued was soon translated in what some were to castigate as museum non-think into everything must be accepted for preservation. While the rescue movement achieved the remarkable feat of prising money from a reluctant government enabling for the first time excavation to begin to match the spate of destruction post-war development had brought into play, the price that had to be paid was indiscriminate salvage excavation, some at least of which was of very limited value and in retrospect can be seen to have made little contribution to our appreciation of the past. But once out of the ground the product of those excavations produced a moral dilemma. Though much appeared of little value, should it not be kept? What criteria could be found for not accepting evidence so laboriously and expensively obtained? Ten years ago a British Museum working party reviewed the problem and found deep divisions within the profession.[2] While the majority of archaeologists felt that all, or almost all, the evidence that could be preserved should be kept, others believed that selection was inevitable. Further divisions emerged between those who considered the onus of making that decision should lie with the director of each excavation and others who argued that decisions over preservation must ultimately rest within the judgement of the recipient museum. That debate remains with us today and the current exercise being undertaken by this Society to look into these matters is very welcome, particularly if it manages to address these problems from the perceived requirements of the different sectors and periods of the discipline and not from entrenched positions either of intuitive belief, or fiscal expediency. At the same time we must ask ourselves whether the role of museums should ever have become one of total acceptance or do museums *per se* have another, perhaps more considered view of why they exist. Should we not be moving away from the idea of the provincial museum as a universal *omnium gatherum* for its catchment area – an area based upon modern administrative convenience rarely relevant to archaeological considerations? Should not collecting policies in future be more selective of the material needed for display, education and research? But if so, what of the rejected material? Should this go into a handy cement mixer, be carefully re-buried or should such material be placed in stores serving much larger

geographic units or specialized needs to be funded by those who have created the problem – the developers, English Heritage or whoever? Such moves would at least have the merit of bringing museums once more back into the world of active decision making rather than that of knee-jerk reaction. Perhaps we could then move on from the current state where at least in England and Wales field archaeology has become largely a response to the planning process rather than a pro-active first stage in a discipline with clear and attainable research aims. We might then avoid the fate of becoming in that memorable phrase of a former Dean of Westminster, mere 'collectors of cashiered nails'.[3]

Curiously, if the presumption has been that museums should act as perpetual guardians of the excavated find a somewhat different response emerged for finds born out of archaeological wedlock, namely those which in increasing numbers were discovered by enthusiasts of another persuasion, the metal detectorists. Metal detecting devices as we all know offer a useful tool for prospecting in the field and in the right hands have provided the archaeologist with invaluable assistance. Faced with a dispersed hoard of metallic objects like coins or a cemetery where foreknowledge of metallic grave goods would offer an important aid to planning and procurement of necessary resources, a field-worker would indeed be crass not to take advantage of its use. The fact that over-enthusiastic hobbyists *can*, and more particularly a hard core of criminals *do*, destroy invaluable evidence has however posed a major problem. Many have felt that the archaeologist could not be seen to use such a device without encouraging its destructive use by others. Early attempts, notably by the CBA (Council for British Archaeology), to brand all users of metal detectors as social lepers, can now be seen to have been both ineffective and ill-judged. The hobby has continued to flourish and even expand while the refusal of some archaeologists and museums even to speak to metal detector users has driven potentially helpful people away into the hands of less than scrupulous dealers with consequent loss both of information and artefact. Due to this policy the falsification of provenance has multiplied immensely and is probably now the norm. Since the problem lies not with the machine but the motives of its users the answer has always lain with persuasion of the majority and prosecution of the much smaller criminal element. In practice, both solutions have proved difficult to follow. Yet the late Tony Gregory's efforts in Norfolk, a hard core area for the problem, or, say, John Williams' continuing efforts in Kent have shown that results can be obtained directly proportional to the amount of effort expended on the task. Regrettably prosecutions for criminal damage brought under the Ancient Monuments and Archaeological Areas Act of 1979 for illegal use on scheduled sites show a success rate only slightly better than skydiving clutching a toy balloon.

The issues raised by metal detecting are none the less important, particularly for the museum archaeologist, since both object and true provenance are basic to museum life. In the UK which lacks the inherent interest in antiquity which one finds in Scandinavia or a system of state control as exercised in France, little progress has been made towards outlawing the non-professional use of metal detectors in sensitive areas or the limitation of this use to projects under professional guidance. Clearly education has failed to get the message across and by nature Britain is not one to promote quickly legislation which curtails freedom of the individual. Nonetheless, continued education seems essential and museums should surely be at the forefront of this effort. If that is so it seems logical for museums to maintain an active dialogue with the metal detector users and be prepared to continue to explain why context, and the reporting of objects, is important, and how common aims can be met to mutual benefit. Hopefully this will stem the current problem of museum archives and SMRs being burdened with totally bogus contextual information.

The rise of uncontrolled metal detector usage has also given rise to a vast increase in the international trade in stolen antiquities both leaving and entering the country. By its very nature this trade is difficult to quantify but the appearance of items openly provenanced to Britain in sales catalogues in the USA and as far afield as Australia documents the trade. Taken with the minuscule number of export licences actually applied for in an area where everything, regardless of value (and including even coins) is so

covered,[4] we have some grounds for feeling that present legislation is grossly ineffective. With the prospect of European harmonisation upon us in 1993 bringing with it the removal of many inter-European customs controls only an extreme optimist would predict anything but increased depredation. Most museums in this country adhere to a code of practice laid down by the Museums Association that stolen antiquities should not be acquired. Some have wished to limit museum acquisition still further by an embargo on any find made by a metal detector user. Where stolen property is concerned the matter is surely beyond dispute but with the resurgence of private collections throughout the world, abstinence from acquiring legally extracted objects would have a negligible effect on their trade while limiting quite illogically the opportunity to acquire important material for museum collections. For this reason having debated the issue at length the Trustees of the British Museum issued a policy statement that selective acquisition of such finds remained not only the practical but also the proper course to take.[5] We must surely applaud their wisdom.

I am of course aware that in making such a statement one is declaring membership of one particular ethical position. It is essentially a pragmatic stance which sees a greater good in museum acquisition of such objects than by disregarding their existence. Such a view will certainly find no favour amongst the fundamentalists who believe that under no circumstances is it right to form any type of relationship with metal detector users whose activities have not been occasioned by or controlled through an archaeological association. By extension, I presume, the same would apply to any who have dealt with them.

A similar but yet starker gulf has appeared in recent years with regard to the retention and occasional display of human remains. Here the questions posed have not been so much the propriety of museums acquiring such material as of meeting counter claims for possession made by religious and ethnic groups. In this area logic has little to offer and we find ourselves in the harsher environment of emotions and beliefs in which opposing positions can be taken with total conviction and sincerity. Here again once purely legal requirements have been met museums must ask themselves the fundamental question: what is the underlying purpose of their collections? If those collections have been built up by design, and retention of carefully selected material for future research is a prime aim, then the dice must be loaded towards retention. This is particularly pertinent in areas like physical anthropology where after some years of relative neglect major advances are now afoot. In turn it would surely be unwise to assume that these advances would be the last and that any analysis made now will be seen as adequate to meet future research needs. The so-called Vermillion Accord[6] may ensure that the contest begins with a respectful bow but casts no light on the subsequent rules of combat.

Questions of re-patriation and return of human remains or indeed of other forms of antiquity raise other fundamental issues which cannot be shirked. What community of interest does the museum serve? We can only begin to answer this question if we accept that museums are not one and indivisible and that their aims and *raison d'être* vary enormously. A local government museum funded entirely by the citizens within its catchment area albeit supplemented by local business interests may have a relatively clear brief to serve the needs of this restricted but often diverse community. An encyclopaedic museum such as the British Museum has no such parochial limitations and is catering as much for the world as it is for the British nation. Such an institution needs to balance interests on a global scale. If preservation for future study remains a fundamental plank on which a collection has been built then sectional interests must be weighed carefully against this goal. It is after all rarely politically disadvantageous for others to lay claim to material under the banner of restitution but though such claims need to be considered seriously by any museum and taken case by case most can be seen as the product of political and diplomatic posturing and treated in that light. Such a view is in keeping with the British belief that museums should remain politically neutral. This view admittedly is not shared by many of our colleagues abroad and is a claim sometimes also disputed within our own profession.

If we accept that one of the prime roles of a museum is the preservation of material, to be studied not only now but also in the future, in order to gain further insights into the past, our displays must be just the visible tip of an intellectual iceberg which supports and enlightens those displays. The way that information is presented, therefore, deserves careful thought. Here museums often stand accused in Britain and elsewhere in northern and western Europe on three counts:- that most if not all displays are biased towards a middle class, essentially sanitized, view of the past; that androcentricity remains embedded in the system; and that it is rare for a museum to offer more than a single interpretation in its displays while knowing that many are possible. Let us take a look at these in turn.

If our displays emerge unbiased it is certainly something of a miracle. Most are created by museum professionals whose vocabulary largely equates with their professional status. All forms of display embody some form of interpretation and the words used in conjunction with the objects in particular often involve values derived more from the familiar present than a conscious attempt to portray an impartial presentation of the past. As one of our contemporary critics put it recently, "It may be that the discipline actually attracts people who prefer to sustain an illusory boundary between their work and the rest of their lives."[7] In turn values are constantly changing. Take the term 'craftsmanship'. To label an object as showing supreme craftsmanship was at least in this country to award a degree of excellence to its manufacture on a scale well-founded in Victorian values. But the cult of crafts and craftsmanship is in the process of being reworked. Excellence in manufacture can now be the preserve of the automated machine tool. Henceforth craftsmanship may come to stand for little more than an idiosyncratic approximation to a perceived ideal.

Of equal concern has been an inbred and largely unthinking male orientation in keeping with past usage but no longer in touch with the current mood of society. I am not calling here for some defensive feminist-provoked neutrality – from Man the Hunter say to Person the Hunter/Huntress. Rather a call for museums to respond to genuine advances in gender archaeology as they occur. Not only should we be embracing this area of increased knowledge but we should also, where we can, begin to pass on to a wider viewing public the results of increased research into the roles that men, women and indeed children played in the societies to which they belonged. I take it that gender archaeology is part of a long-term realignment responding to changing social usage over most of Europe and at least the North American continent. Whatever the origins and motivation the importance of this change lies in questioning an area of sloppy thinking and demanding greater care in how the evidence is analysed. It is also an area of great interest to the public at large, and one which can with a little thought be communicated fairly simply. But how easily can and should museums respond to other shifts in fashion generated within the archaeological discipline itself? I am not thinking here of new discoveries of primary data, though these can be taxing enough, but rather of method and theory in the interpretation and manipulation of the basic data. Setting aside for the moment (and probably for ever) the wilder out-pourings of TAG (The Theoretical Archaeology Group) we would over the past two decades have been asked to respond in quick succession to processual, structuralist, hermeneutic, neo-Marxist and post-modernist interpretations to name but a few. Many of the concepts developed, while explicable in a tract, are not easily transferred to a label and the use of jargon made self-consciously arcane, inevitably confines these approaches to a small, often minute audience of committed disciples. Perhaps one might be more generously disposed to meet this challenge if the theoreticians a) knew a little more about the material culture to which their theories must ultimately relate and b) shared a willingness to accept that almost every approach offers new insights, and that each adds a new facet to our knowledge and understanding but does not necessarily invalidate what has gone before. The process is additive and for some perhaps addictive. What it is not is wholly purgatory. Here the museum faces again the problem of short term fashion. Better I say to take a detached view than embrace each fad with messianic enthusiasm. This is not to say that museums cannot or should not keep the public informed of developments within the profession. But like taking the sun this is best achieved by an occasional temporary display, offering limited rather than total exposure. An excellent example of how this can be achieved was David Clark's exhibition "Symbols of Power" at what was then the National Museum of Antiquities of Scotland.

"Symbols of Power" was essentially a missionary exercise, employing that term for once in its correct usage. It set out to say, look at these objects, some of which you have often seen before, but look at them in this way and you will get new insights. The visitor was guided but was also asked to think and was encouraged to take the study further by reading an accompanying publication which was well written and superbly illustrated.[8] The exhibition was held at a time of year, during the period of the Edinburgh Festival, when a fair whack of thinking visitors might be expected to be in the city over and above its own thinking citizens. Like all good exhibitions it could be enjoyed at more than one level mixing object and context to achieve its aim.

The degree to which museums should embrace context is of course of fundamental importance in the debate as to what museum displays are trying to achieve. For the site museum the task is relatively obvious since the objects recovered have only been removed marginally from their original setting. But for the vast majority of museums, contexts are remote and with space almost always limited efforts to introduce context have perforce called for new techniques ranging from the pre-War use of panoramas and dioramas to the more recent tide of videos, film clips and CD/ROMs. Indeed, in some displays today it is difficult to decide whether one has strayed into a flip-up book or been embraced by some gigantic Nintendo Game Boy. This seems to me to present something of a crux. While in this country the successes of a Jorvik or a White Cliffs Experience have shown that well-researched and well-presented re-creations can be highly successful, such an approach I suggest is neither possible nor desirable for the majority of museums. Here I would draw a distinction between the display of objects as found, presenting the viewer with an actual situation or moment in time – a burial, a manufacturing event with product and waste preserved unadorned, and a re-creation of a complex group of contexts which can offer but one detailed reconstruction. My reasons for this are two-fold. Firstly, museums are and should be principally about objects; about the actuality of what survives from the past. While for many periods, visitors will need help to gain insights into what they see, curiosity and stimulation of the imagination need to be encouraged not eclipsed. For me then the ideal display is one in which the visitor whether casual or entrenched scholar can gain in proportion to the effort that he or she is prepared to put in in terms of mental effort. The paradox of using detailed reconstruction to explain is that since personal effort has been eliminated, the visitor is left to marvel not at actuality but at the designer's artifice. But perhaps the greatest danger of the reconstruction is that few visitors have the background knowledge to validate what they see. For Jorvik and Dover they are in good hands, but in the still burgeoning realms of heritage exploitation from bogus medieval feast and joust to dubious reconstruction of prehistoric village life, the public are at risk. Thus as more of our profession are seduced into using the tricks of Disneyland in the belief that this alone will attract more people so they are moving public appreciation away from education and on towards a world where unthinking fantasy replaces thought-provoking reality. We have in short moved from heightened awareness to simple escapism. Museums I suggest should pause before lemming-like they throw themselves over this particular cliff.

Museums remain extremely popular and those which, like the British Museum, devote a large part of their resources to archaeology are amongst the most popular. Visitor numbers grow steadily and for this institution alone will approach six million by the end of the current year. Many of the visitors are young and in our increasingly mobile environment many come from abroad. We have responsibility therefore both to the future and as a window to the world. It matters then how we present the results of archaeology for we are in possession of formidable powers of communication. Judged on a simple hierarchical basis we can see for example from past performance that scholarly works produced in this country by publishers such as BMP (British Museum Press), the CBA (Council for British Archaeology), the Society of Antiquaries or English Heritage have an initial take-up rate measured in the low hundreds – confined in other words to libraries and a modest penumbra of committed professionals. A readable synthesis aimed at a more popular readership sold through this museum will often sell in the tens of thousands; but the message we convey country-wide in our exhibition galleries reaches out to many millions a year and unlike the transitory visions which occasionally flicker across our television screens these exhibits can be revisited many times and seen in the round.

What then should we be offering the visitor? Should we be responding to public demand, bowing before the yoke of market forces, or should we be creating our own market place? Judged by sales of postcards in this establishment exhibitions devoted entirely to cats, Egyptian mummies and effigies of Mrs Tiggywinkle would be responding to a massive social need, but I am not convinced that many of our visitors would not be missing out. Popularisation, and by that I mean widening awareness in, not vulgarisation, should surely remain one of our principal objectives. We exist to raise standards not to diminish them; to stimulate not to patronise.

It is heartening to think that we have after all already come a long way. When in 1845 William Lloyd smashed the Portland Vase, the Keeper of the day had no doubt that this was entirely and predictably the result (his words) "of exhibiting such valuable and unique specimens to the mob". Museums were, in the mid nineteenth century, for the few and (apparently), if we are to believe our predecessors, the fewer the better. Acts of vandalism are alas still with us but our visiting public is now immense and one of our basic tasks remains education. As Peter Addyman reminded us recently[9] while it is now no longer socially acceptable, at least in this country, to take eggs from birds' nests, we have some way to go before we have changed attitudes to the extent that it would be equally unacceptable to wrest antiquities from their context. If we are to succeed in this task it is imperative that we gain and keep the confidence of our visitors and to do that we must ensure the quality and accuracy of the information we provide.

The ability to provide informative displays, to answer questions posed by those who wish to ask them and not least to respond to the needs of students and fellow archaeologists at home and abroad rests upon the quality and training of the curators;

their knowledge, their scholarship, and the research that they have undertaken upon the collections which they curate. If these collections have been built up with a clear view of their value both for present and future research, then we have the core justification for the museum's on-going existence. Displays can be mounted in exhibition centres. Videos and CD-ROMs can be watched and interrogated at home or elsewhere but the material culture of the past can only be studied effectively in a curated collection. It is how we ourselves view and use our collections that is the key to the future of museum archaeology. We can rightly stress the teaching aspect of the collections. How in Britain as elsewhere in Europe their study has become an accepted and integrated element in the school curriculum. We are all familiar with the generations of students from colleges of art, design and technology who have worked in our galleries and have gained new inspiration from seeing unfamiliar objects in settings outside their normal patterns of experience. But activities such as these, important as they are, dip but slightly into the deeper well of knowledge that our collections represent. The fundamental role of a true museum is to provide a better understanding of the past through on-going research.

It is a regrettable fact, and one felt perhaps more acutely in Britain than elsewhere in Europe, that the amount of research time available to archaeologists working in museums has diminished rather than increased over the years. Yet museums are self evidently ideally placed to undertake artefact research and, for those possessed of the necessary scientific back up, research into many aspects of early technology. Here the National and University museums with their larger staff numbers and opportunities for greater specialisation have an advantage, but research should not be seen as something confined to these institutions. Many of us who undertook research projects before entering museum service caught a useful glimpse from the other side of the counter. The visiting research worker gains immeasurably from the curator who is knowledgeable about the collections, but conversely, can be hindered and excluded from much that might be relevant by ignorance and lack of interest. To encourage others to make use of the collections requires a thorough

knowledge of the research potential of those collections on the part of the museum staff themselves. Active interest leads to on-going research; ignorance and indifference will lead sooner rather than later to oblivion.

Let me offer you a final quotation:

> "What a museum really depends upon for its success and usefulness is not its building, not its cases, not even its specimens, but its curator. He and his staff are its life and soul, upon whom its whole value depends, and yet in many of our museums they are the last to be thought of."

Those were the words not as you might imagine of a former keeper of the V&A but used in an inaugural address given to the British Association meeting at Newcastle-on-Tyne in 1889. They are as applicable now I think, as they were then. It is after all the task of the present day curator to cope with the perplexities of modern life, to run an institution often without adequate funding, to maintain, encourage and improve standards of scholarship, to wrestle and balance conflicting moral issues, while offering a quality service to student, scholar and public alike. Such is the chimaera we all face. You will remember that there was something of the lion, the goat and the snake about this monster. I think we shall find many of its features familiar to our colleagues gathered here from across Europe and I for one am eager to hear how they have met its challenge.

Notes

1. As chairman of the Ratner Group, jewellers.
2. *Selection and Retention of Environmental and Artefactual Material from Excavations* (November 1982), British Museum.
3. Address to the Archaeological Institute meeting at Winchester in 1845.
4. *Export of Works of Art 1990-1991 Thirty-seventh Report of the Reviewing Committee Appointed by the Chancellor of the Exchequer in December 1952.* Appendix G sections 1 and 5.
5. *The British Museum. Report of the Trustees 1987-1990,* 10. BMP (1990).
6. A position statement issued by the World Archaeological Congress in 1989. *World Archaeological Bulletin* 4 (1990).

7. B. Bender reviewing M. Ehrenberg's book, *Women in Prehistory* (1991) *Proceedings of the Prehistoric Society* 57 pt. 2, 213.

8. D.V. Clarke, T.G. Cowie and A. Foxon (1985) *Symbols of Power at the time of Stonehenge*, HMSO.

9. At the 13th Heritage Co-ordination Conference 'Hold on to your heritage' held at the Museum of London in May 1992.

2. The European Community and Heritage Protection: Boom or Bust?

Jeremy Warren

During the past two or three years, a great deal of ink and not a few tears have been spilt in the press about the risk to European countries' artistic heritage by the full implementation of the Single European Act on 1 January 1993, better known as '1992'. In some countries disquiet has verged on the hysterical. One newspaper article headlined 'The sack of Italy'[1] suggested that Italy was in danger of losing most of its cultural heritage once the Single Market was in place. The real debate within the EC has focused, rather more calmly, on attempts to balance recognition of nations' interests in protecting their heritage, with the free trade objectives which are the *raison d'être* of the European Community. My paper concentrates on this topic, although it should be pointed out that the EC has long taken an interest in protection of the architectural heritage. It has recently announced its intention also to seek ways of assisting protection of the moveable heritage, although no policies have yet been formulated.

It is essential to understand as a starting point that the European Community is primarily an economic grouping. The EC is in fact technically an amalgam of three distinct 'communities', the European Coal and Steel Community, the European Economic Community and the European Atomic Energy Community. The Single European Act of 1987 aimed to streamline the EC's decision making processes, but above all to provide a legislative framework for the development of the Single Market, a free economic area with no barriers to 'the free movement of goods, persons, services and capital.'[2] The Maastricht Treaty is really the first attempt by the EC to formal-

ise its competence in a major way in areas of life, including culture, which go beyond the purely economic.

So in many respects as far as the EC as we have known it up to now is concerned, works of art and other cultural artifacts are in most respects goods to be traded like any other. For most EC officials engaged in realising the Single Market, there is philosophically no difference between a Rembrandt or a Renault.

The Treaty of Rome, the founding act of the European Community, does however make provision for the protection of artistic treasures through its article 36, which states 'The provisions of Articles 30 to 34 shall not preclude prohibitions or restrictions on ... the protection of national treasures possessing artistic, historic or archaeological value ... Such prohibitions or restrictions shall not, however, constitute a means of arbitrary discrimination or a disguised restriction on trade between Member States'. The legitimacy of article 36 was confirmed in a General Declaration to the Single European Act, which added 'nothing in these provisions shall affect the right of Member States, to take such measures as they consider necessary ... to combat ... illicit trading in works of art and antiques.'

It is at this point that the difficulties began. The twelve member states of the EC have twelve very different systems for protecting cultural treasures, ranging from highly protectionist legislation, which seeks in effect to eliminate the export of cultural objects, to market-oriented systems which aim no further than to facilitate the retention of a handful of outstanding objects. Although in theory each country can, by invoking article 36, maintain its existing system, how could this be policed, once customs controls virtually cease to exist between EC states, and once national taxation bodies no longer monitor inter-EC trade? And even more difficult, how should the concept 'national treasure' be defined?

Looking briefly at the existing national procedures, it is at once apparent that like much else in the EC, there is a classic 'north-south' split. All twelve countries have some legislative framework, although in the cases of Belgium, Germany and Ireland, the actual procedures in use are considerably more liberal than the law theoretically allows. In broad terms, the northern countries, including Germany, the Netherlands and the United Kingdom, operate liberal export control régimes which attempt to balance the interests of the nation with those of owners or the trade. The Netherlands and Germany use for their moveable heritage listing systems which seek to identify a relatively small number of objects which may not be exported. Denmark and the UK look at export applications on a case by case basis. The UK's Waverley system was, until the freezing of most national museums' purchase funds 7 years ago, a remarkably successful means of balancing the interests of the Nation, owners and the art trade. By contrast, a group of southern countries, Greece, Italy, Portugal and Spain, believe that the national interest in ensuring adequate protection of their cultural heritage should override to a greater or lesser degree the rights of owners. In effect they operate, or try to operate, a system of blanket protection. This is taken to its furthest extreme in Greece, where any antiquity dating from before 1830 is legally the property of the state, private owners have to register their collections with the authorities, and the State may pre-empt the purchase of any object at half its internal Greek value.

The French as often fall between the two stools. France operates procedures which are complex, but in theory relatively liberal. In practice however the French authorities have used consummate skill in ensuring many objects of importance are acquired for French museums, at prices well below their international value. The French have now however, perhaps mindful of their ambition to challenge the UK's domination of the European art market, indicated more clearly than any other EC state their intention to review the whole basis of their export control system.

These differing philosophies have deep geographical and historical roots. Trading nations such as the Netherlands or the United Kingdom have long been accustomed to a free market tradition, in which an active art market plays its full role. For instance, many of the great pictures which entered British collections in the course of the eighteenth and nineteenth centuries may be traced to Dutch or Flemish collections in the seventeenth century, when Amsterdam and Antwerp were the centres of the European art trade. The UK today is by far the most important European centre for art trade in Europe, with an estimated 75% market share. It is determined to maintain its dominant position, although countries such as Belgium and France have recognized that 1992 represents an opportunity for this dominance to be challenged.

By contrast, the ransacking of the great Mediterranean birthplaces of Western civilisation is not simply a phenomenon of the last two centuries. As early as 1471, for instance, Pope Sixtus IV issued an order to the keeper of the castle of the port of Ostia, instructing him to prevent the export of any marble, including statuary. The rate of attrition did of course increase considerably from the eighteenth century onwards. Nineteenth century nationalist movements in the Mediterranean countries identified strongly with their nation's past glories, a sentiment best seen in the newly independent Greek government's 1834 decree to which I have already referred, confirming the State's ownership of all antiquities and ancient monuments on its territory. The demand for antiquities and works of art has, if anything, increased in the twentieth century. Regrettably the Mediterranean countries continue to be a prime source for illegally excavated and exported objects, although the problem in Europe is not confined to these countries. So it is hardly surprising that Greece, Italy, Portugal and Spain should have found themselves making common ground within the EC, in arguing for the maintenance of tight national régimes for export control.

So how has the EC gone about reconciling the

tensions between its single economic thrust, and the multiple views on how to ensure protection of individual states' heritage? Firstly, by recognising the reality that it would simply not be possible for us all to carry on as if the Single Market did not exist. Quite apart from the practical difficulties of this, the European Commission has made clear that article 36 'should be interpreted restrictively, since it derogates from the fundamental rules of the free movement of goods' and '... cannot be relied upon to justify laws, procedures or practices that lead to discrimination or restrictions which are disproportionate with respect to the aim in view.'[3] Inevitably therefore there would have to be some form of harmonisation of procedures and attitudes.

The European Commission has recognized the depth of feelings among individual member states on the topic of export control, and has handled the lengthy discussions patiently and sensitively. Rather than going into the substance of these discussions, I shall concentrate on what has emerged. This consists in effect of two documents, which when finally agreed will form the basis of all EC states' export control policy.

The first is a 'Council Regulation on the export of cultural goods',[4] the second a 'Council Directive on the return of cultural objects unlawfully removed from the territory of a Member State'.[5] A Regulation does not need supplementary national legislation, and therefore comes directly into effect. A Directive on the other hand does require each national government to submit legislation to its own Parliament. With both documents, it remains the EC's intention that they should come into operation from 1 January 1993, although in practice full implementation is likely to be later for most countries.

The Regulation on Exports sets out a principle that export licences must be obtained for exports from the EC to outside countries. A standard export licence application form will be introduced from 1 January 1993, and a licence, once issued, will be valid throughout the territory of the EC. The system will operate on the basis of pre-determined chronological and monetary limits, a procedure which those who have had dealings with the UK's Waverley system will recognize. The limits which look likely to be agreed are indeed in many respects not dissimi-

lar to our own current Open General Export Licence limits. The main categories currently proposed are:

1. Zero limit

    Archaeological objects more than 100 years old, coming from archaeological digs or sites, underwater sites, or archaeological collections.

    Elements forming an integral part of historic, artistic or religious monuments more than 100 years old, and which have been removed from these monuments.

    Incunabula and manuscripts, and archival material more than 50 years old.

2. 15,000 ECU (*c.* £10,000) limit

    Mosaics, drawings, photographs, printed maps over 200 years old

3. 50,000 ECU (*c.* £35,000)

    Sculpture, books over 100 years old singly or in collections, means of transport more than 75 years old.

4. 150,000 ECU (*c.* £100,000)

    Paintings.

There is also a general category with a limit of 50,000 ECU covering most, but not all, other types of object, and finally another 50,000 ECU category for collections, specifically:

Zoological, botanical, mineralogical and anatomical collections, and specimens from such collections

Collections of historic, paleontological, ethnographic or numismatic interest.

This procedure does not cover all types of object. The MGC's main concern is that objects of scientific, technical and industrial importance are inadequately covered under the proposed new system. Unfortunately we have been informed that it is unlikely this can be remedied in the short term. We are also sceptical about how practical it will prove to define collections, although we very much welcome the inclusion of this category. On the other hand, archaeological objects and antiquities do seem to be afforded comprehensive protection, at least in theory.

This set of categories will provide a type of minimum entry point at which, for each category of object, export licences will be required. An important principle is the EC's confirmation, repeated in the draft Regulation, that each EC member state may continue to take reasonable measures to define its own national treasures. This means that each state will be free to continue to make its own arrangements to protect its 'national treasures', so that the Belgians or the Irish may continue if they wish to exercise more or less no control over exports, whilst the Greeks or the Italians may choose to decide that any object falling within the categories is a national treasure, the export of which is automatically prohibited. Therefore the new rules do not necessarily mean convergence of attitudes towards heritage protection, and in the short to medium term at least this is quite unlikely.

Since the only effect of the new categories is to indicate that a licence is required for export outside the EC, member states may also continue to designate as national treasures objects which fall outside the EC categories. A good example in the UK's case is the special category of British Historical Portraits. Such paintings are often of comparatively low monetary value but great historical significance, and so are given additional protection under the Waverley procedure. Also, individual countries may continue to operate their own procedures for controlling exports to other EC countries. It is by no means clear how a dual system will be made to work in practice.

If a country does continue to maintain blanket export control procedures which make it almost impossible for objects to leave the country legally – Italy for instance has claimed it has 30 million 'national treasures' – it is quite likely to find itself challenged by its own art trade to defend its export control procedures in the European Court, once the Single Market is in place from 1993. The EC has already made clear its view that the southern states' interpretation of national treasures goes beyond what could be considered reasonable, and so it would be unlikely to defend them on this point. Such a court case might well turn out to be the catalyst, which pushes EC states towards real harmonisation of their

procedures. This would in effect mean acceptance by the southern EC states of a much more liberal export control regime than they have been prepared to contemplate up until now.

The fears of the Mediterranean countries for their national heritage have already been mentioned. These are primarily based on their expectation that once their markets are opened, they will suffer further heavy losses of antiquities and works of art. The international art market, in which London is a key player, is seen as a major threat, not without some justification. The southern states worry that freer circulation of cultural goods within the EC will legitimize what most authorities acknowledge already happens – the use of countries such as Belgium or the UK as transit points for massive outflows of antiquities and works of art to North America and Japan.

Their position is also informed by a strong philosophical belief in the civilising nature of art, which has formed an important element in the fierce opposition the southern states have maintained to the imposition of a system of categorising cultural objects based on fixed criteria. One Greek government spokesman has stated 'The chronological and especially the monetary criteria are unacceptable, since cultural and scientific interest overrides any financial value'.[6]

It is with these concerns in mind that we should turn now to the 'Draft Directive on the return of cultural objects unlawfully removed from the territory of a Member State.' It is no coincidence that the only EC states to have ratified the 1970 UNESCO Convention on prohibiting the Illicit Import, Export and Transfer of Ownership of Cultural Property are Greece, Italy, Portugal and Spain. The EC Directive is a genuine attempt to quell the fears of the Mediterranean group of countries, by setting up for the first time a formal process to allow recovery of objects from other EC states.

The Directive will require a member state to take effective legal and other steps to obtain the return of cultural goods which have been illegally removed from another EC country, on that country's request. It will be non-retrospective, applying only for cases of illegal export detected after 1 January 1993, and it will only apply for objects designated as national treasures by the state making the request for restitution. However, it will be possible for states to 'declare' objects as national treasures retrospectively, thereby covering objects illegally excavated and exported. There will be a statute of limitations of one year from the date on which the injured member state received information concerning, or was given ample opportunity to note, the location of the artefact in question or the identity of its owner, and a general statute of limitations of thirty years from the date when the object was first removed. This statute of limitations is extended to 75 years for objects forming part of public collections. The Directive goes on to make provision for fair compensation to be paid to bona fide purchasers by the requesting state, which will also be responsible for paying the legal and other costs involved in obtaining the return of the object.

The outline I have given is the position at present. Not surprisingly the Draft Directive has been the subject of some fierce wrangling. The northern countries, in particular the UK, which expects to be on the receiving end of a large proportion of the requests for restitution, have expressed their concern that any system must be workable, and must not impose undue restrictions on free trade. In its present form, the Directive contains provisions which require governments to act at the behest of other states, to seek out and seize objects, where there are reasonable grounds for suspicion that they could have been unlawfully removed from another country. The UK art trade has been most vigorous in expressing its concerns at the impact this could have on its legitimate business activities, if other countries use the Directive to make large numbers of ill-founded requests. One senior member of the London art trade has suggested that the southern states are trying to use the EC procedures, to compensate for the national procedures they have failed to operate.

For the Mediterranean countries on the other hand the Directive goes nothing like far enough. Just as with categorisation for export licences they would like to see no monetary or age limits, and much longer statutes of limitations. They would also like responsibility for meeting the costs of restitution and compensation placed on the shoulders of those responsible for the illegal export. It is quite likely that these

arguments will run on right up to 31 December, and even beyond.

In conclusion, it does seem that the will exists among the twelve to have some sort of system in place by January 1993. I believe that we are unlikely to see very great changes to the proposed procedures as I have outlined them. So will the new rules change very much? Will it mean the sack of Italy, Greece or even Britain?

I believe that overall the proposed procedures represent a satisfactory and rather good compromise between very different philosophical standpoints. For the UK it should improve protection overall, since the number of objects needing to be covered by export licence applications will increase. However, the previous speaker has already rightly pointed out the inadequacy of the essentially voluntary procedure, so far as antiquities are concerned, although the Department of National Heritage has undertaken to introduce for the first time ever effective penalties for contravention of export control regulations. I mentioned earlier that certain categories of object are likely to suffer under the new rules. Also, as the MGC and others have pointed out to the Government many times, without the relatively modest additional funding for purchase funds needed to make them work, our heritage protection procedures will become even more of an empty show.

For some other countries, it could be argued that the situation could hardly be worse than it is now and that for many, smuggling appears to increase in proportion to the severity of the legislation designed to counter it. The Mediterranean countries have most legitimate grievances. But they are burdened with heritage protection legislation which they cannot afford to maintain or enforce. Just one example: Italy has since the early 1970s been engaged in compiling a database of its estimated 30 million treasures in expectation of the single market; after 20 years and untold expenditure, fewer than two million objects are on the Register. We all know the stories of Italian warehouses full of objects excavated decades ago, which have since lain untouched and unrecorded for lack of resources.

If as is quite likely we do see some gradual liberalisation in the southern states, this ought to have the beneficial effect of reducing smuggling. It could also be argued that it would allow these countries to concentrate their limited resources better on protecting the important objects and monuments. Conversely, it would become less easy for national authorities to rely on the threat of pre-emptive bans on export to engineer purchases from owners at favourable prices.

Whilst it does seem as if the European Commission and the northern states may be winning the technical and legal battle, they have not necessarily won the moral argument. One of the most useful outcomes of the debate could be a greater understanding of and sympathy for other countries' positions on this sensitive issue. If all countries can see the new agreements as a basis for sensible and fruitful co-operation, this could go a long way towards calming the fears of the southern states, and could encourage a more helpful attitude towards heritage protection on the part of governments in some of the northern countries.

Ultimately, the EC is part of a wider world, and cannot build a 'fortress Europe' on its external frontiers. The second most important European art market after the United Kingdom, Switzerland, is geographically situated within the very heart of EC territory, a mere hour's drive from Milan. Switzerland has no export controls for cultural objects. Its role as a transit territory for illegally exported goods on their way to London or New York is well-known. The opening of central and eastern European countries is already providing more useful transit points, as well as exposing these countries' heritage to the insatiable demands of the international art market. As in several other fields, the EC may, almost before it has succeeded in harmonising arrangements among its existing twelve members, find itself having to look ahead to the consequences of a wider Europe.

Notes

1. 'Il sacco d'Italia', *La Repubblica* 2 July 1991
2. European Commission, Communication from the Commission to the Council on the Protection of National Treasures possessing artistic, historic or archaeological value: Needs arising from the Abolition of Frontiers in 1992, COM(89)594 final (Brussels 1989), para 1.
3. European Commission, op. cit. para 5.
4. European Commission, Council Regulation on the export of cultural goods, (Brussels 1992).
5. European Commission, Council Directive on the return of cultural objects unlawfully removed from the territory of a Member State (Brussels 1992).
6. Kakouris, Isidore, 'The Circulation of National Treasures in the EEC: the Hellenistic Viewpoint: MDA Conference paper (Canterbury 1991).

3. Archaeology and the National Museum of Antiquities, The Netherlands
(Rijksmuseum van Oudheden, Leiden)

Jan Verwers

When in the 1960s the discussion about objectives and methods in archaeology flared up with great intensity, the debates in Holland were almost exclusively held inside the walls of the university institutes. In the main scholars of European pre- and proto-history took part in this discussion, whereas it passed most of the Classical archaeologists and Egyptologists by.

As the National Museum of Antiquities (RMO) has charge of collections from Egypt, Classical antiquity, the Near East and The Netherlands, there are curators of different disciplines on its staff. Only the curators of the Dutch collections, by means of their university contacts, took part in the debates about such matters as New Archaeology. Only with the 1980s did the shift from object to process become visible in a few exhibitions. The permanent display of the Museum collection was literally permanent: it was primarily focused upon the object.

For the Egyptian and Classical Departments an object-centred display is, to some extent, acceptable. Sculptures, reliefs, vases, jewellery are all objects that can hold an autonomous position based upon their aesthetic values. The museum visitor looks at them and experiences the beauty of works of art.

However, for The Netherlands Department this approach is no longer of any use. Only a limited part of this collection has any artistic value. The power of the greater part of these objects lies in the fact that almost all of them come from well-documented excavations. Object and documentation form a link between the present-day museum visitor and the ancient maker and user. And here we have arrived at the present aim of the Leiden Museum: to be an archaeological museum, which, in our view, means that the human being behind the objects should be visualized.

This autumn a fully modernized department, devoted to the archaeology of The Netherlands, will be opened. In chronological order the museum tells the story of 200,000 years of habitation. The themes of economy, life and death, and material culture recur, ordered in periods. The objects are accompanied by texts, drawings and photographs. At some locations still-video programmes will elucidate in detail subjects such as flint working, early farming and the Roman army, whereas large wall-graphics give an idea of the environment in which the period under discussion has to be placed.

In a few years the Classical and Egyptian rooms will be renovated. One is conscious of the fact that the objects housed in these collections differ in many respects from those of The Netherlands Department. Yet, these are archaeological collections as well and, therefore, the remains of human actions. In the debates between curators one constantly feels the tension between the art-historical and an anthropological approach towards the objects. I am convinced that this very tension will, in the end, lead to a fascinating concept for the new displays.

In addition to the management and the presentation of the collections the RMO has set itself the task of doing research, in the first place the research of its own collection. Thus, research is mostly object-centred, with classification and typology playing an important part. In this way the museum distinguishes itself from much of the present-day research carried out by university institutes. This also means that, in our view, museum archaeologists differ from their colleagues at universities: in the museum the material culture is the central point.

The Leiden museum also organises field research. Every year there are excavations in Egypt, Syria and in The Netherlands; soon fieldwork in Greece will be resumed as well. Mostly being executed as joint-ventures with universities from home and abroad, these excavations help the Museum to maintain its place in the network of scientific insititutions. Taking part in congresses supports this position.

In the 175 years of its existence the staff of the Museum has built up a wide knowledge of the archaeology and, more specifically, the material culture of our collection areas. Of course this knowledge is available to the public through permanent and temporary displays, books, videos and lectures. In the last few years the Museum has also focused on other sectors of the public. The recently founded Archaeological Information Centre (AIC) is entrusted with the passing on of all kinds of archaeological information. Especially the press but also numerous organisations and individual people are beginning to find their way to the AIC. The employees now regularly contribute to specialist magazines, they publish summaries of the results of recent research, and carry out studies on the relationship between archaeology and the public. The museum houses and supports the AIC.

For some time now the RMO has been organizing

Plate 3.1 The Nubian Temple of Taffeh in the entrance hall of the National Museum of Antiquities at Leiden.

Plate 3.2 The Etruscan Galleries in Leiden.

courses devoted to the reading of hieroglyphs, the cultural history of Egypt, Classical mythology, the Roman cities around Vesuvius, etc. The courses are given by internal and external teachers and always take place inside the Museum, so that one may make use of the collection.

Coming to the end of this article I would like to return to something every museum is concerned with: the collections themselves. I have already given some attention to presentation and would yet like to give a few thoughts to those parts of the Museum which are not easily accessible to the public: the stores. And I will restrict myself to The Netherlands Department.

Since the first Museum excavations in 1826 large quantities of archaeological finds from all over the country have come to Leiden. Only in recent times the tradition evolved for excavators to transfer their finds to provincial museums as much as possible; a procedure laid down in the Monuments Act of 1988. From that moment the only objects which come to the National Museum are those of national importance and which fill gaps in the Leiden Collection. Decisions in these matters are taken by the Minister of Culture at the Director's request.

According to agreements all finds from an excavation will be kept together and thus placed in one store. This is leading to the situation that many museum stores are becoming crammed, with the result that university excavators, after publication, cannot dispose of their finds at the provincial museums concerned. At present, among other things, due to this space problem, a national debate has started about the necessity of preserving everything we dig up. Would not a sample suffice for certain types of finds? Such a question causes very emotional discussions. The Dutch museums argue that the observed space-problem should not lead to the setting up of archaeological warehouses outside the existing museum organisations. Archaeologically excavated finds are museum collections: they need museum care which can only be given by museum curators. Of particular importance is the fact that according to the aforementioned Monuments Act of 1988 all excavated finds are State property: the debate between provincial museums and the responsible (State) minister about the financial responsibility for their storage has not yet been resolved.

These notes give an outline of the National Museum of Antiquities (RMO) in The Netherlands. Together with my colleague Jan Baart's words about local museums with archaeological collections an overview is offered of archaeology and museums in the Netherlands. Here no attention has been paid to the rest of the archaeological scene: the university institutes, the municipal archaeological services, the National Antiquities Service and the local archaeological societies. In everyday practice, however, they form a close bond.

4. Archaeology in Dutch Town-Museums

Jan M. Baart

The first archaeological collections in Dutch towns were brought together in the nineteenth century. They are, as it were, still part of the collections of curiosities, or the result of the first more or less scientifically organized excavations.

Although this situation did not change much during the first half of this century, the first collections from systematic excavations became more important. The real explosion of research in town centres dates from after 1970. Systematic excavations were carried out in no less than 65 towns, and extensive archaeological collections were begun.[1]

As there was no clearcut legislation in the Netherlands until 1988 concerning the ownership of finds, this led to a very diverse development in the organization of management and in the presentation of archaeological collections. Until 1988 the legal situation was such that the finder owned half of the value of the archaeological finds, and the owner of the land the other half. Legislation did not concern itself with the ownership of the objects themselves.[2]

Since 1988 a new law has come into operation that specifies where archaeological collections must be kept after excavation. There are now provincial and municipal depots of finds. As this procedure is still new, there is not yet any clear development. Depots of finds may be under the management of a town archaeologist, a municipal museum, a regional museum, a provincial museum, a national museum, or a foundation. In actual fact it is the municipal government of a town that has an archaeological department which can decide where an archaeological depot is kept.

The archaeological collections of museums were of a relatively modest size until 1970. From 1970 onwards there has been – and still is – an enormous expansion. Archaeological collections used to consist of only several tens, hundreds, or at the most several thousands of items; now, however, there are hundreds of cubic metres.

The term 'cubic metres' already indicates the first problem. The collections have not yet been catalogued. One can roughly say that an adequate system for documenting the material by means of the computer is still being developed. However, the problems involved in this, such as selection or disposal, have not yet been solved. Cautious talks about these problems have started. As research of the archaeological findings or collections has been limited until now, selection is not really possible; a rough survey will have to be made on the basis of research and publications before a selection can be made. Excavations follow each other in quick succession each year, and they still have priority within the archaeological framework. As a result of this, the collections are growing fast and we are now faced with this logistical problem; too soon, it seems, because not enough research has been done yet, and not enough studies have been published.

Who manages, or rather who finances the storage of these collections in the various depots? At the moment it is the depot-keeper. Limited financial means, however, can lead to inadequate facilities. In some cases this has already led to a reorganization of the existing situation in a museum. The depot was cleaned out and reduced to half its size. The rest was destroyed. It goes without saying that this procedure, however practical, is a waste of money and energy.

In order to avoid similar situations on a larger scale in the future, it is necessary to find a balance between digging and processing. Quite recently, for the first time, a different note was struck in favour of management over research. Particularly in the towns, this archaeological dilemma has not yet received much discussion. It seems as if discussion of this problem is being avoided because there are no readymade solutions available. If excavations are abandoned, valuable information will be lost.

There are, however, two aspects which seem to come to the aid of archaeologists. Due to an economic recession, large projects in the inner towns are more difficult to realize. Although this does provide a little more time for research, there are still enough projects which demand attention.

There is a second, more important aspect. The signature of the Minister of Culture to the Treaty of Malta of 1992 means that there is now a legal basis for demanding archaeological research-time and the necessary funds from the property developers.[3] The Treaty of Malta has not yet been implemented in practice, nor have administrative regulations been drawn up.

The treaty may offer a possible solution for the preservation of archaeological sites in the future, but it does not of course provide a solution for the unavoidable selection of archaeological finds. On the contrary, the collections will expand at an even greater pace. It will, therefore, be necessary to recover the funding of the excavations, as well as the funding of the research and publication from those who want to destroy archaeological sites in order to realize new projects. After all, these are necessary conditions before the selection process can be started.

Another problem connected with this selection, and with the research and processing of the excavated results in general is the lack of theory or reflection on the excavation results. There will have to be, in future, a certain consensus on the goals of excavating and the levels of processing and research.

In the meantime, there is the everyday reality of archaeology. Large collections have been assembled since 1970. The longer archaeological departments in the towns have been in operation, the larger the collections. Within the foreseeable future every town

with a permanent archaeological department will soon have a very extensive archaeological collection.

What was the reaction in the Netherlands to the interest in the preservation of archaeological finds? How have these collections been shown to the public? A survey of the various ways in which these collections were put together and exhibited does not only show a great variety in ways and means, but it also illustrates the development that has taken place in the Netherlands. I would like to illustrate this development with seven examples.

1. The first example is the municipal museum 'De Lakenhal' in Leiden. The museum is housed in the 17th century clothmakers' hall, built in a neo-classical style (Fig. 4.1).

It is a good example of how museums are housed in many Dutch towns. In almost every case one of the many 17th century monuments has been chosen as the location. On the one hand this provides a handsome historical environment for the collection, and it is a pleasant solution for a building which is often difficult to make use of. On the other hand these buildings have certain limitations for a modern museum. This has its advantages as well as disadvantages.

The Leiden collection has been assembled gradually since 1874, when the museum was first opened.[4] It consists of archaeological finds from the town of Leiden, and from the surrounding area. The number of finds that can be exhibited is about 500, while there are some 50 boxes full of pottery sherds in the depot. The collection contains earthenware, coins, glass, pewter, copper, bone, wood, tiles, floor-tiles and clay-pipes.

Museums like this often have an art-historian, sometimes a historian or an archaeologist as curator. The exhibits in the museum are arranged from an art-historical point of view. Qualitatively interesting objects are placed among other very handsome works of art such as paintings.

A remarkable find of four bronze candlesticks, probably from a monastery, was recovered in the seventies during building activities, and has since been bought by the Museum. It is a very interesting and rare find, not only for Leiden, but also in the framework of Dutch town-centre research. The candlesticks have been carefully conserved after the Museum bought them and are exhibited attractively together with paintings by Lucas van Leiden in the permanent gallery (Fig. 4.2). The aim here has been to create an aesthetic harmony, and not to provide the context in which the objects were found. There is no further information on the use of the objects (where was it produced, what techniques were used in the production, distribution, retail price or method of acquisition) or their meaning (status of the object, or social context).

There are also a few rooms with various finds. Several kinds of earthenware are exhibited from different periods ranging from the 13th to 18th century (Fig. 4.3). In fact, the Museum has exhibited a number of objects from Leiden which have come to light more or less by accident over a century, and that have been acquired by the museum. The museum has not yet made use of results from excavations carried out after 1970. There has been quite a lot of research in Leiden, and there have also been relatively many publications.[5] But as there is still no official municipal archaeology department; the town does not have any storage authority due to the existing legislation. The excavations and publications have been the responsibility of volunteers and specialists from the various universities.

2. An excavation of a single building or complex of buildings has in the past sometimes resulted in the establishment of an exhibition on site. Excavations of the oldest and most important ecclesiastical centre of Holland, the Abbey of Egmond, gave rise to a small display in the present abbey.[6] The excavations took place between 1938 and 1948, and were carried out by the University of Groningen. Some research had already been done previously, in 1904.[7] The abbey dates from the 10th century AD. From 950 to 1150 it was the burial place of the Earls of Holland. The *Chronicles* and *Vitae*, the most important sources for the earliest history of Holland, were written in this abbey.

The abbey was destroyed in 1572 (Fig. 4.4). In 1938 Benedictine monks returned to the site. The monks have shown great interest in the excavation results and research. They have set aside a special room for the finds. The most interesting objects have been arranged according to period in a varied way, even on the windowsill and on the floor (Fig. 4.5). One showcase, for instance, contains finds from the Roman period. Another contains finds from the period between *c*. 1200 and 1600 (Fig. 4.6).

In such an arrangement ceramics, metal objects and sculptures are placed together. Among the finds are several unique ones, such as the floor-tiles with tin-glaze which date from around 1300. These tiles have been found on only a limited number of sites in North-West Europe. The sites where such ceramics have been found are almost exclusively ecclesiastical locations. Such information is lacking in this kind of arrangement. As there have been no more excavations in the last fifty years, there have been no changes in the arrangement and layout either.

There are three musueums that I want to discuss now, because they give an impression of recent archaeological presentation in a province, region and town respectively. These are the museums of Assen, Hoorn and Haarlem.

3. The museum at Assen is housed in a complex of buildings including the Collector's House, a late 19th-century building in a historical style (Fig. 4.7). After the 1962 restoration, the Museum was established here. It has a very important archaeological collection as well as a considerable collection of popular art.[8] The collection consists of some 20,000 objects. The provincial archaeological depot is also housed in the museum. The museum has 70,000 visitors each year.

The collection was put together as a result of an exhibition of antiquites from Drente in 1854. From that time onwards objects have been added to the collection. A great expansion took place after World War II due to systematic research carried out by the University of Groningen.

A considerable part of the museum is dedicated exclusively to archaeology. The various excavations are exhibited by means of site photographs, models of farms, and artefacts in reconstructed contexts and alongside other objects (Fig. 4.8). The new permanent display is arranged along thematic lines with themes such as "working in stone", and "care for the dead" (Fig. 4.9). The exhibition takes up a considerable part of the building. This is not the case with the archaeological galleries in Hoorn and Haarlem, which are both situated in the cellars of historical buildings.

4. The museum in Hoorn is housed in the former seat of the representative council of the Northern Quarter, a regional administrative body, built in 1631/32 (Fig. 4.10). After restoration between 1908 to 1911, during which the entire façade of the building was renewed, the Westfries Museum was established here. Objects related to the region of West-Friesland are shown in a number of rooms.[9]

In the cellars of this building the displays are primarily concerned with the results of archaeological research in the town-centre. Archaeological research has been carried out since the 1950s; at first only at random, but during the last ten years on a more systematic and regular basis whenever extensive new building projects have taken place. The museum receives around 40,000 visitors each year.

The arrangement in the cellars consists of collections and information panels placed against the walls, in a chronological and thematic scheme. To illustrate an excavated Bronze Age settlement a handsome model is used, surrounded by information and artefacts (Fig. 4.11). There are photographs of the excavations, as well as, for instance, miniature earthenware animals, very unusual finds, and other aspects of the excavations which were carried out by the Unversity of Amsterdam.

The Rijksdienst voor het Oudheidkundig Bodemonderzoek (the national archaeological service) excavated a castle built by the Earl of Holland in the 13th century outside the town of Hoorn. Objects from this excavaton are presented together with photographs, reconstruction drawings, and a short historical description. The existence of a town-centre research department has led to regular excavations in the town. The excavations are represented by individual assemblages (Fig. 4.12). Some showcases contain leather finds, such as shoes ranging in date from the 12th to 17th centuries. Special attention is given to the discovery of a 16th century jacket. Where space is available the museum has attempted to show as many interesting objects from the collections as possible. For instance, there are decorated sarcophagus lids from the 11th and 12th centuries, originally from a village near Hoorn that was flooded in the later Middle Ages.

5. At the initiative of the town archaeologist of Haarlem the cellar of the Meathall, a handsome building in Dutch Renaissance style, dated 1603, was fitted out as an archaeological museum (Fig. 4.13). This museum was opened only recently. The results of excavations carried out by the department in the last ten years are presented here.[10] Before this, only limited archaeological research took place, mainly by amateurs.

The museum decided to use showcases of a modern design, which were adapted specifically to low vaulted cellars (Fig. 4.14). The various displays are arranged thematically, and according to material: pottery waste from the 13th century is placed next to leather objects. On a broader level the museum pays attention to excavation itself. There is, for instance, a completely reconstructed excavation site (Fig. 4.15). Information is available on the excavation techniques used. The public has shown a lot of interest. During the first half of the year, the museum welcomed 20,000 visitors.

The museum was established mainly with the help of sponsors and the cooperation of many volunteers. The municipal government offers structural assistance with a modest contribution. Within the general museum developments of the last decades, the specialized historical museums have taken up a separate position. These museums with their intention of showing the history of the town, have made use of all possible disciplines and means available. Archaeological research is merely one of these. In such a case the aim is not simply to show archaeological results and collections, but to use these to illustrate the town's history. Archaeological data are integrated into a wider context.

6. The Amsterdams Historisch Museum is an example of this. The museum is housed in a complex of medieval buildings, the Luciën-convent. This convent was converted into an ophanage after the Reformation. A Renaissance-style gate was added during the 1581 reconstruction works. This gate now serves as an entrance to the Museum. The large inner courtyards were created in 1632 and the middle of the 17th century (Fig. 4.16). The whole has grown into an attractive complex of buildings with, however, difficult spaces for a museum. The history of the city from 1200 to 1950 is displayed in seventeen rooms.

For the medieval material, in particular, the choice has been for a presentation accompanied by maps, photographs, and origingal documents (Fig. 4.17). There has been some discussion as to whether too many maps and photographic material have been used. The subject of discussion is then the border-line between museum and book. Elsewhere in the arrangement the choice has favoured archaeological objects. A fireplace has been rebuilt using building material found on the excavation (Fig. 4.18). It is furnished with objects dating from *c.* 1400; on the wall is a collage of objects from daily life. The shipping trade is illustrated by means of an excavated rudder and a number of inventories from shipwrecks, together with a cast-iron pitch cauldron. Generally speaking, this reconstruction comprises parts of a larger whole, incorporating archaeological finds. Other examples of the approach include a town-gate with the figure of a guard wearing an excavated helmet (Fig. 4.19), and parts of houses from the 14th and 15th centuries combined with drawings.

In some rooms the showcases contain a thematic arrangement, for instance with leather objects (Fig. 4.20). Several special finds, such as the fragment of a statue, are shown by themselves, just as objects of art are exhibited elsewhere (Fig. 4.21). The rooms have been arranged carefully and aesthetically. The need to show a larger part of the archaeological collection has made itself felt, however.

To meet this need one of the attic rooms has been arranged in a special way. Here, attention is given to the limited finds of the Bronze Age, the Iron Age, and Roman times (Fig. 4.22): building materials (Fig. 4.23), and clusters of finds consisting of imported earthenware (Fig. 4.24) or metal objects. The museum welcomes 180,000 visitors a year.

7. Another and very special example of the use of archaeology in a museum is the recently opened department of ancient and modern industrial art and design at the Van Beuningen-De Vriese pavilion of the Museum Boymans-van Beuningen, Rotterdam (Fig. 4.25).[11]

The composition of the collection of archaeological objects is equally unique.[12] After the war, Mr Van Beuningen began to collect finds from the 12th to 19th centuries. The objects were collected mainly on building sites in Rotterdam and Delft, and also from various other Dutch towns. The collection was donated to the Museum Boymans-van Beuningen in 1983, on the condition that a separate building would be erected. This museum was built in 1990. This is one of the few examples in the Netherlands of an archaeological collection exhibited in a modern, purpose-built, building.

There is one floor for contemporary exhibitions, and a floor for the permanent gallery (Fig. 4.26). In the centre of this arrangement is a unit which gives an impression of the quantity and variety of objects illustrating daily life. In this presentation, finds have been juxtaposed with objects of similar function from the 19th and 20th centuries that have not been exca-vated, but were bought from antique dealers and from modern designers. There are showcases with 14th-century cutlery and drinking glasses. Sub-division by century and by function defines the scheme. Other examples are 15th century jugs and other tableware made of earthenware, stoneware and pewter (Fig. 4.27), and 15th-century red earthenware decorated with white slip (Fig. 4.28).

The museum has an attractive atmosphere. The collection consists of some 10,000 objects, 2,000 of which can be seen in the permanent exhibition; 200,000 people visit the museum each year.

The case studies chosen demonstrate that museums have managed to incorporate the latest data from modern town research in a variety of ways into their displays. Surveys have shown that audiences greatly appreciate the revamped archaeological display in the Amsterdams Historisch Museum and the Drents Museum.[13] The placing of archaeological objects in a wider context is particularly popular. One conse-quence of this style of exhibition has been, however, that the many objects exhibited by former methods have been relegated to the depot. A recent develop-ment that has been observed is a request for more objects on show.

In summary it can be said that a vast amount of archaeological data and objects collected through excavations since 1970 have been given a place in Dutch museums in a variety of ways. A future im-provement could be made by training and appoint-ing archaeological curators in museums.[14]

Acknowledgements

W. Krook, Afdeling Archeologie/Stedelijk Beheer Amsterdam: Figs. 4.2, 4.3 and 4.5–4.24. Museum Boymans-van Beuningen, Rotterdam: Figs. 4.25–4.28.

Notes

1. H. Sarfatij (ed.), *Verborgen steden, stadsarcheologie in Nederland* (Amsterdam, 1990), 163.
2. Riemer Knoops (ed.), *Archeologische Almanak* (Abcoude, 1992), 29–34.
3. W.J.H. Willems, Hoofdstuk I Algemeen in: *Jaarverslag 1991*, Rijksdienst voor het Oudheidkundig Bodemonderzoek (Amersfoort, 1992), 5–15.
4. Information: I.W.L. Moerman, curator of the Stedelijk Museum "De Lakenhal", Leiden.
5. *Bodemonderzoek in Leiden: archeologische jaarverslagen 1978–1992*, jrg. 1–14 Leiden, Dienst Civiele Werken, Leiden.
6. Information: Father P.J. Berkhout, Keeper of the collection.
7. E.H.P. Cordfunke, *Opgravingen in Egmond. De abdij van Egmond in historisch-archeologisch perspectief.*
8. Information: W.A.B. van der Sanden, curator of the Drents Museum.
9. Information: T.Y. van de Walle-van der Woude, town-archaeologist of Hoorn and curator of the Westfries Museum, Hoorn.
10. Information: J.M. Poldermans, town-archaeologist of Haarlem.
11. Information: A.G.A. van Dongen, curator of the Van Beuningen-De Vriese collection "Pre-Industrial Utensils 1150–1800", Museum Boymans-van Beuningen, Rotterdam.
12. A.P.E. Ruempol and A.G.A. van Dongen, *Pre-industriële Gebruiksvoorwerpen/Pre-industrial Utensils 115–1800*, Museum Boymans-van Beuningen (Rotterdam, 1991), 3–11.
13. Folkert Haanstra, *Beleving en waardering van museumbezoek. Een onderzoek in drie historische musea.* SCO rapport 313 (Amsterdam, 1992), 21, 24.
14. Susan Pearce, *Archaeological Curatorship.* Leicester Museum Studies (London and New York, 1990), 198–203.

Fig. 4.1 The Clothhall, Leiden, Suzanne van Steenwijk, 17th century, Coll. Stedelijk Museum "De Lakenhal", Leiden.

Fig. 4.2 Part of the permanent exhibition at the Stedelijk Museum "De Lakenhal", Leiden.

Fig. 4.3 Part of the permanent exhibition at the Stedelijk Museum "De Lakenhal", Leiden.

Fig. 4.5

Fig. 4.4

Figs. 4.4–4.6 4.4, From: A. Horaeus, Kronyck ende
historie van het edele en machtige geslachte van den
Huyse van Egmont (Alkmaar 1630). 4.5, Part of the
permanent exhibition at the Abdij van Egmond,
Egmond. 4.6, Part of the permanent exhibition at the
Abdij van Egmond, Egmond.

Fig. 4.6

Fig. 4.7 "Collector's House", 19th century, Drents Museum, Assen.

Fig. 4.8 Part of the permanent exhibition, Drents Museum, Assen.

Fig. 4.9 Part of the permanent exhibition, Drents Museum, Assen.

Fig. 4.10 Seat of the Council of the Northern Quarter
1631/1632, Westfries Museum, Hoorn.

Fig. 4.11 Part of the permanent exhibition, Westfries Museum, Hoorn.

Fig. 4.12 Part of the permanent exhibition, Westfries Museum, Hoorn.

Fig. 4.13 The Meathall, 1603, now the Archaeological Museum, Haarlem.

Fig. 4.14 Part of the exhibition, Archaeological Museum, Haarlem.

Fig. 4.15 Part of the exhibition, Archaeological Museum, Haarlem.

Fig. 4.16 Part of the "Amsterdams Historisch Museum", 17th century.

Fig. 4.17 Part of the permanent exhibition of the "Amsterdams Historisch Museum".

Fig. 4.18 Part of the permanent exhibition of the "Amsterdams Historisch Museum".

Fig. 4.19

Fig. 4.21

Figs. 4.19–4.21 Part of the permanent exhibition of the "Amsterdams Historisch Museum".

Fig. 4.20

Fig. 4.22 Part of the permanent exhibition of the "Amsterdams Historisch Museum".

Fig. 4.23 Part of the permanent exhibition of the "Amsterdams Historisch Museum".

Fig. 4.24 Part of the permanent exhibition of the "Amsterdams Historisch Museum".

Fig. 4.25 Van Beuningen-De Vriese pavilion, Museum Boymans-van Beuningen, Rotterdam.

Fig. 4.26 Permanent exhibition in the Van Beuningen-De Vriese pavilion, Rotterdam.

Fig. 4.27 Part of the exhibition of the Van Beuningen-De Vriese pavilion, Rotterdam.

Fig. 4.28 Part of the exhibition of the Van Beuningen-De Vriese pavilion, Rotterdam.

5.   A Facelift for the Royal Museums of Art and History, Brussels

Francis Van Noten

The Royal Museums of Art and History was one of the 10 National Science Institutions of Belgium to be granted a self-supporting status in 1989. This entirely new development is not to be confused with the concept of *privatisation*, indeed the 10 Institutions remained state-controlled and the majority of its personnel retained civil service status. This new situation is simple. Formerly the directors had to justify how the budget had been expended, with possible benefits to the Treasury, and how deficits were covered. Now the budget remains more or less the same, but with a board of trustees, appointed by the King, which prepares the annual budget and controls it. On the negative side one should mention the impossibility of obtaining extra income, e.g. a special grant to organize a temporary exhibition. On the positive side chance benefits can be kept. The board of trustees keeps the budget under control throughout the year and gives advice.[1]

Being self-supporting means that the directors have to deal with a completely new type of management, whereas before they were very much civil servants or "administrators" with not so much freedom, and with restrictions on taking any initiative. Now they are "director-managers".[2] This evolution was not taken easily by "traditional curators", who maintained that the Government had to fulfil its responsibilities towards science and art institutions by providing an annual budget. The far greater liberty, however, makes it possible to address a number of possibilities formerly not profitable for the institutions. Within two years the directorate of the Royal Museums of Art and History took sole responsibility

for the museum shops, the museum restaurants and the replicas department. They were reorganized and were soon financially rewarding for the Museums. This new system of self-government greatly encouraged the museum personnel as they became soon aware that an extra input produced direct results. Thus new possibilities of collaboration were opened up with the private sector.[3]

The Royal Museums of Art and History, more than any other of the larger museums in Brussels had, or dare I say, still have, the irritating reputation of being the "old lady", or should I say "the sleeping beauty": namely dusty, inactive, gloomy and, especially with the main building, difficult for access.

After a period of one year as acting director, nominated as such since April 1990, I have taken on the task of trying to wake up this sleeping beauty. This process proved slow. First of all one had to mobilise within the museums themselves all forces capable and willing to act towards rebirth. Firstly a group of colleagues with enough courage and willingness to tackle the renewal of the buildings was motivated and mobilized, their actions opposed to some extent by the inevitable group of "traditional curators". The latter judge that museums are places of learning, safeguarding collections (in the first place for themselves, and eventually for a few other colleagues); in reality the public was not really wanted or expected. The result of this attitude, was a number of galleries being closed to the public, others open only one day a week, all others on even and uneven dates. Two other of the six buildings, The Japanese Pagoda and the Halle Town Gate, were closed for many years. In addition all Museums were closed to the public at lunchtime. This policy sounds strange if one knows that the main building, the *Cinquantenaire*, has 100 galleries housing collections from prehistoric times to the present, covering the World, except for Black Africa and the Fine Arts. It should be mentioned here that the Royal Museums of Art and History launched an education department in 1922, and a *Museum for the Blind* in 1975, pioneer work in both cases.

The first thing to do was to convince the Minister of the absolute necessity to open all galleries to the public, including over lunchtime.[4] A number of additional warders made this possible. Their status is temporary, as their contracts are renewed on 31st December every year. This situation is not exactly ideal for motivating the staff.

The next step was to remind the Ministry of Public Works that building works had been carried out in nearly all of the nine National Science Institutions over the last 25 years, and that now our turn had come! This philosophy worked. Unfortunately by March 1992 it transpired that the Ministry of Works saw its financial means within the Government being reduced. Consequently some of the works started and could be finished, others were stopped, and others, although planned, never started. At present the situation is most alarming.

***

The Royal Museums of Art and History consist of 6 buildings in Brussels. They are:

The Cinquantenaire (Fig. 5.1)

This is the main building with not less than 100 galleries. One third of them cover Egypt, the Near East, Greece, Rome and the Islamic world (together they are known as the Antiquity Department.) The Decorative Arts Department mainly covers Western Europe and fills a second third of the galleries. The third department groups Belgian archaeology, folklife and the transport collection, along with the archaeology and ethnography of America, Asia and Oceania. Again these collections are spread over about one third of the building.

The Royal Museums of Art and History have a longstanding tradition of organizing temporary exhibitions: some are large and attract the crowds (*Aztecs*: 380,000 visitors; *China, Heaven and Earth*: 250,000; *Inca-Perú*: 248,000); others are on a medium or a small scale. The way these are organized today may appear of a complex nature: some are organized by ourselves, (eventually travelling through Europe), sometimes we receive packaged exhibitions from elsewhere; others consist of special arrangements as in the case of *Europalia*,[5] and a fourth possibility consists of somebody outside organizing an exhibition in our galleries. In this last case we charge for the space and the services we offer. One of the major problems in organizing temporary exhibitions is that they have to be organized in galleries normally occupied by permanent collections. As in so many other museums, these have to be stored temporarily elsewhere. This situation was obviously heavily criticised by the traditional curators, whose criticism was often justified. Until quite recently, the showrooms normally showing China, Japan and the America's were closed to the public as the major temporary exhibitions took their place. New building improvement has abbreviated this problem.

Hence the building of an entirely new special exhibition room of 1600 sq. metres, of which the central part (900 sq. metres) can be used separately, can be proudly announced (Fig. 5.4). The entrance to these new galleries has been fully refurbished with facilities making it possible to receive a large number of visitors. Included are a new lecture hall with 230 seats (Fig. 5.5) and a lobby and exhibition shop, which now make it possible to organize large-scale exhibitions without disturbing the rest of the Museum.[6]

Close to the new exhibition galleries, in one of the former interior gardens, another gallery of *c*. 500 sq. metres will be built and equipped in order to house what will be called *The Russian Museum* (Fig. 5.3). Every year the intention is to show (over a 6-month period), collections from the great museums of Russia. Agreements have been signed with three museums contributing to the creation of a window on Russian art and archaeology.

With the commencement of refurbishment in

Fig. 5.1 The Cinquantenaire Museum complex. The Royal Museums of Art and History occupy the south-eastern part.

order to house large-scale temporary exhibitions liberating all galleries, attention has now turned towards the permanent galleries themselves. In order to open up large parts of these showrooms, entrances are being rebuilt. Today only one of the three main entrances is in operation, a second one is for the time being reserved for personnel only; a third one has been closed for a very long time. Three entrances will be in full operation in the near future. Each of them will serve a section of the Museum, without excluding the rest of the galleries.

The Parc entrance, today the main entrance, will continue to be the main access to the Near East, Egypt and the Classic World galleries. The Esplanade entrance, closed for dozens of years, will be reopened and will be rebuilt with new facilities. From this entrance the access will lead, on the one side to the new Transport Museum, which is to be shown in an unused space underground; on the other side it will guide the visitors to the main Museum, through

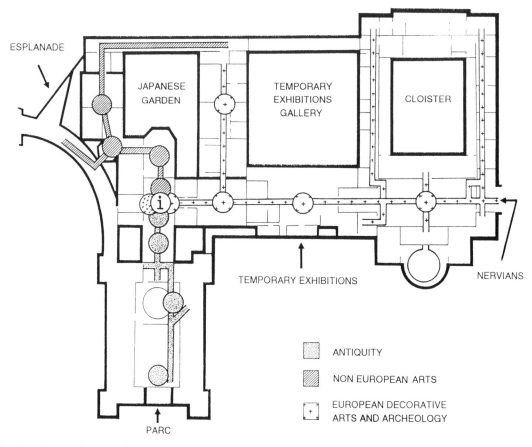

ESPLANADE

JAPANESE GARDEN

TEMPORARY EXHIBITIONS GALLERY

CLOISTER

i

TEMPORARY EXHIBITIONS

NERVIANS

ANTIQUITY

NON EUROPEAN ARTS

EUROPEAN DECORATIVE ARTS AND ARCHEOLOGY

PARC

*Fig. 5.2 General map with new "routes". The **i** indicates where the new information desk will be located.*

Fig. 5.3 The interior garden chosen to become the gallery for temporary exhibitions.

Fig. 5.4 The roof of the new exhibition gallery.

Fig. 5.5 Work in progress on the new lecture hall underneath the exhibition gallery.

Fig. 5.6 The Large Narthex in 1992, before redecoration.

Fig. 5.7 The Large Narthex in 1993, redecorated.

a gallery where a display of techniques and art-styles represented in the collections will be shown. From here the visitor reaches an existing rotunda where today a collection of Christian Art from the Orient is displayed.[7] This rotunda will become the main junction for public orientation and information. A central information desk will be built.

This newly organized information centre is the point where three circuits will start and end (Fig. 5.2). These have been devised by experts and will offer to the visitor the choice of the three following routes: Antiquity as described above; archaeology and arts from America, Asia and Oceania; and finally European decorative arts and archaeology from Belgium. The non-European parts will be completely reorganized.[8] On the ground floor coming from the central meeting point one will be able to visit the American archaeological collections (8 galleries), ethnography (1 gallery) and a 19th-century *collectors cabinet*. These series of showrooms will lead to the Oceania and Easter Island gallery. The Asian collections (China, India and South-East Asia) will be reorganized on the first floor, right above the Americas. Here, a gallery will be devoted to Buddhism, one to the Hinduism. Four galleries will present the Chinese collections, one of them on textiles, one a house interior, two on Vietnam and Thailand, and two on Indonesia. This part of the Museum, twenty galleries all told, together with the reopening of the Esplanade entrance, was the subject of a large-scale and expensive project including a new self-service restaurant with 300 seats and a more sophisticated one of 150 seats. With the air-conditioned rooms for textiles, one for the American collections, one for China, the project is considered as vital for the future of the Institution. This is especially so because on the Esplanade three other museums have their main entrance: The Army Museum, The Air Museum, and the Vintage Car Museum *Autoworld*.

However, this project promised by the Ministry of Works for implementation in 1992 and 1993, is now being postponed for a number of years.[9] We have therefore decided to reinstall the American and Asian galleries using our old showcases which we had thought of discarding. Too bad for the new entrance, access gallery, new restaurants and new

Transport Museum, the rebuilding being far beyond the present financial resources. The carriages, sledges and bicycles not shown to the public will be stored temporarily in six galleries, recently refurbished in order to have extra, much-needed storage space below existing galleries.

The reorganization of the Asian collections, moving from one part of the Museum towards another, liberates six galleries in that wing. It has been decided that the Royal Museums of Art and History should not become a fossil museum. The decorative art galleries now terminate (except for ceramics and glass) with the Art Nouveau movement. The six new galleries will be devoted to the decorative arts of the 20th century: Art Nouveau, Art Deco, the 1930s and the Brussels World Fair of 1958. One gallery will be devoted to temporary shows on contemporary creations. Important World Exhibitions of the 20th century will be axed.

Finally, the Nervians entrance, for many years only in use for personnel, will again become a public entrance. It will lead to an entirely redesigned national archaeology room, dealing with prehistoric times to the early Middle Ages, . These galleries are on the gound floor. The prehistoric section received new showcases thanks to a special arrangement.[10] This entrance leads into Decorative Arts on the first floor. This important part of the existing exhibition which shows furniture, sculpture, tapestries, metalwork, ceramics, etc. are not being redesigned for the time being. Next to these galleries three others have been refurbished: textiles and costume, lace and coptic textiles. Also new is a chapel to house Christian Art from the Orient. These collections cover all periods from medieval times to the present, and are located in a central part of the Museum on two floors. These galleries are situated next to large open hall, the Large Narthex (Fig. 5.6). This is being redecorated and will remain from now an open space, where smaller temporary exhibitions will be organized (Fig. 5.7). The walls will be hung with 16th-century Brussels tapestries. On the first floor the Large Narthex will show 19th- and 20th-century glass collections. Next to this hall a smaller one called the Small Narthex is also being refurbished. On the ground floor a collection of film-cameras and projectors covering one century of film history are being shown.

This was a recent gift to the Museum. Close by is one of the lecture halls where amateur films may be shown on request.

From the Nervians entrance one will be able to reach the new *Museum for the Blind*. This *Museum for the Blind* houses a special exhibition once a year, sometimes along the same lines as the large temporary exhibitions. The educational Departments (French and Flemish speaking) organize the exhibitions in turn.

The Japanese Pagoda and the Chinese Pavilion (Figs 5.8 and 5.9)

The Pagoda was closed to the public in 1947. The exterior, entrance hall and ground floor were refurbished at the occasion of the Japan *Europalia* in 1989. The reopening of a well-known monument of Brussels as a museum is quite an experience. After the Europalia exhibition, everybody thought that the Pagoda had been closed again. There were hardly any visitors and we decided to attract the public by organizing temporary exhibitions. Its special character, being a mixture of Japanese architecture and Art Nouveau style, does not suit temporary exhibitions, although *The Dragon King of the Sea*, *Chinese and Japanese Cloisonné*, both private collections, have been shown. Now the Pagoda houses our own Chinese export porcelain collection. This collection is normally housed in the Chinese Pavilion on the other side of the street, but as it is being refurbished, we took the opportunity of showing it elsewhere in the meantime.[11] In 1989 the Chinese Pavilion was closed for restoration; at first it was expected to be ready in 1991, thereafter in 1993. Now it has been decided that the Ministry of Works responsible for the restoration will stop all activity after the completion of the exterior of the building. They will probably return to us a building of which only the outside can be shown to the public, as there is no money left to refurbish the interior; thus it will not be possible to use it as a museum. The interior will remain a store for the time being.

The fact that the Chinese Pavilion will not be in use for some years (and that it now appears that the basement of the Japanese Pagoda is in poor shape while the five upper floors still wait to be restored),

Fig. 5.8 The Japanese Pagoda.

reduce the hope we had to create at Laeken a *Centre of Asian Museums*. Nevertheless, with a new museum for Japanese Art, the Far East will be well represented.

Bellevue (Fig. 5.10)

This museum, part of the Royal Palace, is situated in the centre of Brussels. Its 18th- to early 19th-century architecture contains *salons* of the Louis XV, Louis XVI, Napoleon I and Napoleon III styles along with silver, porcelain and preciosa. It houses also a recent gift of: *The Museums of Hearts*. The Ministry of Works redecorated the second floor in order to house

Fig. 5.9 The Chinese Pavilion.

temporary exhibitions. After a short time it was decided it should house the *Museum of the Dynasty*. An alternative means of organizing temporary exhibitions at Bellevue seems to be needed urgently.[12]

La Maison Saintenoy and *Old England* (Fig. 5.11)

Both these important buildings, the *Maison Saintenoy*, a well-known Art Nouveau building, and *Old England*, next to each other, have been chosen to house a new museum for musical instruments. This collection is considered as one of the most important in the world and is housed today in 10 small houses in Brussels, most of them in appalling condition. One of these buildings, although far too small, is still in use as a musical instruments museum. Years ago it was agreed that this collection deserved a new larger building. The houses *Saintenoy*, and *Old England*, located next to each other in the Royal Palace

grounds, were thought to be ideal. The Ministry of Works started to renovate the buildings a couple of years ago with a view to housing the music collection. The exteriors had been restored. The interiors were demolished in order to create more space. In the meantime the façade of the complex is being completed. There is, however, no money to finish the interior. It will be a case comparable to the Chinese Pavilion: the outside will look good, but the interior will be empty.

The Halle Town Gate (Fig. 5.12)

If the Japan *Europalia* had been at the origin of partly restoring the Japanese Pagoda, the *Portugal Europalia* 1991 has helped to rebuild and refurbish the Halle Town Gate. This Gate is the last town gate of Brussels and dates from the 13th century. It was the original Royal Museums of Art and History, when it was set up as such in 1835. The main collections

Fig. 5.10 Bellevue Museum.

Fig. 5.11 The Saintenoy House and Old England.

shown before its closure in 1975 consisted of arms and armour; unfortunately these were given to the Army Museum in 1975. Since then, the building remained empty until we could organize its refurbishing for *Portugal Europalia*. At that time an exhibition *Azulejos* was shown. While the exterior of the building was restored, as well as the inside, and archaeological excavations were undertaken, a new location had to be found. It was finally thought that the Town Gate was ready to house the folk art collection. In the meantime the Ministry of Works handed over a nicely restored building, but without any museum equipment(!) There is today very little hope to get the promised showcases and further arrangements. This fine building has impressive cellars and a large gothic hall. Most of the floors will house folk art collections, one floor being available for temporary exhibitions. The top floor right under the roof is a magnificent open space where cultural events can be organized. According to plans, the walls of this room are going to be decorated with our important collection of *Ancien Régime* corporation silver.

In summary we can say that our new self-supporting status is a tremendous challenge. But the challenge needs to be seen as an enormous advantage, and can be seen as a guide for other institutions. As long as the State is ready to sustain its financial support, the new system of complementing the annual budget by extra income has many advantages. In running these income producing activities (temporary exhibitions, bookshop and giftshop, restaurant and expo-snack, cast department) it has become clear that a benefit is possible. The net gain is, however, not so obvious and the personnel needs to be motivated. This motivation of mostly low-rank civil servants is not easy, as it often implies that their new jobs do not necessarily correspond with the ones for which they have been engaged. Therefore, it does not a seem bad policy to have a certain proportion of the personnel under contract. The Belgian law indeed protects civil service personnel for life. Contract personnel on the other hand can be replaced much more easily if necessary. The present 2/3 civil servants to 1/3 contract personnel seems a reasonable ratio.

Fig. 5.12 The Halle Town Gate.

The challenge of being self-supporting enables us to promote, thanks to extra income, all our facilities ourselves, not least the large temporary exhibitions, but also to research, provide educational programs, and refurbish the galleries with permanent collections and new material. It should, however, be made clear that the Government has to accept its responsibilities. Being self-supporting does not mean privatisation. Self-supporting here means that the Government provides the minimum support. The ideas of privatisation, however, cannot but make us afraid of all that could follow. Without charging any entrance fee, the Royal Museums of Art and History wish to remain a public museum with an important educational and social role. We are the custodian of a cultural heritage that has come down to us over a very long period of time. Privatisation would mean to look after ourselves and our budget; this could only be possible by selling objects. You might know where you start but it would perhaps be more difficult to decide where to stop. The Royal Museums of Art and History must remain the largest group of government museums, with a certain number of personnel belonging to the civil service. The new independent status makes "extra" income possible but this could never replace the annual State budget. Never, even with an admission fee, could enough income be guaranteed to run the various sites. If privatisation should mean that museum collections are sold, this would be a shame for the role of cultural heritage custodian which is, and will, remain ours.

Notes

1. The 10 National Science Institutions have been organized in 5 "groupings". The group "Museums", includes the Royal Museums of Art and History and the Royal Museums of Fine Arts. The board of trustees nominated per group consists of the directors of both institutions, one representative of the staff of each institution, the accountants of each of the institutions, two directors of the central administration, the inspector of finances and four exterior members, representing possible private sponsors (e.g. banks and businessmen).

2. We strongly advise that director-managers come from the academic sector. They should first of all be scholars having activily taken part in research before moving into a directorship, where scientific research is no longer possible. We have recently seen a non-scientist administrator in charge of a similar institution. This was a disaster.

3. Within the new system, however, the Belgian State did not go as far as some other countries did. The ownership of the buildings remained with the Ministry of Works. The Institutions rent the buildings from the Ministry of Works and are entirely dependent on them for all works to be done on the buildings.

4. At this time it was the Minister of Interior Affairs, as there is no Belgian Minister of Education or Culture anymore. The State is evolving towards a federation. There is today a Flemish Minister of Education, a Flemish Minister of Culture, a French speaking Minister of Education and a French speaking Minister of Culture. The country today is split into 3 communities: Flemish, French and German.

5. *Europalia* is a biannual festival, where a country is the special guest of Belgium; exhibitions, theatre, dance, music, and other cultural events take place between September and December. In 1989 it was Japan, in 1991 Portugal, and in 1993 Mexico.

6. In the last quarter of 1992 an exhibition *Treasures from the new World* (a private enterprise) containing some 600 artefacts from all parts of the Americas. It attracted 185,000 visitors. In the Spring of 1993 an exhibition *Splendor of the Sassanids*, organized by the Museum itself brought together some 180 artefacts from major museums owning Sassanian collections.

7. The Christian Art from the Orient will move to a Chapel, within a gothic cloister. This chapel has never been in use and will now become an exhibition room.

8. Earlier Japanese collections were shown in these galleries. It has, however, been decided recently to present them in a new Museum for Japanese Art in Laeken, close to the Japanese Pagoda.

9. The Ministry of Works has changed its programme and now proposes two stages: firstly the entrance would be reopened and the access to the new central meeting point created. The new Transport Museum will be built at a later date.

10. Beginning in 1991 we organized a temporary exhibition on *Scythian Gold*, based on the collection from the Hermitage, St Petersburg. For this occasion, the Ministry of Works rebuilt the gallery and even included new showcases. The bank Crédit Communal sponsored the exhibition and let us keep the profits, which went into modelling of the gallery designated for the prehistoric collections.

11. The collection has been exhibited in the Ashmolean Museum (Oxford), the National Museums of Singapore and Taïpei, as well as in Hong Kong and Groningen.

12. From our experience, and this is a general remark for all our Museums, we know that the general public prefers to come to museums when there is something "special to see". And as they are spoiled with 70 museums in Brussels, (with only 1 million inhabitants) and 650 in Belgium (under 10 million inhabitants) this task is not easy.

6.   Museum Rescue-Archaeology in Duisburg, the Lower Rhineland

Günter Krause

From early times the city of Duisburg at the confluence of Rhine and Ruhr has been a suitable area for
human settlement. On the fertile lower terrace of the
Rhine an almost uninterrupted sequence of occupation can be traced from the Neolithic period. Especially numerous are relics of the first millennium BC
(Duisburg 1990, 12–62).

The Lower Rhine region (Fig. 6.1) does not appear before the first century BC in the consciousness
of the Ancient World. The conquest of Gaul by Julius
Caesar and the following consolidation of Roman
power created the Lower Rhine frontier of the Roman empire (Kunow 1987). The Duisburg area was
strategically important. Roman camps as well as
earlier and later installations were constructed to
control the Rhine and the mouth of the Ruhr and the
major crossroads (Fig. 6.2). The Roman camp of
Asciburgium in the modern urban area of Duisburg
and Moers to the left of the Rhine is well known
from ancient sources. In the second century it was
followed by the small stone-built camp in Duisburg-
Werthausen (Bechert 1987).

Clearly visible besides modern disturbances are
the remains of earlier river-courses of the Rhine and
the Ruhr (Fig. 6.2). The first datable shift of the Rhine
occurred at the end of the 1st century AD (Scheller
1957, 66–68). In the hollow of the Rhine-bed of the
2nd to 12th centuries (Gerlach 1992a) lies the modern "Innenhafen" (inner harbour basin) of the large
barge-port of modern Duisburg (Fig. 6.3). It is the
waterfront of medieval and modern Duisburg. In
front of the late medieval "Stapeltor" (The Staple-
gate) the river Ruhr ran in a large curve into the

Rhine. The medieval harbour is to be found along
the old Rhine front in the area of the modern
"Innenhafen", not far from the central market place,
the *Alter Markt* (Fig. 6.3), and in the former mouth
of the Ruhr in front of the "Stapeltor". The port was
as vital for early Duisburg as it is today.

Until about 1200 the main course of the Rhine lay
directly in front of the Old Town of Duisburg, underneath the castle hill and the *Alter Markt*. From the
castle hill the other side of the Rhine was only about
500 metres away (Binding & Binding 1969, 5).

Fig. 6.1 Duisburg and the Lower Rhineland.

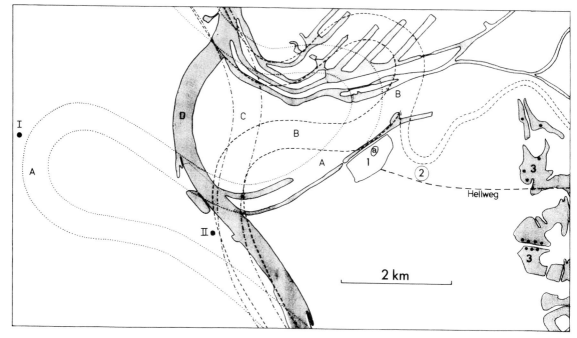

Fig. 6.2 Duisburg and its surroundings. Earlier courses of the Rhine and the Ruhr.

I: Roman camp of Asciburgium, 1st century AD.
II: Stone-built camp, Werthausen, 2nd century AD.
A: Course of the Rhine before 100 AD.
B: Course of the Rhine between 100–1200 AD.
C: Course of the Rhine after its breakthrough near Essenberg, after 1200 AD.

D: Current course of the Rhine.
1: Duisburg within the town-wall at the end of the 13th century (a: castle hill).
2: Late Carolingian pottery kiln.
3: Clay deposits and clay sources.

The formation of Duisburg in the Middle Ages according to historic sources

The first clear historic record of Duisburg dates from the year 883/4. The Danish vikings occupied the "oppidum diusburh" in the Winter of 883 and stayed here until Spring of 884 (Rau 1969, 267–269). At the end of the 9th century a church with a priest, a royal court and a colony of Frisian merchants were recorded for Duisburg (Milz 1985, 3). It is quite certain that they existed earlier and attracted the Vikings in AD 883/4.

The medieval royal palace that developed out of the royal court on the castle hill above the Rhine (Fig. 6.3), is recorded for the first time in 1145 (ibid., 2–3). The importance of Duisburg for the Saxon and Salian German kings of the 10th and 11th centuries

suggests a much earlier date for the existence of the royal palace (ibid.). Since the end of the last century remains of the palace and of the fortifications of the castle hill have been found and recorded. Their beginnings can be dated back at least to the early 10th century (Krause 1992a, 3; 39).

At about 1120 the first town wall in stone was erected, one of the earliest in the Rhineland. However, the shift of the Rhine during the 13th century (Fig. 6.2C) gradually cut Duisburg off from its main lifeline. In 1290 the Imperial town of Duisburg was pledged to the Count of Cleves and would never be redeemed. So Duisburg changed into a Clevian country-town. To this period belongs the extremely detailed map of Duisburg from 1566 (Fig. 6.4) by the young Johann Corputius, a pupil of the world-famous scholar Gerhard Mercator, who spent most of his life in Duisburg and died there in 1594. Included in the map is the fortification of the late 13th century (Milz 1982; Müller 1992) and the moats and outer walls that were built in the 14th century after the shift in the Rhine was completed. It marks the widest extension of the town up to the early 19th century. In 1821 the first house was built outside the medieval town-walls. At that time Duisburg had about 4 to 5,000 inhabitants (Fig. 6.5). In 1900 about 100,000 people lived there. The advantageous geographical position of Duisburg and the natural resources of the Lower Rhine/Ruhr area led to the formation of one of the largest centres of heavy industry in Germany.

This rapid development from a small rural town still within its medieval town-wall into one of the centres of heavy industry in the European community with more than half a million inhabitants, has completely changed the nature of pre-industrial Duisburg and its surroundings (Milz 1985). It could not have taken place without the influx of hundred thousands of people from different parts of Germany and the East and, for the last thirty years, mainly from the Mediterranean. Their identification with Duisburg has often been not very expressive.

Duisburg's past and the public

Nevertheless a permanent interest in the history and archaeology of the city of Duisburg and its surroundings arose shortly after the middle of the 19th century (Krause 1990a).

In 1853 the first Frankish cemetery was found during construction works near the Old Town (Fig.

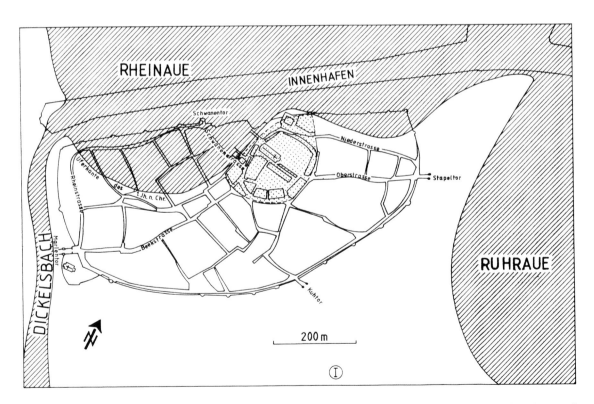

Fig. 6.3 The Old Town of Duisburg with the course of the Rhine in the Roman and medieval period; medieval Rhine within the area of the modern Innenhafen. I: Frankish cemetery.

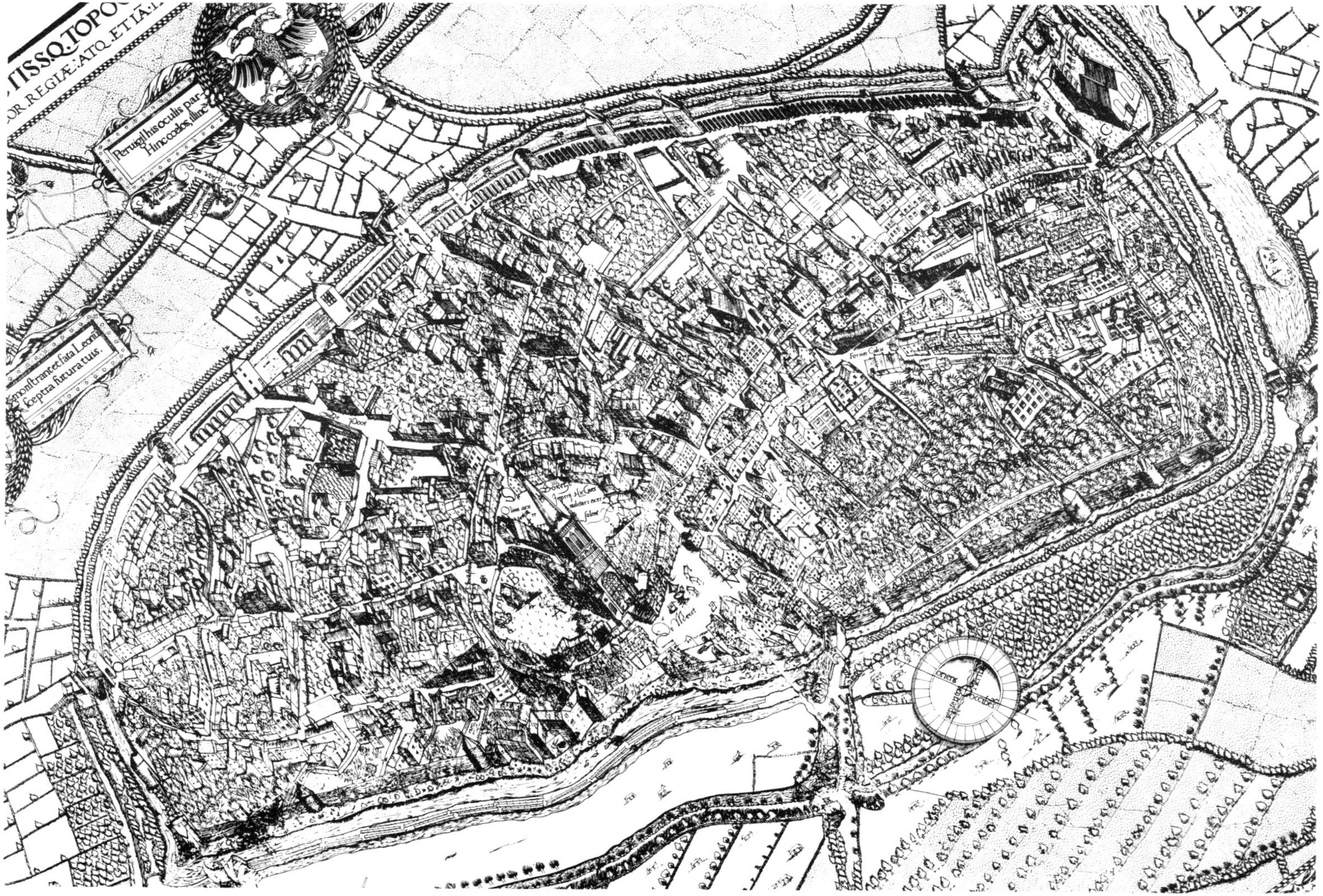

Fig. 6.4 Map of Duisburg in 1566 by Johann Corputius.

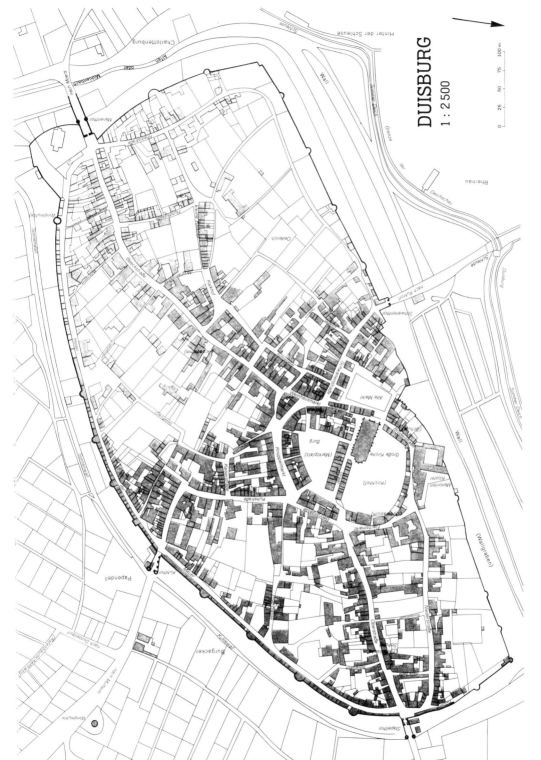

Fig. 6.5 First town census map of Duisburg (1823 to 1824).

6.3). The finds were kept in the local grammar school. In the next decade, Moritz Wilms, a teacher at that school, led numerous excavations in the vicinity of Duisburg on behalf of the local academic society. He published the results of his work in *Bonner Jahrbücher* 1872 (Wilms 1872). In 1881 the headmaster of this school, a professional archaeologist and a member of the board of the Römisch-Germanisches Zentralmuseum in Mainz published a paper entitled "Duisburger Altertümer" (Duisburg's antiquities), the first complete inventory (and the latest until now) of the archaeological finds from the Duisburg area (Genthe 1881).

At the beginning of the 1890s the engineer Anton Bonnet excavated more than 120 burial mounds of the late Bronze to early Iron Age in Duisburg. These were the first scientific excavations in Duisburg. In 1896 he offered the numerous finds from his excavations and his notebooks to the newly-founded Museum Society in Duisburg. This Society cared for the collection of historical and archaeological remains of international, regional and local provenance. The collections of the Society, including finds from the grammar school, were exhibited in the attic of the new town-hall, built from 1897 to 1902 on the castle hill on top of the former medieval royal palace. A guide to these collections was published in 1902 (Averdunk 1902). In 1913 the Society donated its collections to the city of Duisburg. Thereafter the new owner promised to build a new museum. This happened only in 1990 with 90% financial support from the federal government and the state of North-Rhine Westphalia (NRW). In the meantime these collections – which form the basis of the present-day Kultur- und Stadthistorisches Museum were kept in various buildings. From 1927 the directors of this museum have always been prehistoric specialists in archaeology.

Inspite of all the changes the structure of the Old Town of Duisburg survived until the Second World War. Even at the end of the war about 80% of the medieval town wall, the old pattern of the streets and properties including the medieval royal palace area were still intact (Milz 1982, 149–163; 1985). The years 1950 to 1970 saw a period of almost constant rebuilding in Duisburg, regardless of the existing historic substance of the town. More than 50% of the

medieval town-wall was dismantled and most of the pre-wartime buildings disappeared (Fig. 6.6; Pfotenhauer & Müller 1992). New roads were built to facilitate the modern traffic flow (Fig. 6.7). Only one vernacular building of late medieval origin survived. The peak of this attitude was the destruction of a part of the town-wall between 1966 to 1968 in order to rebuild it again (Fig. 6.8).

At that time the local museum archaeologists tried at least to record parts of the disappearing town-wall and to run rescue excavations. This was done by Prof. Fritz Tischler, and was not at all appreciated by the administration. This initiative marks the beginning of urban archaeology in Duisburg (Binding & Binding 1969, 35–66).

By about 1970 the monuments of Duisburg's past were mainly reduced to those hidden underground. But even these remains have not survived untouched. Severe destruction of the archaeological record has been caused by the removal of old buildings and the construction of underground garages, supply mains, roads etc. This has contributed to the generally predominant but erroneous impression of Duisburg as an industrial centre of the 19th to the 20th century: faceless and without any relevant history of its own. Perhaps this impression has even been intended. As a consequence everything seems to be freely disposable in the interest of economic growth as the best guarantee for an even better future. This attitude has been advantageous for the industries as long as they boomed.

At the end of the 1970s the decline in local heavy industries began and the euphoria of an ever-growing economy came to a standstill. New, not so materialistic values were needed. A new image seemed to be helpful to attract more diversified industries, since structural change has become the new slogan. Almost at the same time large scale developments, mainly financed by federal funds and the State of NRW, began to threaten the surviving parts of the town-wall and the remaining archaeological evidence for Duisburg. New monument legislation, a growning interest in the city's past and substantial financial support from the government (90% to 100%) have provided an opportunity for an interdisciplinary programme of rescue excavations in the course of these building activities, for urban archaeology in general and for better protection and conservation of historic and archaeological monuments. All this had become obligatory through the new monument protection legislation of 1980, though at that time nobody was really aware of the potential and consequences of that law.

Excavations since 1980

Since 1980 the construction of an underground railway in the inner city has caused the shifting of main gas and water supplies, sewers and cable lines. This was the beginning for large scale rescue excavations and urban archaeology on a more and more systematic basis in Duisburg. It was the expressed will of the City Council's Cultural Affairs Committee that the museum archaeologists should be granted access to the construction sites in order to expose, document and rescue the archaeological evidence of Duisburg's past and to make this available for academic research and public view.

From the beginnings of the urban excavations in Duisburg the public has taken an active interest stimulated by a continuous information policy provided by the museum archaeologist. The local, regional and occasionally even the international press, radio and television have reported on the Duisburg excavations. Tens of thousands have been reached by lectures, guided tours, general publications, permanent and special exhibitions in local museum and other local institutions, and loan exhibitions to German and European towns (Duisburg 1983; Krause 1983a; 1986; 1988; 1990b–d; Naumann 1988), for instance, in the former Soviet Union, Finland, Hungary and in Great Britain. The archaeological site of the *Alter Markt* has been since transformed into a small open-air museum (Krause/Untermann 1990).

In the Summer of 1980 a line of construction crossed the castle hill and the *Alter Markt*. It revealed a wall of the medieval palace on the slope of the

Fig. 6.6 Demolition of the town-wall at the Marienkirche (Church of St Mary) in 1967.

Fig. 6.7 Archaeological sites (excavated or monitored during destruction) in the Old Town up to 1991.

1: Modern town-hall; medieval royal palace. **9**: Castle hill; moat of the royal palace. **12**: *Marienkirche* (Church of St Mary); precinct of the Knights of St John and earlier remains. **13**: Franciscan friary. **15**: *Alter Markt* (Old Market Place).**16**: Schwanenstraße, excavation in the area of the department store "C&A". **17**: Innenhafen, excavation adjacent to the inner harbour basin. **28**: Poststraße, court of the royal castle. **31**: Universitätsstraße; Gothic stone building. **37**: *Alter Markt*, Pfeffergasse. **38**: Untermauerstraße; excavation in the area of the department store "Galeria". **44**: Town-wall: Friedrich-Wilhelm-Platz to Josef-Kiefer-Straße; remains of the medieval town-wall; Mühlenturm (mill tower). **47**: Town-wall: Marientorstraße to Schwanentor; noble estate (12th/13th century): western corner tower; town-wall. **48**: Town-wall: Schwanentor to Johannes-Corputius-Platz; medieval town wall; Romanesque house; large latrine building of the Friars; Aachener Turm (Aachen tower). **51** and **52**: Klosterstraße; remains of the monastery of the 3rd order of the Franciscans from the later 13th century and earlier settlement. **57**: Schwanenstraße; excavation of the underground railway tunnel. **65**: Niederstraße, block D. **68**: Steinsche Gasse; excavation in the area of the department store "Galeria": two noble estates (12th/13th century); remains of medieval to modern settlement.

Fig. 6.8 Medieval town-wall, rebuilt in 1968.

tions, is chairman of a regional archaeological society, founded in 1921, with some 120 members of which about a dozen have been actively trained and engaged in archaeological fieldwork, rescue excavation and post-excavation work. The support of these volunteers was essential to obtain rapid results in the investigation of the construction line. Another important factor should not be forgotten: the technical director of the city's large power and water supply company, charged with the construction work, was chairman of the Duisburg Archaeological Society for many years and supported the investigations in 1980 and later.

Equally supportive were Prof. Walter Janssen and his successors from the Rheinisches Landesmuseum, later Rheinisches Amt für Bodendenkmalpflege in Bonn, the State institution in the Rhineland which controls archaeological field and post-excavation work in the region and distributes State funds for these investigations.

At that time there existed a plan to build an underground garage under the *Alter Markt* (Fig. 6.7, no. 15). This was one more reason to begin regular excavations there in 1981. The aim was to investigate the market stratigraphy in smaller trenches to get an overall view of the formation and the potential of the site, later to excavate larger market areas and the medieval market hall complex which originated in the late 13th century (Figs. 6.9–6.11). These excavations took place on a continuous basis until 1990. Archaeological deposits of more than 5 metres thickness were found under the *Alter Markt*. They provide a detailed stratigraphy that ranges from the 5th century AD, the early Frankish settlement, to the present (Fig. 6.12). Layers from the early to post-medieval times were excavated with equal interest and accuracy (Krause 1983b, 29–77; 1992a, 9–21, 64–65; 1992b, 93–105). Numerous features such as pavements, layers containing foot prints and cart tracks were revealed (Fig. 6.13), along with the remains of market stalls, of craftmen's activities and the foundations of the market hall itself (Untermann 1992a).

Already by 1980 it was clear that the market layers were quite well preserved. The underground is formed by the waterlogged silt of a former bed of the Rhine. Organic and other finds are abundant (Krause

castle hill and stratification in the market area which dates back to the early days of Duisburg, at least to the 9th century, the time of the Viking attack (883 AD) and early settlement (Fig. 6.9; Krause 1983a, 20–29; Krause 1983b, 29–77). This caused a sensation. Early Duisburg, long sought after, had not been expected here, though it was quite reasonable to suppose that it lay in the centre of the Old Town next to the castle hill and the former Rhine. On the basis of the first historic mention of Duisburg relating to the Viking invasion of 883/4 the city celebrated its 1100th anniversary in 1983. This discovery came just at the right time, therefore (Krause 1983b).

There are some other logistical factors worth considering here: the local museum with limited funds for excavations, run by three archaeologists, assisted by a technician and a conservator; an excellent medieval historian as director of the important local archives. The writer, director of the excava-

1983b, 29–34). So it was very obvious that the archaeologists alone would not be able to extract the maximum results out of that excavation. An interdisciplinary approach had to be chosen including the history, architecture, geology, historic geography, dendrochronology, botany, zoology, technology and so on. This was and has been until now quite difficult to achieve. Mainly in response for large scale construction developments, but also with the aim of answering relevant historical and archaeological questions, many excavations and field observations have been conducted in other parts of Old Duisburg. This has been possible only through close cooperation with various municipal departments and construction companies (Figs. 6.7; 6.9; Krause 1992a; Müller 1992). Funds for these excavations have to be provided year by year from the City and the State of NRW. Permanent staff, besides the writer, were not granted by the municipality. On the contrary, staff numbers were reduced in spite of rapidly growing archaeological threat, caused by large-scale development. More than 1,400 different persons have been engaged in the Duisburg excavations between 1980 and 1992. Institutions and specialists in various fields, and many students from Germany and other countries were invited to take an active part in the excavations and post-excavation work. A number of University dissertations and papers have resulted from this participation.

Volunteers from the local Archaeological Society have always played a very important role and at least partially compensated for the lack of permanent staff. This illustrates the weakness of the project. It has depended almost completely on the dedication and motivating power of the project director, and despite the unwillingness of the Duisburg and State authorities to fund and encourage these investigations in the long term. It is unfortunate that the Duisburg authorities wish only to make the maximum profit out of the project for the new image of their city without risking permanent costs, while also denying the scientific value of that work. Unfortunately most of the Council members have never been interested in the protection and investigation of Duisburg's cultural heritage as a valid policy in its own right.

At this stage it is worth reviewing the most significant results of the Duisburg excavations to date.

Results of the excavations in Duisburg

Earliest settlement

The first known settlement evidence in the Old Town of Duisburg belongs to the 4th and 3rd centuries BC. It consists mainly of pottery (Krause 1992a, 44) from Iron Age settlements at the northern and southern ends of the town (Figs. 6.7, nos. 44, 65).

Roman settlement

A continuous occupation, as well indicated in the pollen diagramm from the *Alter Markt*, begins in the second quarter of the 1st century AD (Knörzer & Meurers-Balke 1992, 177–192). The finds hint to a Roman settlement for the control of the important road and water junction. The centre is already on the castle hill. A column fragment of limestone, marble and brick, along with mortar pieces were found at the foot of the castle hill in a Frankish layer of the 7th century (Krause 1992b, 94–105 with overall plan on p. 95).

Frankish settlement

Frankish finds of the 5th to 8th centuries have been excavated in the last years in the same area as Roman finds (Krause 1992b). The centre of Frankish Duisburg is certainly on the castle hill, presumably the site of a Merowingian royal court, and in its surroundings.

The Frankish settlement finds are of outstanding importance, because there exists so little evidence from that time besides burials. For the first time the early Frankish colonisation can be identified and dated in the Rhineland. It falls in the time of the beech pollen climax that marks the recovery of the forests after the collapse of the Roman occupation of the Rhineland (Figs. 6.15–16; Berke 1992; Knörzer/Meurers-Balke 1992, 195–197). Settlers from outside the Roman world with their specific lifestyle, so different from the Roman one, occupied the strategic site of Duisburg by the first half of the 5th century (Krause 1992b).

Carolingian and Ottonian Duisburg

In the 9th and 10th centuries Duisburg was already

Fig. 6.9 "Alter Markt", Schwanenstraße and surroundings. Overall plan of excavations from 1980 to 1990 with earlier evidence (key numbers see Fig. 6.7).

Fig. 6.10 Centre of medieval Duisburg with the Salvatorkirche (Church of Our Saviour), town-hall, market place with market hall (N), Minoritenkloster (Franciscan friary) and Schwanentor (town-gate). Detail from the Corputius map 1566 AD.

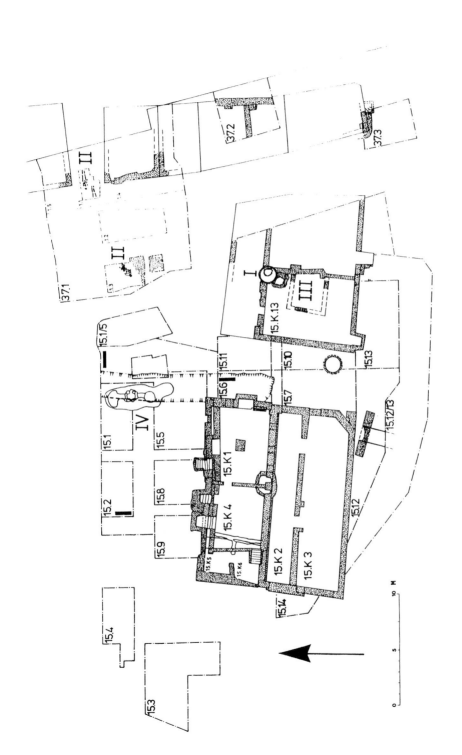

Fig. 6.11 "Alter Markt" (Old Market Place). Overall plan of excavated areas (15.1 to 15.14) with the foundations of the market hall and the building east of the market hall.

K 1 to K 6:	Cellars of the market hall complex.	I: Well of the 5th century.
37.2 and 37.3:	Remains of the medieval palace.	II: Carolingian skeletons.
		III: Cellar of previous building, 13th century.
		IV: Bell-casting pit.

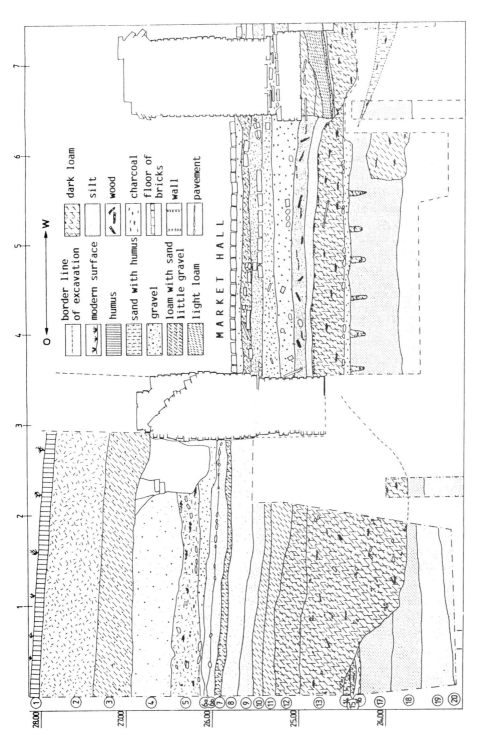

Fig. 6.12 Overall plan of the "Alter Markt" (Old Market Place) stratification (heights above sea-level).

1: Present-day to post-war period.
2: Destruction rubbish of Second World War.
3: Pre-war period to the 17th century.

4 and 5: Medieval market, 2nd half of the 13th century.
6 to 12: Market layers, 13th to 10th century.

13 to 16: Market layers, 10th to 9th century.
17 to 19: River bank, 8th to 5th century.

6.9, no. 1) and in 1990 remains of the earliest royal palace presumably from the beginning of the 10th century were investigated between the town-hall and market place. It is obvious that the medieval palace, the Church of Our Saviour next to it, as well as the modern town-hall, lie directly on the former riverside of the early Roman Rhine (Figs. 6.2–3; 6.9; Gerlach 1992a, 70–75) which still determines the townscape of modern Duisburg.

Fig. 6.13 Frozen moment of a busy market day in Duisburg, showing footprints of men and animals, tracks of carts and carriages, 2nd half of the 13th century.

an important trade centre. Parts of that settlement, "the oppidum diusburh", have been excavated in many parts of the later town near the Rhine waterfront. By about 1000 AD the first large-scale fortification was built between the Ruhr and Dickelsbach, consisting of a wall and a moat (Figs. 6.3; 6.17; Krause 1993).

The medieval royal palace (Fig. 6.7, no. 9; Binding & Binding 1969, 35–66; Berghaus 1983.)
The new excavations began in 1980 (Krause 1983b, 24–29) with the discovery of the outer wall of the palace precinct dating to the 12th and 13th centuries. Completely surprising was the discovery of a fortified bailey of the castle going back to the 10th century at the foot of the castle hill above the *Alter Markt* site (Figs. 6.7, no. 37; 9, no. 37). The approach from the Rhine was formed by a roadway with a stone-built bridge crossing the moat (Fig. 6.11, no. 15.12/ 13). In 1989 the south front of a palace building from the 12th century was found during the paving of a passage underneath the town-hall (Figs. 6.7, no. 1;

Noble estates built of stone in the 12th and 13th centuries
Five estates of noblemen that may go back to the 10th and 11th centuries have been investigated in the last 12 years. They lay around the royal castle (Krause, Müller & Müller 1994a). At least two of them were later incorporated within the fortifications (Fig. 6.7, nos. 12, 17, 47, 68).

The precinct of the Knights of St John, the friary of the Franciscans and the monastery of the 3rd order of the Franciscans
The Knights of St. John erected their first church, hospital and other domestic buildings in Germany in a moated noble estate. The church, consecrated in 1150, was partly excavated, and remains of buildings belonging to the earlier moated estate and the moat itself were found (Fig. 6.7, no. 12; Krause 1992a, 26–27).

Investigations on the site of the friary of the Franciscans uncovered building remains of the 2nd half of the 13th century and later ones, and the large latrine building of the friars from the 14th century, situated in front of the town-wall (Figs. 6.7, nos. 13, 48; 6.9; Müller 1992).

The monastery of the 3rd order of the Franciscans from the later 13th century was recorded in small service trenches in the modern Klosterstraße (Fig. 6.7, nos. 51–52). Several hitherto unknown building phases and a predecessor from the 12th/13th century, presumably another noble estate, could be established (Krause, Müller & Müller 1994b).

Early stone-built private houses
Especially remarkable is the dense first phase of private stone-built houses on both sides and above the Schwanenstraße dating to the 12th and 13th cen-

turies, which were investigated during the building of the department store "C & A" and the construction of the underground railway (Figs. 6.7, nos. 16, 57; 6.9; Untermann 1985; 1992b). Underneath, remains of earlier wooden and wattle and daub houses were found that date back to the 9th century. Other early stone buildings were located at the sides of the Niederstraße in the direction of the town-wall (Fig. 6.14, no. 1). They are important testimonies of early stonebuilding in the Rhineland and have changed our conception of the town in the 12th and 13th centuries completely. It became evident that the pattern of the Old Town, destroyed after the Second World War, has its roots at this time or even earlier (Figs. 6.4–5; 6.9).

Commercial buildings on the waterfront
Quite different are the stone buildings on the waterfront which date to the 12th and 13th centuries, which were uncovered in the winter of 1989 below the Niederstraße (Fig. 6.14). They are long extended warehouses at street level with thin foundations of stone or brick, bordering each other with massive facades on the Rhine. These warehouses and others, using the town-wall as a retaining wall, disappeared at the end of the 15th century or even earlier when the Rhine trade came to an end. A comparable situation is found at the south-western side of the Rhine waterfront.

The town-wall as an important characteristic of the medieval town
The investigation of the fortification in the eastern "Innenhafen" area (Rhinefront) and Springwall (Ruhrfront) with its moats and walls (Figs. 6.14; 6.17) led to surprising results. Underneath the *Koblenzer Turm*, not only the foundations of at least one earlier tower were found, but the corner of an earlier fortification from the 12th century appeared (Müller 1992, 467–476). This wall of tufa stone, which can be dated historically to about 1120, is partially preserved to a height of more than 5 metres. Its foundations are only 40–50 cms deep. This caused unstability, so that in the second half of the 13th century deeper foundations had to be dug and pillars were erected to support the wall. The reason for this constructional flaw became obvious only in the last

months: the first stone wall stands on an earlier wall made from the unstable natural clay. This wall, and the large moat in front of it, date to about 1000 AD (Krause 1993).

Geological and ecological investigations
The numerous excavations have been used for intensive geological investigations (Gerlach 1992a). Shifting river-courses of the Rhine and Ruhr (Figs. 6.2–3), partially well dated by archaeological evidence, had to be recorded exactly so that their impact on human living conditions could be studied.

Data for the historic ecology enable us to determine the scale of environmental pollution and the quality of the drinking water. The first results from the market place for the last 1500 years are already available (Gerlach, Radtke & Sauer 1992). Other interesting data have been gathered to determine ground and river-water levels for medieval and later Duisburg (Gerlach 1992b).

Finds from the urban excavations
The excavations have furnished an extremely rich quantity of objects: all currently being conserved and documented by the Museum's archaeological staff. They span the last 1500 years without major gaps.

Plant and animal remains
The recovery of plant remains has instigated intensive botanical investigations that still go on (Knörzer & Meurers-Balke 1992; Knörzer 1992). Human nutrition, agriculture and gardening as well as the composition of the natural environment and their changes have been studied intensely. With the same attention bone and fish remains, insects etc. have been collected and partially analysed. Already by the 9th century hunting played no role at all in the region. In contrast to the 5th century, domesticated animals were the main source of meat (Berke 1992; Nobis & Ninov 1992). Some of the fish come from the North Sea and even the Atlantic Ocean (Heinrich 1992). Young turkey was present on the menu in Duisburg in about 1550 (Reichstein 1992).

Material culture
Objects produced and utilized by people, made of

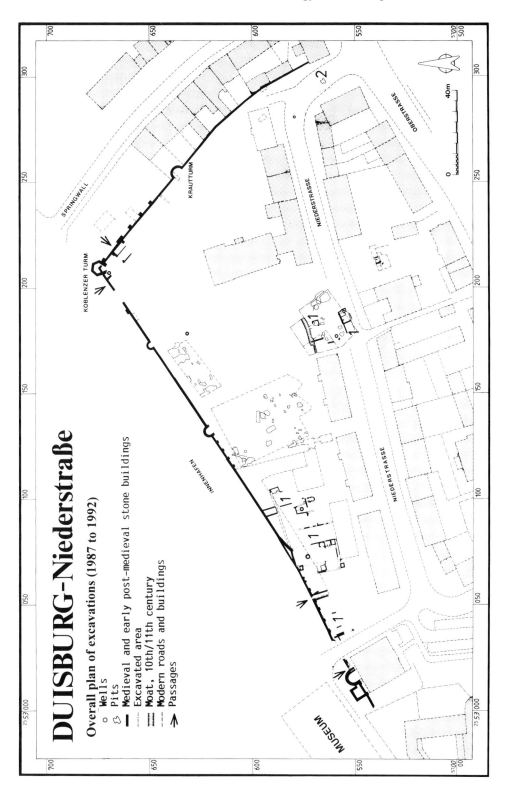

Fig. 6.14 Niederstraße. Overall plan of excavations from 1987 to 1991. 1: Commercial buildings, 12th to 14th century. 2: Waster heaps of a faience ceramic manufactory, 2nd half of the 18th century.

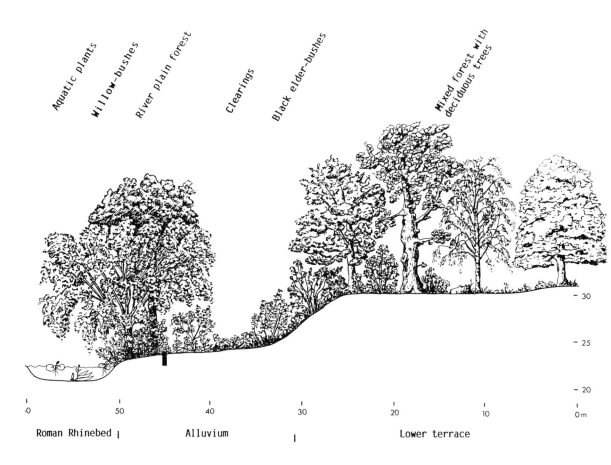

Aquatic plants   Willow-bushes   River plain forest   Clearings   Black elder-bushes   Mixed forest with deciduous trees

- 30

- 25

- 20

,0   50   40   30   20   10   0 m

Roman Rhinebed | Alluvium   Lower terrace

Fig. 6.15 Development of local vegetation before the 5th century AD.

various materials, represent numerous spheres of life. They demonstrate the general level of civilization, the exchange of goods and the change of human needs and taste in the locality over more than 1500 years (Krause 1983b; 1986; 1988; 1992a; 1992b). The pottery represents a good example (Fig. 6.18). The assistance of specialists in the investigation of this material is essential.

Rhenish pottery had been for centuries one of the most important traded goods in northern Europe. The Duisburg excavations have helped to establish a firm chronology for these wares and their context. It is a valuable basis on which to solve various cultural-historical questions in the area of its distribution (Gaimster 1992a; 1992b; Löw 1992).

Summary

Since 1980 the excavations in the Old Town of Duisburg have developed into a large scale research project. Excavations have revealed a stratigraphy that goes back to Antiquity and may soon reach the late Iron Age without a gap. The project is exemplary, not only in the region, for the study of human life in its natural setting.

In spite of numerous problems, insecure financial resources, lack of permanent staff etc., continuous and systematic work has been done by the Museum. The growing public interest has led to a new consciousness of the community's past. According to the wishes of the City Council the *Alter Markt* site, with the remains of the market hall, was transformed

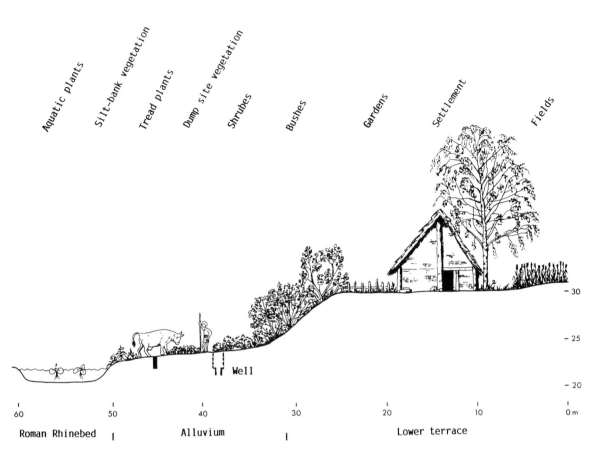

Aquatic plants

Silt-bank vegetation

Tread plants

Dump site vegetation

Shrubes

Bushes

Gardens

Settlement

Fields

Well

— 30

— 25

— 20

| 60 | 50 | 40 | 30 | 20 | 10 | 0 m |

Roman Rhinebed   Alluvium   Lower terrace

Fig. 6.16 Development of local vegetation, 5th century AD.

into a small open-air museum (Fig. 6.19). The extant parts of the medieval town-wall have been cleared, partially excavated, conserved and restored. These activities are still in progress under the supervision of the writer, and are incorporated in future town planning policy (Figs. 6.20–6.21). At the same time in 1990 a new museum opened its doors, one which has been especially designated to the history and archaeology of Duisburg.

When in September 1990 the annual archaeological congress of the Nordwestdeutscher Verband für Altertumskunde took place in the new Museum, the head of the civic cultural department stressed the importance of the urban excavations and promised the continuous support and expansion of these activities in the name of the City. Shortly afterwards

the author was awarded the emblem of honour of the Duisburg Civic Society for long-lasting and outstanding services to the City and citizens because of his work.

Despite these positive developments, at the same time the civic administration began to deal a number of heavy blows to the Museum's archaeological investigations.

The civic planning department has since attempted to gain control of all future excavations, neglecting existing laws and rules. A new, non-permanent unit has been established to clear away archaeological remains in order to develop plots owned by the municipality. The unit is part of the civic department of underground engineering, and will operate for two or three years. It was argued that the

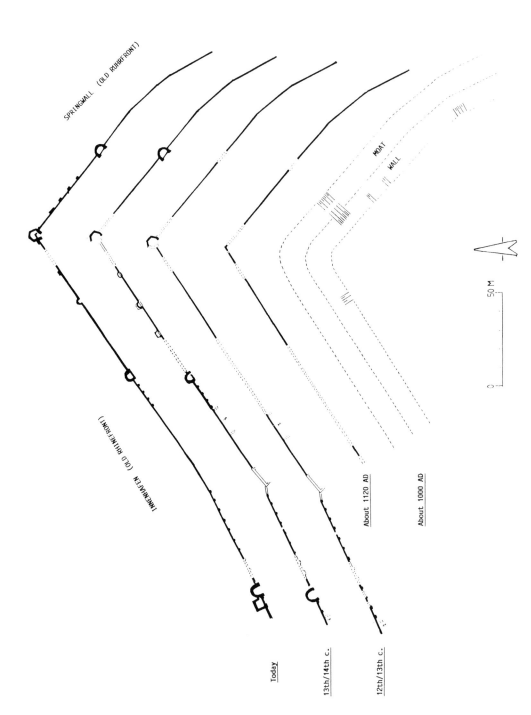

Fig. 6.17 Development of the medieval fortifications of Duisburg.

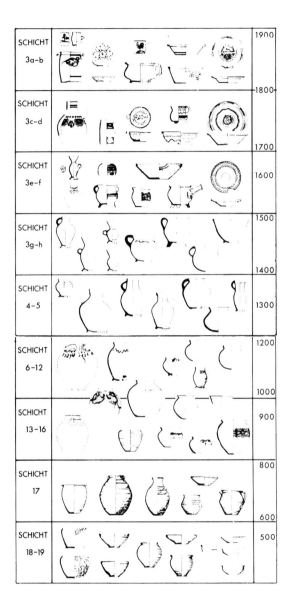

Fig. 6.18 Duisburg pottery sequence, 5th to 20th century, based on the "Alter Markt" layers. Layer 3: Pre-war period to 14th century. Layers 4 to 5: Medieval market, 2nd half of the 13th century. Layers 6 to 12: Market layers, 13th to 10th century. Layers 13 to 16: Market layers, 10th to 9th century. Layers 17 to 19: River-bank, 8th to 5th century.

urban excavations are much closer to that department than to the Museum. Before, the construction department had been repeatedly interrupted in their work by the Museum and State authorities because of the numerous unauthorized destructions of scheduled archaeological deposits in the City. The unit consists of an underground engineer as supervisor, a classical archaeologist as field director, three technicians, a palaeolithic specialist to care for the small finds "that are worth keeping in the Museum" and about 40 completely inexperienced, partially disabled people, payed by the labour exchange. The two archaeologists lack any qualification for their jobs and have, for instance, no experience of medieval or post-medieval pottery and architecture. That is the reason for their selection. Continuous interdisciplinary concept-orientated archaeological research will cease in Duisburg, though most of the institutions and scholars engaged in Duisburg have participated at their own cost.

Private developers are forced to charge profit-bound archaeological contractors for excavations that are much more expensive, because the Museum is no longer allowed to excavate. There exist extremely vague regulations for such work, introduced only recently. Some contractors do not own a single trowel, yard-stick or helmet when starting their work. They are not obliged to publish the results of these excavations, but own the copyright for publication.

At the same time the civic administration has begun to divide the Museum personnel, to descredit the Museum's archaeological work and to block its efficiency in order to make room for the above-mentioned unit and private contract archaeology.

The administration hopes to dry out the work of the Museum in the near future by denying adequate personnel and funding for excavations and post-excavation work. The author remains the only one in the Museum permanently employed and occupied with the urban excavations. He is treated in quite an oppressive and illegal way.

The reason is not because of higher costs of professional Museum archaeology. The new unit and "business archaeology" are much more expensive and ineffective. They lack experience, continuity and a research concept. But the civic administration wishes to minimize the importance of urban archaeology, to exclude the volunteers and the public from that work, to suppress the publication of results, all in the interest of undisturbed economic growth. It accepts the profound knowledge of the author but calls it unprofitable for the City. It has not allowed the results of the urban excavations to be presented in the new Museum that was at least partially built for this purpose. To date, however, the Museum has not been displaced: it is still involved in town planning and most of the construction projects in the City of Duisburg that lead to archaeological investigations. Private business archaeology has proved to be too expensive and to have only a weak legal basis.

The sadly permanent philosophy is: Duisburg is the city of steel and iron, once again and forever; history is irrelevant here prior to industrialization. Archaeology annoys and obstructs structural change, whatever that is.

A new monument, symbolizing Duisburg's past (and replacing it), was erected in the Autumn of 1992 at the modern (artificial) confluence of the Rhine and Ruhr (Fig. 6.22), a site declared as the "basis of Duisburg's urban history". This sculpture "of extraordinary artistic choice", called the "Rheinorange", a monumental red (glowing) iron block (25m in height), is "the symbol of the everlasting dominance of these industries", a "piece of the future", as much a "monument for Duisburg as it is the Statue of Liberty for New York, the Opera House for Sydney or Cologne Cathedral for Cologne", and so on (Fritsch 1992). That the inauguration of such a monument takes place at the outbreak of a new economic crisis for these industries is not surprising, nor is the banning of professional archaeological investigations and the view of our cultural heritage as a possible obstacle to unlimited economic development. This monument is no sign of "innovation" and "awakening" but a fetish and a diversion from the real problems of our day: here manifested in the wanton destruction of our unique historical resources, which should be cared for and preserved for future generations.

Postscript

Since the end of 1992 the situation concerning urban archaeology in Duisburg has continued to deteriorate. The treatment of Duisburg's archaeological heritage has led to an open conflict between the civic administration and the Civic Society of more than 11,000 members. The Society believes that Duisburg's archaeological heritage is in great danger and continuously sold dirt-cheap to the detriment of its citizens. It exhorts the head of the civic administration to follow existing monument legislation and not to obstruct the Museum's archaeological activities any longer. The Society refers to the State constitution of NRW which protects the archaeological heritage as the property of society as a whole. According to the constitution and monument legislation of NRW the City of Duisburg is jointly responsible for its protection and has no right to overrule these public interests.

The inadequate handling of Duisburg's archaeological heritage by the civic administration has caused the withdrawal of State funding for archaeological activities in Duisburg since 1993. In the end this is another blow against the Museum, and has been followed by a complete cut in the City's funding for 1994 in favour of developer resources for excavation and the non-permanent unit. This may eventually cause the loss of Duisburgs' archaeological heritage, rescued and documented through excavation since 1980. Already since the beginning of the project the administration has been unwilling to pay for post-excavation work so that there is still an enormous backlog. Even the curation of the archaeological material and documentation of the urban excavations since 1980 can not be guaranteed by the single remaining archaeologist. He is to be separated from the Museum that houses all the facilities for his work or even forced to give up his job he has held since 1971 as a curator of the archaeological collections of the City. To obtain the necessary permission for various archaeological excavations caused by the City's activities, the civic administration still names the author without consultation as field director and does not procure the necessary personnel and funding demanded in the permits. This behaviour risks both endangering vital projects for Duisburg's urban development by the controlling State institutions and the destruction of further archaeological deposits.

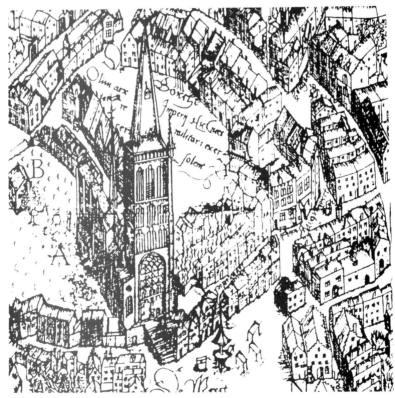

Fig 6.19 The archaeological zone "Alter Markt" in 1991; below the same site with market place, market hall and church shown on the town map of 1566 by Johann Corputius.

Fig. 6.20 Demolition of a building incorporating the town-wall at the Innenhafen and, in front, the construction of the Kultur- und Stadthistorisches Museum in 1989.

Fig. 6.21 View of restored town-wall from the new Museum. In front, town model of the Corputius map.

Fig. 6.22 The "Rheinorange" monument.

The non-permanent, well-funded unit under the control of the civic planning department has proved to be even less qualified than expected. Since Summer 1992 they have been excavating the largest and only one remaining, nearly-intact city quarter (about 8,000 qm). It is the most important archaeological site in Duisburg which dates from the early Iron Age and shows an uninterrupted sequence from Merowingian times. This was established by a watching-brief conducted by the Museum shortly before as main basis of the excavation licence. The field director denies the importance of the site and has been excavating so as not to find anything of importance which obstructs the projected underground garage and cellars. The unit operates completely free of the Museum's archaeological activities, standards and accumulated knowledge in that field. This seems to be the best recommendation to get a permanent job and to ultimately take over the Museum's archaeological activities. The work of private contractors in Duisburg generally follows the same lines. Often a builder hires an archaeologist regardless of

specialization and experience, a technician and some workmen to make quick money. This is completely opposed to the code of conduct and the code of approved practice for the regulation of contractual arrangements in field archaeology of the Institute of Field Archaeologists in Britain, which refer to proper and honest archaeological practice.

The work of the unit and the use of private contractors reflect the low standard of Rhenish archaeology in general. The State authorities which do most of the archaeological work, and licence and control all other archaeological activities, lack a general working concept and experience in urban archaeology which has only been practiced on a permanent basis in Duisburg. Relations of that institution to colleagues in private companies and units seem sometimes too friendly, so that nearly any permission for archaeological excavation is granted. Too often its members act by virtue of their office and not on the basis of expert-knowledge, sometimes even denying accepted values and ethics for archaeologists. For an onlooker they seem not always to be aware of their responsibilities.

The state of archaeological heritage management in Duisburg is deplorable and an example of the difficulties still only rarely encountered in German urban archaeology. But it is evident that a solution has to be found. The outcome is still quite uncertain. The same is due in regard to the personal fate of the author, who falls between all stools. The civic administration treats him as a traitor of Duisburg's interests. He feels committed to honest archaeological practice which is indispensable for an academic discipline and in the handling of the archaeological heritage. It must follow this course and loses its right to exist when instrumented for other purposes.

Acknowledgements

The author wishes to thank Dr David Gaimster for collaborating on the English translation of this essay.

Editorial note
As of June 1994 the author has been forced to give up his position as director of excavations in Duisburg which he has held since 1971. He continues in the post as Deputy Director of the Kultur Stadthistorisches Museum, Duisburg.

References

Averdunk, H. 1902. *Führer durch die Sammlung des Duisburger Altertumsvereins*, Duisburg.

Bechert, T. 1987. Moers-Asberg und Duisburg-Rheinhausen. In: H.G. Horn (ed.) *Die Römer in Nordrhein-Westfalen*, Stuttgart, 559–568.

Berghaus, P. 1983. Duisburger Münzen. In: Duisburg 1983, 89–113.

Berke, H. 1992. Tiernutzung in Duisburg im frühen Mittelalter. In: *Duisburger Forschungen* 38, 207–222.

Binding, G. & Binding, E. 1969. Archäologisch-historische Untersuchungen zur Frühgeschichte Duisburgs. In: *Duisburger Forschungen*, Beiheft 12.

Duisburg 1983. *Duisburg im Mittelalter*. Begleitschrift zur Ausstellung, Stadtarchiv und Niederrheinisches Museum der Stadt Duisburg (ed.), Duisburg.

Duisburg 1990. *Duisburg und der untere Niederrhein*. Führer zu archäologischen Denkmälern in Deutschland 21, Stuttgart.

Fritsch, L. 1992. *Rheinorange*. Begleitschrift zur gleichnamigen Ausstellung des Wilhelm Lehmbruck-Museums, Duisburg.

Gaimster, D.R.M. 1992a. *Pottery supply and demand in the Lower Rhineland c. 1400–1800: An archaeological study of ceramic production, distribution and use in the city of Duisburg and its hinterland*. Unpublished Ph.D. dissertation, London University.

Gaimster, D.R.M. 1992b. Frühneuzeitliche Keramik am Niederrhein. Ein archäologischer Überblick. In: *Duisburger Forschungen* 38, 330–353.

Genthe, W. 1881. Duisburger Altertümer. Ein Beitrag zur Geschichte der Stadt Duisburg und zur prähistorischen Karte Deutschlands. *Beigabe zum Programm des Gymnasiums Duisburg* Nr. 377.

Gerlach, R. 1992a. Die Entwicklung der naturräumlichen historischen Topographie rund um den Alten Markt. In: *Duisburger Forschungen* 38, 66–92.

Gerlach, R. 1992b. Rheinwasser, Grundwasser, Trink- und Abwasser in der Duisburger Altstadt seit dem Frühmittelalter. In: H. Schuhmacher & B. Thiesmeier (ed.), *Urbane Gewässer*, Essen, 476–491.

Gerlach, R., Radtke, U. & Sauer, K.-H. 1992. Historische Bodenbelastungen in Duisburg. In: *Duisburger Forschungen* 38, 365–379.

Heinrich, D. 1992. Fischknochen aus mittelalterlichen Siedlungsabfällen in Duisburg. In: *Duisburger Forschungen* 38, 295–305.

Knörzer, K.-H. 1992. Vorbericht über paläo-ethnobotanische Untersuchungen in Duisburg. In: *Duisburger Forschungen* 38, 223–236.

Knörzer, K.-H. & Meurers-Balke, J. 1992. Pflanzenfunde aus dem 5. nachchristlichen Jahrhundert in Duisburg. In: *Duisburger Forschungen* 38, 169–206.

Krause, G. 1983a. Zu den Anfängen Duisburgs. In: *Duisburg und die Wikinger*. Begleitschrift zur gleichnamigen Ausstellung, Niederrheinisches Museum der Stadt Duisburg, Duisburg, 15–29.

Krause, G. 1983b. Archäologische Zeugnisse zum mittelalterlichen Duisburg. In: Duisburg 1983, 23–77.

Krause, G. 1986. Übersicht über die mittelalterliche Keramik am Unteren Niederrhein (ca. 800–1500) nach den Funden aus Duisburg. In: *Volkstümliche Keramik vom Niederrhein, Töpferware des 8. bis 20. Jahrhunderts*, Duisburg, 7–28.

Krause, G. 1988. Keramikproduktion am Niederrhein. Zur Duisburger Abfolge vom 5.-14. Jahrhundert. In: Naumann 1988, 37–53.

Krause, G. 1990a. Zur Geschichte der archäologischen Forschung in Duisburg. In: Duisburg 1990, 24–29.

Krause, G. 1990b. Stadtarchäologie in Duisburg. In:

Archäologie in Nordrhein-Westfalen. Geschichte im Herzen Europas, Mainz 1990, 294–303.

Krause, G. 1990c. [Catalogue numbers] 343, 345–351, 362–364, 367, 369, 371–372, 381, 383. In: *Vergessene Zeiten. Mittelalter im Ruhrgebiet*, Vol. 1, Essen.

Krause, G. 1990d. Stadtarchäologie in Duisburg. In: *Vergessene Zeiten. Mittelalter im Ruhrgebiet*, Vol. 2, Essen, 284–289.

Krause, G. 1992a. Stadtarchäologie in Duisburg. In: *Duisburger Forschungen* 38, 1–65.

Krause, G. 1992b. Archäologische Zeugnisse zum ältesten Duisburg. In: *Duisburger Forschungen* 38, 93–168.

Krause, G. 1993. Archäologisch-bauhistorische Beobachtungen zur frühen Duisburger Stadtbefestigung. In: *Archäologie des Mittelalters und Bauforschung im Hanseraum*, Eine Festschrift für Günter Fehring, Rostock, 193–200.

Krause, G., Müller, J. & Müller, P. 1994a. Zwei mittelalterliche Adelshöfe in der Duisburger Altstadt. In: *Bonner Jahrbücher* (forthcoming).

Krause, G., Müller, J. & Müller, P. 1994b. Das Kloster Peterstal in der Duisburger Altstadt. In: *Bonner Jahrbücher* (forthcoming).

Krause, G. & Untermann, M. Der Alte Markt mit der archäologischen Zone Alter Markt. In: Duisburg 1990, 171–177.

Kunow, J. 1987. Die Militärgeschichte Niedergermaniens. In: H.G. Horn (ed.), *Die Römer in Nordrhein-Westfalen*, Stuttgart, 27–109.

Löw, L. 1992. "Bunzlauer" Keramik aus Duisburger Bodenfunden. In: *Duisburger Forschungen* 38, 354–364.

Milz, J. 1982. Untersuchungen zur mittelalterlichen Stadtmauer von Duisburg. Mit einem Beitrag von Günter Krause. In: *Quellenschriften zur westdeutschen Vor- und Frühgeschichte* 10, 135–171.

Milz, J. 1985. *Rheinischer Städteatlas*, 2nd edition, Lieferung IV, Nr. 21, (bearbeitet von J. Milz), Duisburg.

Müller, J. 1992. Zur Baugeschichte der Duisburger Stadtmauer am Innenhafen und am Springwall. In: *Duisburger Forschungen* 38, 463–519.

Naumann, J. (ed.) 1988. *Keramik vom Niederrhein. Die Irdenware der Düppen- und Pottbäcker zwischen Köln und Kleve*, Köln.

Nobis, G. & Ninov, L. 1992. Zur Haustierwelt des Mittelalters. Nach Studien an Tierresten aus der Altstadt von Duisburg. In: *Duisburger Forschungen* 38, 237–294.

Pfotenhauer, A. & Müller, J. 1992. Die Duisburger Stadtmauer – rekonstruierte Geschichte als Denkmal der Gegenwart. In: *Duisburger Forschungen* 38, 520–537.

Rau, R. 1969. Regino von Prüm, Chronica. In: R. Rau (ed.), *Quellen zur karolingischen Reichsgeschichte* III, 2nd edition, 179–319.

Reichstein, H. 1992. Vogelknochen aus mittelalterlichen Siedlungsabfällen in Duisburg. In: *Duisburger Forschungen* 38, 306–315.

Roden, G. von 1970. Geschichte der Stadt Duisburg 1. Duisburg.

Scheller, H. 1957. Der Rhein bei Duisburg im Mittelalter. In: *Duisburger Forschungen* 1, 45–86.

Untermann, M. 1985. Neufunde romanischer Häuser in Duisburg. In: *Hausbau im Mittelalter II*, Jahrbuch für Hausforschung, Sonderband, 127–137.

Untermann, M. 1992a. Der Baukomplex der Markthalle am "Alten Markt" in Duisburg. In: *Duisburger Forschungen* 38, 394–450.

Untermann, M. 1992b. Das Steinhaus auf dem ehemaligen Grundstück Oberoederich 18 (jetzt Kaufhaus C&A) in Duisburg. In: *Duisburger Forschungen* 38, 451–462.

Wilms, M. 1872. Alterthümer der Umgegend von Duisburg. In: *Bonner Jahrbücher* 52, 1–38.

7. Archaeology and the Museum of National Antiquities, Stockholm

Hans A. Lidén

Introduction

The Museum of National Antiquities is a part of the State administration together with the Central Board of National Antiquities. It is also the central museum in Sweden responsible for archaeological matters. It is, however, not an excavating institute. At the Museum Department, where I work, you find most of the archaeological competence of the Museum: 15–20 trained archaeologists with field experience. I happen to be one of the very few who more or less frequently conduct archaeological field research – I am not talking about large expeditions, just a couple of weeks each summer.

My paper will deal with basically two questions: why does the Museum not conduct excavations and what are the terms of my own field projects? A number of supplementary questions occur as well, such as why don't my colleagues dig and doesn't the museum have any interest in field projects? Finally, what could the Museum gain by conducting excavations?

The historical background

Perhaps we first of all should examine the statement, that the Museum is non-excavating, even if this sounds a little strange.

The basic elements

In contrast to other countries archaeology is not a very old science in Sweden, but collecting ancient objects (preferably with inscriptions) and notes on remains has in fact been going on since the end of the 16th century. In 1599 Johannes Bureus, later appointed King's Custodian of Antiquities, began crisscrossing the country with a notebook on behalf of the King. In 1630 an "Instruction of the Antiquarians of the Realm" was proclaimed, and Bureus received two assistants. The first legislation respecting ancient monuments was made in 1666, the same year as the College of Antiquities, the first such academy of its kind in Sweden, was established. The first inventory of ancient monuments was carried out during the following decades. These are the basic elements in what we see today.

The Academy of Antiquities played an important role in the following development. It was totally reformed a few times before 1786, when King Gustav III established his Royal Academy of Letters, History and Antiquities, and after some decades of it teething troubles it became a firm and powerful scientific institution. This development led to the appointment of a Principal of the King's Custodian of Antiquities, who was connected to the Academy as its permanent secretary. This relationship lasted until the reorganisation of 1975.

The birth of the Museum

The Museum of National Antiquities (*Statens Historiska Museum*) was established late in the 1840s with the King's Custodian of Antiquities as its head. The initiative was taken by Bror Emil Hildebrand, one of our most renowned Custodians, who organized the collections scientifically and created – for the time – a modern display. Thus the cabinet of curiosities became a museum. Hildebrand's staff was no larger than Bureus' had been 200 years earlier, but the collections had grown, mainly by purchases and large private collections.

The provincial museums

Hildebrand was also a pioneer in another respect. By the middle of the 19th century the public interest in archaeology and cultural history had grown significantly, and many societies of local and regional history had been established. Hildebrand encouraged cooperation with these societies; soon they developed collections of their own and later on many of them became provincial museums. Today they are 24. The historical background is still reflected in the very special relationship between these (museums) and the central Museum.

Field archaeology and collection studies

A few excavations were conducted as early as the 17th century, but these were more or less treasure-hunting episodes. During the second half of the 19th century field archaeology was gradually developing, and a number of large and important excavations were taking place, conducted or supervised by officials of the Museum. The most renowned internationally is probably Hjalmar Stolpes' excavations at Birka, which began in 1871. The Museum had effectively become an executive arm of the King's Custodian of Antiquities.

However, field archaeology was just a minor part of the obligations of the Museum. This was emphasized later on with such artefact-orientated scholars as Oscar Montelius, Berhard Sahlin and many others.

The birth of the Central Board of Antiquities
(Fig. 7.1)

This early concentration on artefact studies in our collections has, I believe, influenced the research policy of the Museum ever since.

During the 1920s, large changes along the same line were taking place, resulting in the birth of the Central Board of National Antiquities – a new institution connected to the Museum and under the direct leadership of the King's Custodian, at the time Sigurd Curman, the man behind this development. At the

same time the Museum got its own chief – the Museum Director, subordinate to the Custodian. Under the directorship of the Academy, the Board and the Museum collectively make a civil service department, the *Riksantikvarieämbetet och Statens Historiska Museum*. In this authority the responsibility of the Museum is limited to the collections, while the Board is responsible for the monuments. (Many important functions of the Board were decentralized to the provincial state government when the Board was reorganized in 1975.)

In the beginning the main task of the Board was the systematic recording and documentation of cultural resources. This included some excavation activities, which increased with time and meant fewer excavations for the Museum. Still the Museum was, or at least some officials were, conducting a number of field projects. The very last of these, the Helgö excavations, was completed only some 17 years ago. Many of these projects seem to have been performed in collaboration between the Board and the Museum, and in many cases it is difficult to tell which part of the organisation had the main responsibility.

The Museum as a part of an excavating institute
(Fig. 7.2)

Today the Museum does not even own a spade, but it is important to remember that it is, in fact, a part of an excavating institution. The organization is not dissimilar to any other. For instance, in provincial museums we usually find one department corresponding to the Board with responsibility for the monuments, and another department corresponding to the Museum with responsibility for collections and exhibitions.

The birth of contract archaeology

The field activities of the Board have been growing steadily since the 1940s; during the post-war period, very much due to the construction of water-powered dams in the lake systems of northern Sweden, hundreds of Stone Age settlements and other remains were recorded. During the 1960s the expansion of Sweden demanded even greater capacity with the development of new roads, new industrial areas, and above all new suburbs. This meant fewer excavations for the museums. The 1970s was the time of

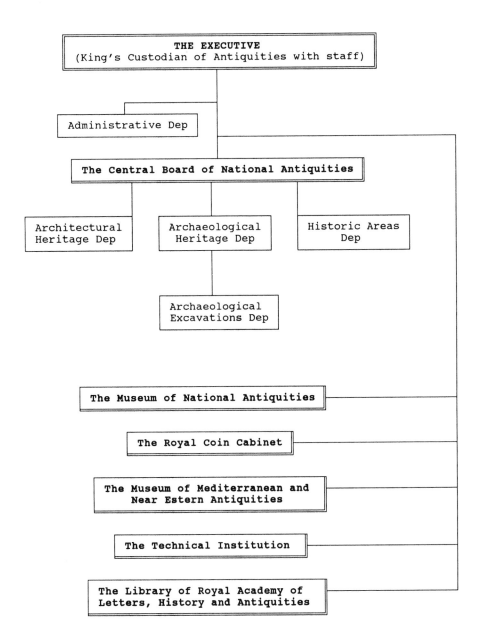

Fig. 7.1 Organization scheme: "Riksantikvarieämbetet och Statens Historiska Museer" (The Central Board of National Antiquities and The Historical Museums).

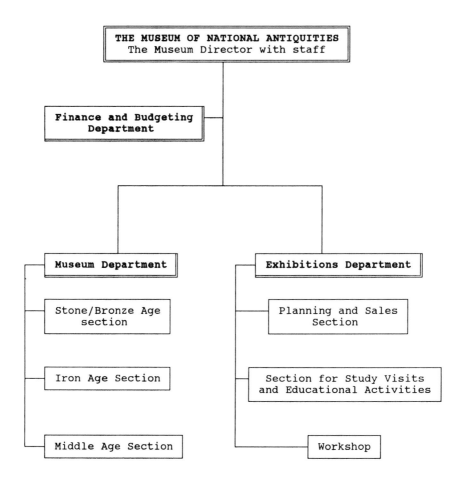

Fig. 7.2 Organization scheme: The Museum of National Antiquities.

town re-development schemes and urban archaeology.

Quite early on the archaeology of the Board became an institution in its own right, today known as the Archaeological Excavations Department. It is a contract archaeology section, with its own budget based upon the income from excavation-commissions. Today this large organisation has one central and six regional offices (see map, Fig. 7.3); permanent employees are about 150, and to this must be added at least 120 seasonally employed or employed for special projects. Forty years ago the number of employees were perhaps ten or even twenty times smaller.

Today the section has a position in Swedish archaeology that could be described as next to a monopoly; it is responsible for more than two-thirds of all excavations in Sweden – almost exclusively rescue excavations and pre-excavation surveys. Other players on the archaeological scene are the provincial museums. Universities also conduct fieldwork, but only exceptionally rescue excavations.

In 1991 the Excavations Department of the Board produced 420 reports; 360 commissions were carried out and 101,000 hours were spent in the field. A large number of these commissions were, however, investigations without any or with a minimum of excavations.

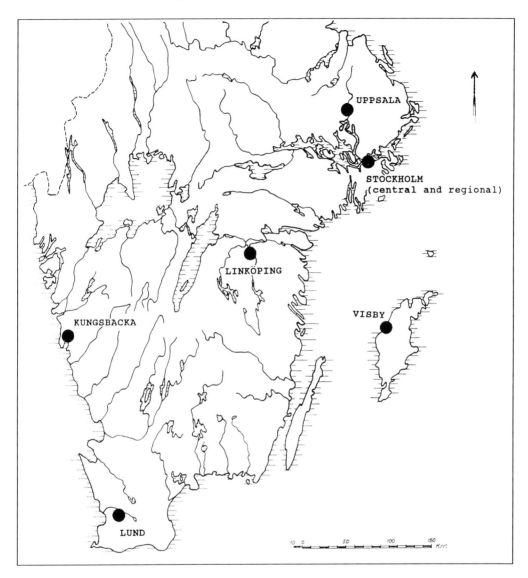

Fig. 7.3 Map of Sweden with the offices of the Archaeological Excavation Department.

The role of The Museum of National Antiquities

In spite of being a non-excavating museum our collections are constantly growing. As a central museum our collections and exhibitions are intended to be representative of all parts of the country, and the tool given to us here is the legislation. The law not only protects the remains; it also claims that the State is the owner of objects from these, and that the Museum of National Antiquities is the custodian of these objects.

All excavations in Sweden have to be reported to the authority, and the objects, with certain exceptions, are to be sent to the Museum for further treatment. The legislation also permits the Museum to transfer ownership to provincial museums, and this is rather common today.

A future separation

Now we have looked at the past and at the present, so what about the future? Developments are naturally difficult to forecast, but there are some very interesting indications of a possible scenario.

Right now Sweden is in the middle of a heavy sequence of changes, not least economical. There are cut-backs everywhere, especially in the public sector. Here we also find a political change; what formerly was understood as public affairs are now turning more and more into private business. At least one private archaeological firm has been established, also a number of archaeologists are working on a freelance basis, and the position of the Archaeological Excavations Department of the Board has been questioned.

Besides the main argument that a public authority can or should not superintend what it is performing itself, the new economical and political wave salutes the principle of unrestrained competition and suggests that the "archaeological monopoly" of the Board must be broken. The basic idea is to separate the department from the responsibility of the Central Board, allow it to reorganize and then, under a new principal, act on a market like any other company competing for contracts.

Some people regard the Museum of National Antiquities as the "natural" archaeological institution, which again would make us an excavating institution. Others claim that this would be unrealistic with too many consequences, especially for the Museum administration, and that a more realistic solution would be to organize the section as a self-dependent company with the Museum as one of its main partners.

Advantages and disadvantages of this separation have become a hot topic of discussion in Sweden. If the separation is necessary it has to be done without disturbing the stability of the structure of Swedish archaeology. Whatever happens, there will be an impact even in the Museum. For the moment a government committee is studying this "divorce" and all questions concerning a reorganisation. I do not want

to forestall its results, so I will leave it here as an open scenario.

Personal projects at the museum

Let us instead quickly look at my own projects and start with the budget. As far as the Museum is concerned finance is a major problem. Our budget has no column for field projects, but the Museum pays my field-period salary.

Most of the archaeological equipment is at my disposal, free of charge, thanks to a favourable agreement with the Central Board. Labour is usually the heaviest part of the costs. I would be totally helpless without a large number of local volunteers: we consume about 450–500 hours in a two week period with about 15 amateur archaeologists, often in a three shift system. In my group at present there are some high-ranking officers from the nearby military camp; and the army supports the excavation with tents, caravans and other useful things.

Now, to the side questions: why for example do so few – or rather – none of my colleagues conduct excavation projects? Well, of course they envy me in what I am doing and declare that they would do the same if they could. But the answer to the question might be very simple: they look at their field archaeological background as a road into the museum; safely inside they sit still and do their research work.

Now, to the question as to whether the Museum is interested in field projects? This has already been answered indirectly: the permission for me to dig on duty I take as a positive indication. From colleagues and superiors on all levels I am fully encouraged in what I am doing, but I can not detect any obvious interest in establishing field projects under the directorship of the Museum as a responsible institute. Anyhow, materials are constantly coming in from other excavations.

Then, what could the Museum gain by supporting or conducting excavations? Well, here the Museum and I have a mutual interest. Looking at the pattern of our growth we find that the incoming items during the last decades – this hugh mountain of artefacts, fragments, test-materials – almost exclusively come from rescue excavations. That is fair enough, but we have not been able to "control" our growth, or to keep up a distinct policy according to an agreed research programme. Materials from prehistoric cemeteries and settlements are predominant, as well as medieval and later urban materials. There is, however, a clear under-representation when it comes to objects or materials from sites outside the redevelopment areas, such as late medieval fortifications, in which I am particularly interested. In former years excavations were carried out with methods and, above all, goals which today seem quite out of date.

New excavations would not only re-new and balance up these parts of the collections, they could also create new platforms for further studies of these materials.

Finally I am convinced that it is essential for an "armchair archaeologist" to keep in touch with field archaeology. If you lose contact here you also lose a great part of your ability to approach materials coming in to the museum from excavations. This might sound like a truism, but then it is a golden one.

8. Excavations in the Medieval Centre of Malmö and in the Surrounding Area: Museum Archaeology in Practice

Ingmar Billberg

Malmö is situated in south-western Scania (Skåne) (Fig. 8.1). Scania belonged to the Kingdom of Denmark until 1658 as did Halland and Blekinge. At the Peace of Roskilde in 1685, however, Denmark had to surrender these provinces to Sweden. Malmö has, therefore, been affected to a very great degree by developments in Denmark during the Middle Ages.

From the early written sources we learn that the built area of the town expanded very rapidly. The town also became an important trading centre. Two Malmös are mentioned in the written source material: an Upper Malmö and a Lower Malmö. On the basis of the source material, Upper Malmö would seem to have been an ordinary village, and it was Lower Malmö which later developed into the town (Fig. 8.2). The earliest mention of Malmö is in Lund Cathedral's donation book. From about the year 1170 a prebend is mentioned with an estate in Malmö belonging to it. This record indicates that it is a village and not the town of Malmö which is meant here. Archdeacon Erland Erlandsen gave two marks to the church in Upper Malmö and 4 marks to the church in Lower Malmö in a donation of 1269. There was thus a settlement on the coast with a church of its own as early as this date. In the excavations of 1864, when a small lake was being enlarged (Pildammarna), graves of the medieval period were discovered. Both wooden and stone coffins were found. To date this is the only evidence for activity

which could be linked with the village of Upper Malmö.

In 1275 mention is made for the first time of the citizens of Malmö. In that year, Bishop Peder of Roskilde gave the burghers of Copenhagen the freedom from customs duties in Malmö provided that the same right was secured for burghers of Malmö trading in Copenhagen. In 1296 King Erik Menved laid down that the Dominicans from Lund had the right to collect alms in Malmö among other places. In 1353 King Magnus Ericsson granted Malmö its town charter.

When discussing the written sources, mention should be made of the map drawn up by the city archivist of that time, Isberg, as early as 1875. By examining the written source material and observing excavations in the town, he was able to piece together the information on a map (Fig. 8.3). The various medieval buildings mentioned in the written sources are indicated here. The map also contains a reconstruction of the plots of ownership, especially town land owned by the church. The map also shows the development of the town's defences, i.e. the fifteenth century wall as well as the more elaborate system of bastions built in the sixteenth and seventeenth centuries. The map is of very high quality and it still serves as an aid for acquiring information about an area in preparation for forthcoming archaeological investigations.

The town grew up along the coast situated on a

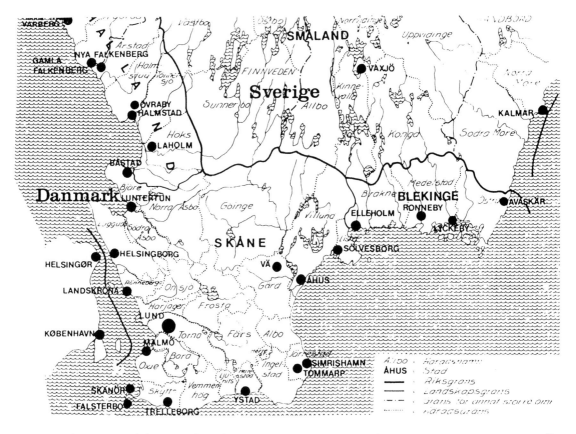

Fig. 8.1 The territorial division of southern Sweden during the Middle Ages. Taken from the "Atlas Över Sverige".

number of sandbanks. Some sizable marshy areas provide the town with natural protection on the landside. The building of St Peters, the town church, was probably started in about 1300. Larger brick houses were built along the main street, the Västergatan-Östergatan. The medieval market-place and the court house are also located here. Along this street there is also evidence in the form of clay-lined pits of trade prior to the establishment of the market-place (Fig. 8.4). It was also here that the monasteries were built, the Grey Friars and the Black Friars. The present Stortorget (main square) was created in 1540. In order to build the square the Heligands Klostret (Monastery of the Holy Spirit) was demolished along with a large number of other buildings. Four blocks of the medieval town more or less disappeared. This

is today Malmö's only continuous area of archaeological interest for the medieval period, which has been largely preserved under the present square.

As far as archaeological activities are concerned, they have fluctuated very much in their level of ambition. Malmö's oldest excavation-report originates from the second half of the nineteenth century. Apart from some minor observations and the donation of finds from various excavations in the medieval town, it was in connection with the laying of a main sewer in 1907 that a record was made of the medieval remains. The sewer was dug along Norra Vallgatan where the sea-wall ran, erected during the fifteenth century. The sewage-works took place along both sides of the wall and it was possible, therefore, to document the various gates in the wall.

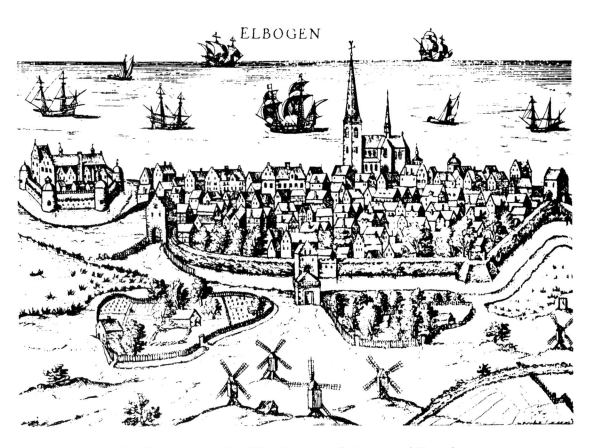

Fig. 8.2 Malmö in the 1590s. Engraving by Braun and Hogenburg.

In 1909, Malmö's Forniminnesförening (Antiquarian Society) was founded. One of its first steps being to appoint a person who could document important medieval remains when construction work took place in the town. This activity ceased at the beginning of the 1920s.

Like many other museums, Malmö's was created as a result of private initiative in the second half of the nineteenth century. Initially, the Museum was indeed a private collection. In its early days, the Museum was located in the town's grammar school. A museum building was erected in 1903. This soon became too small. In its stead the medieval Malmöhus Castle was made available, which had previously housed the prison. Plans for restoraton began during the 1920s. It was not until 1939, however, that the new Museum was opened (Fig. 8.5).

In about 1930 an assistant was employed at Malmö Museum. This resulted in a more systematically organized archaeological documentation of the city area. Proper measured drawings were made of remains which were discovered. The possibilities to record declined rapidly with the introduction of digging-machines. Archaeological efforts were concentrated instead on documenting excavations in connection with cable and pipelaying, which were still dug by hand until well into the 1950s. By the close of the nineteenth century, the potential of archaeological records made in connexion with pipe and cable-trenches for the purpose of reconstructing the medieval topography of the town areas had already been realized.

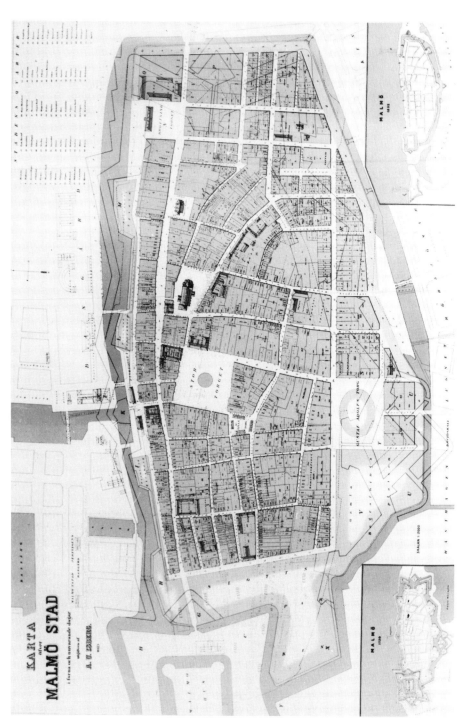

Fig. 8.3 Isberg's map of medieval Malmö, 1875.

At the end of the 1960s and the beginning of the 1970s, major development took place in the city of Malmö as in a number of other medieval towns in Sweden. In Malmö's case, these involved a large part of the area with the oldest medieval settlement i.e. the thirteenth-century town. This development led to the creation of a special position at the Museum oriented towards medieval archaeology and, moreover, a general legislative tightening-up, which has meant that after 1974 all development must be preceded by an archaeological investigation.

From 1974 onwards about 200 excavations of varying duration have been carried out ranging from a few days to years. Besides excavations carried out on land occupied by houses, a very large number of excavations have taken place on streets. Since the town in the main still has its medieval street pattern, only a few street excavations have concerned remains of buildings. Despite this street excavations have been invaluable for topographic studies, particularly for the dating of the successive expansion of the street network and for linking up with the structure of the cultural layers in the various excavation areas.

Despite the large number of demolitions in the 1960s or perhaps as a result of this, interest for preservation and restoration of older buildings grew. This took place above all on the initiative of private owners of property. The municipality first became involved in restoration projects at the end of the 1960s. This has meant that the majority of preserved medieval houses are in private ownership.

The archaeological investigations during the recent decade have provided a number of important findings as far as the development of medieval settlement is concerned and the demarcation of the medieval town area. The very extensive finds material has still not been completely processed. Signs of market activity have been documented from investigations in the western parts of the town. It has been possible to establish that the market area extended along the seafront and also comprised a couple of blocks to the south during the early part of the four-

Fig. 8.4 Evidence of market activities comes from the areas close to the coast, also from so-called "lerbottnar" or clay-lined pits containing fish bones.

teenth century. It can further be seen that a regulated settlement with a clear division into different plots and a street network was established in the first half of the fourteenth century when the market area had its hey-day. The archaeological results indicate intensive building activity. Trade was probably concentrated close to the shore.

It has been possible on one occasion to carry out investigations in the areas in which the older part of the town was located, that is the thirteenth century town. One of the oldest houses found in the town to date was discovered here. At the same time the trenches indicate a regulated town settlement. The house can be dated to the end of the thirteenth century (Fig. 8.6). It contains a number of prehistoric characteristics, such as a saddle-backed roof extending down to the ground. The walls were made of thin layers in a sill-frame. Moreover, an open fireplace was situated centrally in the house.

As the town is built on sandbanks, wood has only been preserved in very rare cases. Instead clay floors and post-holes are often the only indication of a house construction. Another kind of house which has been found above all in the outer areas of the medieval town is the sunken house. This should not be confused with the *Grubenhäuser* of the Viking period and the early medieval period. The sunken house can be dated to the first half of the fourteenth century. The walls are erected of wood with clay as filling. The houses probably also had saddle-backed roofs. Some of these houses were found in an investigation of the southern outer area. In the same investigation a brick-kiln was found (Fig. 8.7). Isberg was able to locate the brick-kiln in the area in 1875 on the basis of the written sources.

It could be established that the oldest brick-kiln was erected at the end of the fourteenth century. It was rebuilt and altered on five occasions and was still in use by the beginning of the sixteenth century when we know through written sources that it was owned by the town and that the brick-master was called Jörgen. It could also be established that in these outer areas, building was regulated with property demarcations and a street network during the

Fig. 8.5 The "Malmöhus" Castle. The earliest parts date from around 1438. Extended during the late 16th century. Today a museum.

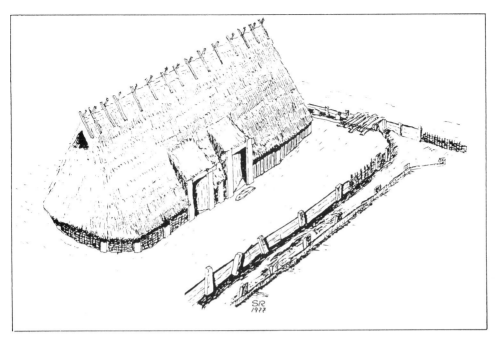

Fig. 8.6 Reconstruction of a late 13th-century house uncovered in excavations at St Peter's Church. Property boundaries visible as narrow ditches.

first half of the fourteenth century.

At present a very large investigation is taking place in the southern part of the town. During the Middle Ages St Jörgen's Chapel was situated here, with a churchyard. Here at the most fifty graves have previously been documented. The investigation now in progress has so far resulted in recording of over 1,200 graves. This provides for the first time evidence for the distribution of sexes and ages at death, and also various illnesses which can be recognized in the skeletel material.

St Jörgen's is first named in the written sources when it was demolished between the years 1517 and 1520. Through dendro chronological dating of the coffins and coins in the floor layers in the chapel and in the graves, it can be established that the chapel was erected at the beginning of the fourteenth century. It was, therefore, in use for about two hundred years. During this period St Jörgen's functioned both as an institution for the treatment of leprosy and probably, during the fifteenth century, as a more general hospital. We have no clear evidence for this change

yet. An examination of more than 800 skeletons, however, has so far shown none with indications of leprosy.

As far as investigations of medieval rural settlements are concerned, the Museum carried out excavations in a number of villages at the end of the 1960s. During the 1960s, the aim was often to examine the earliest phases of the settlement, that is the late-Viking to early-medieval period. During the later years some well-preserved house remains from the period 1200–1300 were also recorded. There is, as far as Sweden is concerned, very little comparative material. It has, therefore, been important to document house-length, breadth, room-plan and also the position of the stove. From the scanty evidence a very preliminary interpretation can be made concerning the transition from longhouses of post-construction to houses built on sills. This change seems to have occurred at the end of the thirteenth century on the basis of the available material. It is also from this period that we can note the appearance of clay floors which have not been found in the long-houses.

Fig. 8.7 The town brick-kiln. The oldest part dates from the late 14th century. The kiln was in periodical use until the early 16th century.

There is evidence from a number of sites that long-houses and sunken buildings existed at the same time during the late Viking to early medieval period. It can also be established they they disappear as a house-type at the same time as the long-houses. Red earthenware is not found in the long-houses nor in the *Grubenhäuser*, while it is plentiful in the houses erected on sills.

What we now have ahead of us in the 1990s is the bridge project linking Denmark and Sweden. This will mean major works above all in the countryside with new terminal buildings, a new railway and a new motorway. As far as the medieval town is concerned, a tunnel is planned from the existing railway station to the bridge. This will affect large areas of the eastern part of the medieval town, which have not previously been investigated. The area today is

a park and is to be restored after the completion of the building works.

The archaeological department in the Malmö Museum operates as a self-financing operation. According to existing legislation for the protection of ancient remains, the owner of the land is responsible for the costs of the archaeological investigation. Since 1979 the department has had 25 permanent employees. There is also a permanently employed palaeo-osteologist. During the excavation season, students are employed. The number depends on the number of projects and their scope. The area of responsibility of the Museum is limited to the municipality of Malmö. This also means that the staff work both on the prehistoric and the medieval periods. The head of the department is also the city archaeologist. This means that the department is also in charge of matters concerning building and demolition and has the responsibility of supervising restoration and rebuilding work in medieval houses, which are protected buildings. Research excavations are carried out if these can be externally financed.

One of the museum departments is responsible for special exhibitions when these concern archaeology or cultural history. This often takes place in collaboration with our own department. There is also a conservation department for the achaeological finds.

9. A New Archaeological Museum on Funen as an Example of Current Trends in Danish Archaeology

Henrik Thrane

This paper can only present some personal views and experiences. My background consists of continuous employment in museum archaeology over more than 30 years.

I began as Bronze Age keeper at the National Museum, but took over the Museum in Odense in 1972, and have been working as a generalist ever since. I should add that working at one of the four purely archaeological museums in Denmark I am privileged, compared to most of my colleagues who work in local museums with a broad historical field.

Firstly, I wish to present four points as premises for the ensuing discussion:

1. In Denmark archaeology has always been an amateur as well as a museum affair. We do have university departments of archaeology at Copenhagen (1941) and Århus (1949) and some of their staff have dug quite a lot, but always in cooperation with a museum, at least nominally, because in Denmark museums are the only institutions permitted to excavate.
2. My generation discovered 30 years ago that it was living in a state of archaeological crisis.
3. The comprehensive approach to museum work which Dr Longworth stresses in his paper here is to me a condition *sine qua non*, rooted as I am in the Danish archaeological tradition. Research should be integrated with the other museum tasks.
4. Museums should be centres of knowledge. Our

task is to provide access to this accumulated knowledge for the public in various ways.

The Museum at Odense was founded 1860 as one of the mini-versions of the universal museum which the educated citizens of that period thought a suitable way of educating the people. From the start the Museum has had responsibility for the whole province of Funen (Oxenvad 1985). Amateurs cared for archaeology, and proper excavations did not take place until the 1930s, when a wealthy local pharmacist, Poul Helweg Mikkelsen, did practically all the digging. He discovered the Ladby Viking ship burial and financed its excavation and preservation (Thrane 1987).

The first archaeologist was appointed in 1940, and from then on we have had an archaeological section operating independently of the other museums under the umbrella of the "Municipal Museums of Odense". This group of individual museums is financed by the City of Odense, an anomaly in Danish museum circles. The first keeper, Erling Albrectsen, was made an honorary FSA for his work on the Iron Age graves of Funen published by him in 5 volumes between 1957 and 1973 (Thrane 1991). Albrectsen was only the second university-educated archaeologist appointed to a job outside the National Museum.

His period marked a gradual change from the amateur period with limited money and mobility due to the war conditions. The real change came in the

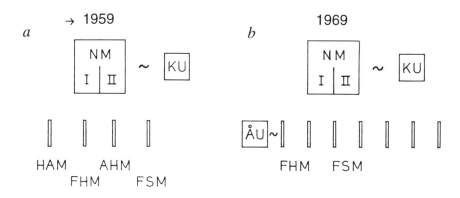

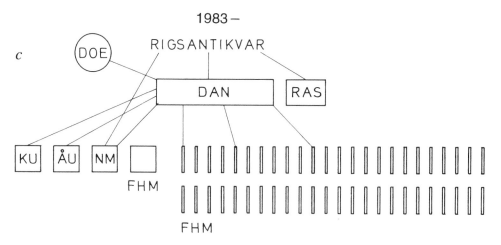

Fig. 9.1 The organisation of Danish archaeological museums. a, the situation around 1959. b, the situation after the law revision 1969. c, the present situation.

The abbreviations on Fig. 9.1 are:

NM	National Museum, HAM Haderslev Museum	DOE	Miljøministeriet
FHM	Forhistorisk Museum Moesgård	KU	Copenhagen University
ÅHM	Ålborg Museum	DAN	Det arkæologiske nævn
FSM	Fyns Stiftsmuseum	RAS	Rigsantikvarens arkæologiske sekretariat.
ÅU	Århus University		

late 1950s when the first museum law of 1958 institutionalized the old museums with advisory duties over the small local museums (Fig. 9.1a). A hierarchy was established with the National Museum at the top but resentment inherited from the very strong central rule of Sophus Müller provoked the local museums to an ever-increasing demand for inde-

pendence, which has continued to the present day.

By the mid-1960s it had become clear that the new affluent society put different demands on archaeological museums, and in 1969 the new law of environmental preservation revolutionized Danish archaeology. It prescribes that public institutions must pay for the damage which they inflict on ancient monuments and it also provides an annual sum for the excavation of sites on private land, as no similar obligation could be placed on private owners. This meant a lot of money compared to old times when the annual budgets of the better museums, like ours, only allowed for small excavations.

Money means power, and soon the major conflict in post-war Danish archaeology broke out between the National Museum and the new Ministry of the Environment. The latter succeeded in snatching the administration of the new law in 1973 (Fig. 9.1b) and was only forced to return it in 1983. During that decade an advisory committee "The Ancient Monuments Board" was nominated and tried to distribute the available money to the museums according to the merits of the individual excavation cases (as it is now done by the Board of Danish Archaeology (DAN) under the chairmanship of the Rigsantikvar, i.e. at the National Museum). The current state is that about one quarter of the applications for grants for rescue excavations on private land is granted – where the law intends full coverage (see *Arkæologiske udgravninger i Danmark* 1984 & ff.).

By 1976 fourteen local museums had professional academic archaeologists on their staff and the National Museum had the maximum number of staff (Fig. 9.1c).

An impression of the financial situation may be gained from the graphs (Figs. 9.3–9.4). Data for the situation prior to the new law are not available but the total sum spent on fieldwork outside the National Museum could be counted in 6 figures. 1976 saw a new museum law and it has been revised continually since then, so that now the rules regulating rescue functions are incorporated in the museum law and the administration resides with the National Museum. Now we have 48 museums each in charge of their own geographical area and, of course, with professional staff. The network is illustrated by Figures 9.1c & 9.2.

This enormous expansion of local museums has meant that we "old museums" have seen new rivals popping up, demanding their own territories. I will not say that fights over territorial rights have been evaded, but a working situation has been reached, sometimes more like an armed truce. For our situation it means that the southern and eastern islands as

well as the southeastern corner of Funen are now covered by the museums in Rudkøbing and Langeland, but we still have the right to work in the whole territory of 3,474 square kilometres.

From this brief look at the national situation I return to my local base. I succeeded as director in 1972, when the staff consisted of 2 part-time posts. We worked in the old museum building of 1885 in very crowded conditions busily planning the future. We were lucky in our timing and managed to enlarge the staff before the recession, but felt frustrated when the plans collapsed in 1978. Now, however we can see how fortunate we were. In 1979 the city acquired the estate of Hollufgård just outside the city boundary and we were asked whether this might solve our problems. Of course it was an offer which no sane curator could have refused, and since 1981 Hollufgård has been our residence and we have spent most of our time planning and building.

The aim of the Hollufgård Museum (Fig. 9.5) is to present archaeology in its natural surroundings, i.e. in the countryside and to allow the public to generate their own ideas besides digesting ours. We realize that we cannot compete with the big museums like the National Museum or the Moesgård Museum (FHM), but hope that the combination of lower rank elements may, nonetheless, give our Museum a special quality which will compensate for the quantitative shortcomings.

In order to do this we work with a 4–pronged concept. The main one is the open store where all our finds are on display. They are arranged according to 10 geographical units, of course coinciding with the current administrative division of the island. Each unit is divided chronologically into Thomsen's 3 Ages plus post-medieval. The idea is to provide visitors interested in their own home parish or town with the opportunity of finding the relevant things. We still have the problem of labelling to solve, but otherwise managed to gather everything from 4 different temporary stores during the winter 1990–991 and opened the 350 square meter hall in May 1991. We are rather proud of this achievement.

The second aspect is to provide a permanent exhibition introducing our visitors to the Prehistory of Funen under the heading of "Man the Creator".

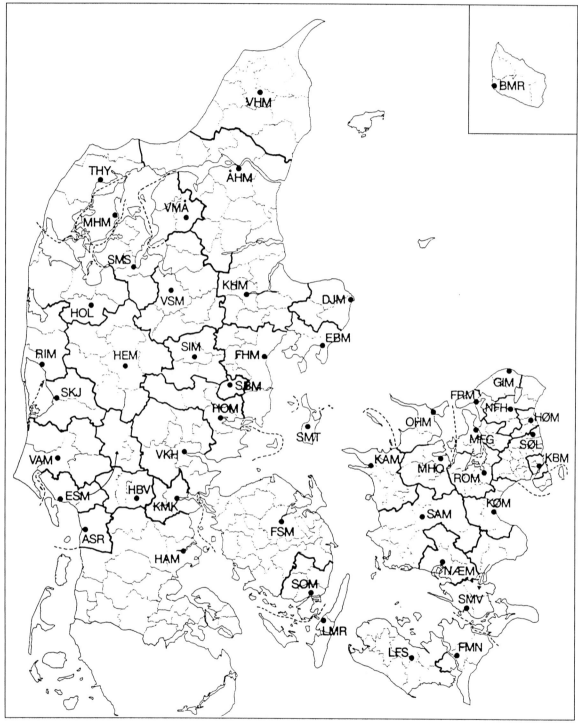

Fig. 9.2 *The division of Denmark into areas of antiquarian responsibility for museums (after Arkæologiske udgravninger i Danmark 1990).*

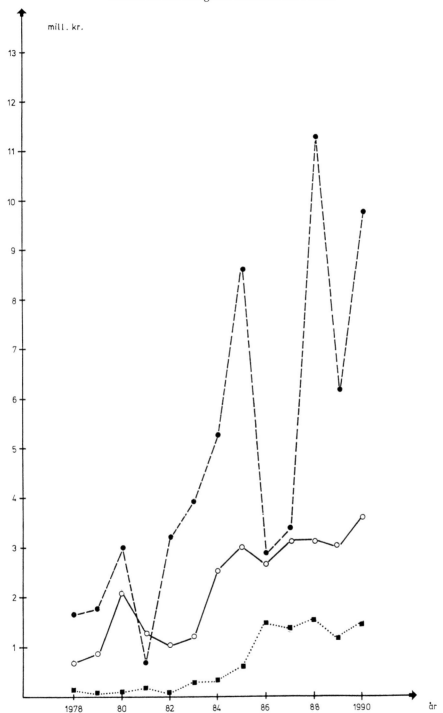

Fig. 9.3 The money available for fieldwork (excl. the wages of the permanent staff and the museums' own budgets). Bottom curve: The grants available for excavations on private property (the Rigsantikvar budget); Middle curve: The grants from the Carlsberg Foundation; Top Curve: Excavation financed by public authorities e.g. natural gas companies (after Thrane 1992).

We have a hall of 200 square metres and plan to open in 1994, so at the moment this is where our resources go.

The third is meant to elucidate major issues or current topics under the heading "Man and Nature". This theme has been our main topic for many years and is also the topic for the research centre opened this spring by the Danish Research Council and the Ministry of Environment – as our neighbour at Hollufgård. So far we have shown four special exhibitions in our 400 square metre hall, the first was opened by our Queen in 1988 and was on the Bronze Age under the title "Power and Glory", the second was on the population and landscape of Funen over 10,000 years. Last year we attracted a record number of visitors (50,000) to the exhibition on the rain forest. The latest was made at a record speed this Spring. It is simply called "Europe" and covers the whole period from 1400 BC to 1992 (Fig. 9.6). We hope to be able to join a European network so that we could take in foreign exhibitions of the size mentioned, because we do not have the resources for producing our own exhibitions every year.

Finally, there is a fourth approach which we consider indispensable to our concept of an archaeological museum. It stands outside the Museum, however. We have at our disposal about 20 hectares where a Prehistoric Park is growing slowly. Since 1987 the flat, farming landscape of the 1980s has

been transformed into an undulating mixture of grass and forest with a Bronze Age farm and a Viking Age farm under construction. The final goal is to have a path from the Neolithic to Medieval times winding past a series of farms surrounded by the vegetation, both wild and cultivated, characteristic of the individual periods. Each farm reconstruction is based on excavated plans from Funen and on the concept that Prehistoric man knew what he could do and had a high technical ability. Incidentally this programme revives one of the local traditions of which we are reasonably proud. In 1878 the first attempt at building a house with original Stone Age tools was carried out at Broholm by Frederik Sehested. This house now stands in the park at Hollufgård.

Another local tradition is amateur archaeology. This has always been important for Danish archaeology but reached a low status in the 1960s to 1970s. I tried to persuade our local amateurs that fieldwalking was just as important as excavation – and better suited for amateurs and we have seen some very good work, of a high professional standard. In 1976 the first post was created at our Museum for a liaison archaeologist – a former amateur – with the result that we have had about 10 groups of amateurs working dilligently. The pressure on the exhibition side, to fill the buildings, has unfortunately meant that the amateur work has been set aside during the last couple of years where we have had to invest all

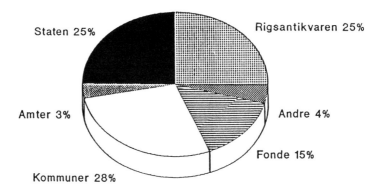

Fig. 9.4 The funding of excavations during 1990–1991 in percentages (after Albrethsen et al. 1993). State 25%; The State Antiquary 25%; Counties 3%; Municipalities 28%; Private Funds 15%; Others 4%.

Fig. 9.5 The Hollufgård museum complex seen from north-west 1991. The big L-shaped building houses the exhibitions and the open store. The offices are in the 1577 manor-house in the background.

resources in new displays – as mentioned above. These plans have taken most of our resources, human and otherwise, but we have managed to do some fieldwork too, especially during the years when we were virtually cut off from normal museum work (before 1986). It remains a problem, however, to have a permanent staff ready to cope with all chal-

lenges. The last 20 years have seen some very wide variations in budget, in tasks and in performance.

The basic idea is that we are best qualified to look after Fyn because we have an accumulated knowledge of local conditions which other museums cannot have. There is no more the difference in quality between the staff of the National Museum and the

Fig. 9.6 From the "Europe" exhibition 1992.

provincial museums which was used to excuse the exclusive role of the National Museum before 1959. This attitude does not exclude external museums from working here. The National Museum particiates in the Gudme project and the Moesgård colleagues have done most of the research into the Ertebølle culture.

We now have a permanent staff of nine, three of us being archaeologists, but one having to raise his own salary from the excavation projects that we manage to finance from outside. Our own excavation budget is less than 100,000 dKr. In fact, we have had several years where the final accounts showed that more than a million had been spent on archaeological fieldwork. We have dug all the year round in the mild years, so quiet winters are no longer the case. Practically no excavation has comprised pure research, but we have tried to use the rescue funds in our research.

The western half of the motorway across Funen was constructed between 1963 and 1971 without any notice being paid to archaeology. The eastern half was built between 1972 and 1985 and we were involved from the start, the most interesting site being the Viking Age settlement and cemetery complex at Rosenlund. The largest archaeological untertaking in Danish history was the natural gas pipe line which hit Funen in 1980–85, with the Late Bronze Age settlement and hoard at Lindø as the star find. This enormous project created a major rift in Danish archaeology because of the autocratic line taken by the Department of Antiquities of the Ministry of Environment against the local museums. Looking back I have wondered whether these costly projects were worth all the trouble? I see much more profit in the other projects which we have undertaken at significantly lower cost. We chose them ourselves, and that really makes all the difference.

We have had three major research projects with Odense University as partner in the first two. They are all elements of what I call settlement archaeology (Thrane 1989). The Southwest Funen project was an attempt to break the archaeologist's evil circle – his perpetual running after the bulldozers, ploughs etc., never being able to pick and chose what seems most important from a research point of view. The major benefits have been the Early Neolithic C situation with the Sarup causewayed camp and contemporary dolmens (Andersen 1981), the Late Bronze Age centre of wealth epitomized by the Lusehøj tumulus and the contemporary Voldtofte settlement (Thrane 1984). A methodologically interesting feature is the extended Pre-Roman Iron Age hamlet which was a byproduct of the 7–hectare excavation at Sarup (Andersen 1984). The Late Iron Age remained enigmatic.

The Origin of the Medieval Village was a doctoral project for two of my students and was financed by an employment scheme for young people. Its purpose was to elucidate the central problem of Danish settlement history, i.e. when the villages were fixed in their present positions. The project has been an inspiration for similar studies elsewhere in Denmark and Scania (Sweden) and indicated that this major shift in the settlement structure should be placed at the end of the Viking Age (Jeppesen 1981; Näsman 1991, 174).

We are still active in the third project at Gudme with a variety of other museums – and ensuing problems. Incidentally, this project was triggered off by treasure hunters using metal detectors. A major donation from the A.P. Møller Foundation has enabled a fine programme of surveys, trial excavations and final excavation of the largest Danish Iron Age cemetery at Møllegårdsmarken during the last 5 years, concentrating on the period 200–800 AD when this area was the richest in Scandinavia. An extraordinary wealth of metal objects indicate a central settlement with a coastal landing site beginning in the third century AD and ending in the sixth century. Money for an exhibition next year, for an international symposium and for the final publication is included (Nielsen, Randsborg & Thrane 1994).

These 3 projects have each in their own way important implications for Danish archaeology. They prove the importance of being earnest and of working scientifically on specific problems. Apart from the Gudme project they have been relatively inexpensive. The maps figures 9.7–9.8 show the geographical coverage. The distribution of the different types of sites excavated is illustrated in Thrane 1991. The excavation reports are in our archive, which after all is something, and the finds have been conserved and stored. Between 1971 and 1985 we have published 3 books (final publications) and 33 papers presenting preliminary reports on individual sites or projects, for some years comprising joint symposia of the university and the museum on settlement archaeology and history: the net result ten volumes.

This is certainly not below the average Danish rate of publication and yet it is clearly not good enough. Preliminary reports are fine, especially if the general public read them, and some sites clearly do not deserve a detailed report, but there are too many important excavations which do not cross the doorstep to the final report. The basic problem of Danish – and indeed European archaeology as I see it – is the discrepancy or even gulf between input and output (Thrane 1992).

The excuse that we always bring up is that we cannot possibly cope with the publication issue as long as we have to go on rescuing on a round-the-clock schedule. Our scientific conscience prevents us from setting the field-glass to the blind eye as Admiral Nelson did at the Battle of Copenhagen, so we have to go on digging all these threatened sites. It may not be irrelevant that rescue archaeology is where most of our jobs and money come from. At a certain level the archives have been opened to a previously inconsidered degree by the work of the Danish Central Sites and Monuments Record (Larsen 1992). The site indices for Fyn are currently being computerized so that by 1994 all known sites will be easily available and up to date.

I have said already that my generation lives in a perpetual state of archaeological emergency, but so apparently does the next one. How long will this go on? Is Europe going to remain in this state all through the next century too? I do not see any signs of change, so we shall have to adapt to this state of perpetual pressure, but how? It is, needless to say, much easier

Fig. 9.7 Distribution of excavations carried out by Fyns Stiftsmuseum 1940–1971. The large dot marks the cemetery of Møllegårdsmarken, otherwise no distinction has been made between small and large excavations.

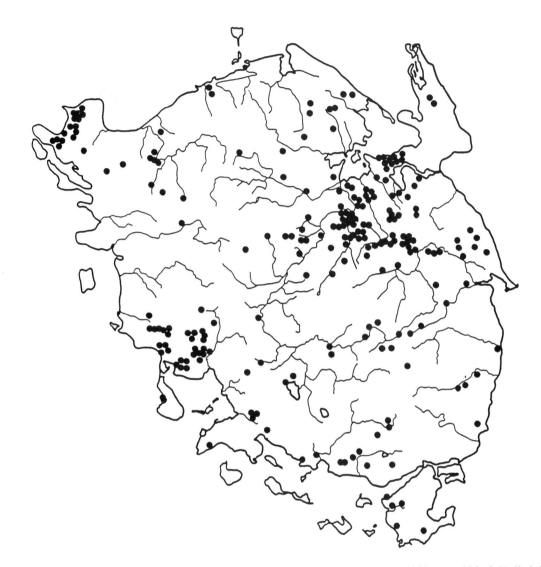

Fig. 9.8 Distribution of excavations carried out by Fyns Stiftsmuseum (from 1990 Fyns Oldtid, Hollufgård) 1972–1991.

to describe the problems than suggesting solutions or improvements.

To sum up, we have a functioning system catering for the rescue archaeology. There is never enough money available, but I doubt if there ever would be, even if the wildest archaeological dreams came true. Rescue archaeology is practically the one and only sort of archaeology practised in Denmark which means a general lowering of the standard to meet the economic level.

The structure with less than a handful of institutions having more than one archaeologist in a permanent position has become a problem. It is virtually out of the question to free the one man-one museum archaeologist from the daily chores to prepare a final publication. It is deeply unsatisfying for them to have to watch as students come and take over their unpublished excavations. Something has to be done to increase, or rather establish, the mobility between universities and museums.

The pressure from outside – and even inside the museums – to produce success is growing. This year my first 5 months were spent on the "Europe" exhibition and my next 9 months will have to be reserved for the introductory exhibition. Of course it is not just my time, but nearly the whole staff has to be geared for this work on a round-the-year basis. We really need a moratorium for 5 years, with a full stop to excavations. This is of course out of the question due to our high ethical standards, and the economic consequences. We could begin by raising the demands for rescue excavations so that we only dig what is significant. We should excavate cemeteries and short-lived settlements completely, and preferably we should excavate settlements with their associated cemeteries. We need a general awareness that important excavations must be published by the excavator. Finally, when we dig there should be time

for thought. The few excavations which bring us forward are those where the excavator had time to consider what he was doing.

References

Albrethsen, S.E., Hertz, J. & Nielsen, S. 1993. The Excavations, in S. Hvass & B. Storgaard eds, *Danish Archaeology during 25 Years* (prelim. title).

Andersen, N.H. 1981. Befæstede neolithiske anlæg og deres baggrund, *Kuml* 1980, 63–l04 (Engl. summary).

Andersen, N.H. 1984. Jernalderbebyggelsen på Saruppladsen, *Hikuin* 10, 83–90 (Engl. summary).

Arkæologiske Udgravninger i Danmark 1984 & ff. København 19854 ff (Danish summaries).

Jeppesen, T. Grøngaard 1981. Middelalderlandsbyens opståen, *Fynske Studier* 11, Odense, German summary.

Larsen, C.U. (ed.) 1992. *Sites & Monuments National Archaeological Records*, Copenhagen.

Nielsen, P.O., Randsborg, K. & Thrane, H. (ed.) 1994. The archaeology of Gudme and Lundeborg, *Arkæologiske Studier*, in press.

Näsman, U. 1991. The Germanic Iron Age and Viking Age in Danish Archaeology, *Journal of Danish Archaeology* 8, 1989, 159–187.

Oxenvad, N. 1985. Othiniensia, *Fynske Minder* 1985, 5–128 (Danish only).

Thrane, H. 1984. Lusehøj ved Voldtofte – en sydvestfynsk storhøj fra yngre broncealder, *Fynske Studier* 13, Odense (Danish only).

Thrane, H. 1987. The Ladby Ship revisited, *Antiquity* 61, 41–49.

Thrane, H. 1989. Siedlungsarchäologische Untersuchungen in Dänemark mit besonderer Berücksichtigung von Fünen, *Prähistorische Zeitschrift* 64, 5–47.

Thrane, H. 1991. Fyns første fagarkæolog, *Fynske Minder* 1990, 19–29, Odense (Engl. summary).

Thrane, H. (ed.) 1992. *Dansk forhistorisk arkæologi – gennem de sidste 25 år, nu og i 2001*, Odense.

10. L'acquisition des Objets Archéologiques par les Musées en France

Jean-Yves Marin

In France laws protecting the natural heritage were first drawn up during the nineteenth century, but they concentrated mainly on the preservation of existing monuments. Few archaeological finds were catalogued or published, and it was not until 1941 that the first archaeological legislation was passed dealing with such topics as permission to excavate and ownership of finds. The fate of excavated material depends upon its legal status and the circumstances of discovery; the State can claim all or part of the finds.

Given the increase in archaeological activity since the Second World War the situation is not ideal, and the problems posed by such material are discussed. The author considers how objects are acquired by museums, which museums acquire what, the particular difficulties of archaeological stores, the financing of object acquisition and conservation, the exhibition of material, and its publication. A legal document drawn up by the Museums Association offers a way of tackling some of the issues raised.

Le choix du theme

Beaucoup de chercheurs étrangers arrivant en France, ignorent, a priori, où trouver les objets provenant de telle ou telle fouille archéologique. L'organisation du système français apparaît complexe – voire désordonné.

Il m'est souvent arrivé d'accueillir des chercheurs qui ne parvenaient pas à trouver le lieu de conservation d'une série d'objets dont ils souhaitaient faire l'étude. Or, même pour un conservateur français, il n'est pas toujours aisé de retrouver le lieu de dépôt "provisoire" ou même définitif du produit d'une fouille.

Malgré des tentatives d'amélioration sur lesquelles nous reviendrons, cette situation perdure et parfois s'amplifie dans certaines régions du fait de la multiplication des fouilles.

C'est à partir de cette approche concrète que j'ai proposé de traiter ici des modes d'acquisition des musées français tant d'un point de vue juridique que de celui de la pratique quotidienne.

Origine de la règlementation

Les règles de la protection du patrimoine s'élaborent au cours du XIXe siècle. Elles sont la réaction à deux sentiments antagonistes issus de la Révolution française: d'une part, la volonté politique d'anéantissement des vestiges de la féodalité et des restes de la monarchie, mais aussi le désir de faire du peuple non seulement le propriétaire des oeuvres d'art mais aussi de le rendre apte à les connaître et à en jouir.

En fonction de ces exigences antagonistes plusieurs mesures sur le patrimoine monumental ont été prises. Elles sont caractérisées par une absence de prise en compte du patrimoine archéologique. En cette période où l'urgence est d'empêcher l'effondrement de monuments brutalement privés

Pl. 10.1 Aprés chaque campagne de fouilles plusieurs milliers d'objets arrivent dans le musée. Leur classement est la condition d'un véritable travail scientifique.

d'entretien, la conception monumentale prédomine. Malgré les efforts louables des Sociétés savantes qui essaient de valoriser les vestiges mis au jour, cette conception demeure tout au long du XIXe siècle. Les inventaires d'objets archéologiques restent rares, leur publication exceptionnelle. L'intérêt de mener des fouilles archéologiques apparaît dans les circulaires ministérielles comme le souci de mettre au jour de nouveaux monuments pouvant apporter un enrichissement des connaissances de l'histoire de l'art.

L'émergence d'un statut scientifique des fouilles apparaît pour la première fois au début du 20è siècle à travers une tentative de législation archéologique qui ne sera pas menée à son terme.

Il faudra attendre la loi du 27 septembre 1941 pour que soit mis en place ce qu'un juriste a pu récemment appeler "le noyau dur de la protection du patrimoine archéologique". En effet son innovation majeure est d'avoir instauré de manière formelle un régime d'autorisation préalable.

La législation sur la propriété des objets découverts

Le régime des objets révélés par les fouilles dépend de leur nature juridique et des circonstances de leurs découvertes. La loi du 27 septembre 1941 se réfère au droit commun pour définir et attribuer les découvertes archéologiques. Ce n'est pas le lieu ici de proposer une exégèse de cette loi mais il faut savoir que les travaux d'un juriste de l'Institut de Droit de l'Environnement à l'Université de Lyon III, Vincent NEGRI, dont on trouvera la liste des travaux en bibliographie, ont récemment apporté une vision rajeunie de ce texte plus souvent évoqué, qu'étudié.

Pour ce qui concerne notre sujet, rappelons simplement que la loi prévoit deux modalités différentes pour la réalisation des fouilles terrestres. Les fouilles sont, soit surveillées et autorisées par l'Etat, soit exécutées par l'Etat. Enfin les découvertes fortuites font l'objet de mesures particulières. Dans chacune de ces hypothèses, la loi précise les mesures à prendre à l'égard des découvertes immobilières et règle l'attribution des trouvailles à caractère mobilier.

En fonction des cas de figure, l'Etat peut revendiquer tout ou partie des découvertes, demander l'abandon des droits du propriétaire ou se rendre acquéreur de la part qui revient au propriétaire. Bien entendu dans les faits de telles dispositions posent de nombreux problèmes d'application. On doit cependant signaler que cette situation n'a provoqué qu'un nombre infime de contentieux porté devant la justice d'où une absence de jurisprudence qui serait pourtant bien nécessaire.

Les modes d'acquisition des objets

Sans préjuger des droits de propriété sur les objets nous devons rappeler qui peut acquérir les objets d'une fouille et à quelles conditions. Normalement tout objet doit dès sa sortie du sol ou à l'issue de son étude entrer dans un musée où son inaliénabilité est assurée de fait. Il faut toutefois que ce musée soit un musée national, un musée de collectivité territoriale classé ou contrôlé par le Ministère de la Culture ou encore un museum d'histoire naturelle appartenant ou contrôlé par le Ministère de l'Education Nationale.

Il est fréquent lorsque l'Etat est propriétaire de la moitié des découvertes que les objets soient déposés dans un musée de collectivité. Afin de définir clairement les droits et devoirs de chacun on établit généralement une convention qui traite de la propriété des collections de leur dépôt, des mesures de conservation, de la propriété scientifique, du prêt des collections ainsi que des analyses et études complémentaires pouvant être effectuées. Un document type – que l'on trouvera en annexe – a été élaboré à l'initiative de l'Association générale des Conservateurs des Collections publiques de France en concertation avec la Direction des Musées de France et la Direction du Patrimoine. De très nombreux conservateurs de collections archéologiques ont également été consultés pour la rédaction du document.

Pl. 10.2 L'existence d'inventaires informatisés est devenu indispensable à une bonne gestion des collections.

Quels musées acquierent quoi?

Les fouilles ou découvertes ne s'effectuent pas nécessairement dans des lieux où il existe déjà des musées; se pose alors le problème de l'acquéreur ou du lieu de dépôt quand une part est propriété de l'Etat. En ce domaine le choix de la collectivité propriétaire du musée et des conservateurs est déterminant car nul ne peut obliger un musée à acquérir le produit d'une fouille mais a contrario s'il souhaite l'acquérir le musée doit accepter certains engagements définis dans le texte de la convention évoquée ci-dessus. Ces conditions remplies, l'acquisition dépend du "territoire scientifique" du musée qui diffère souvent de son cadre institutionnel. Sans formaliser à l'excès on peut dire qu'une classification des musées archéologiques s'est progressivement mise en place depuis la Seconde Guerre Mondiale. Ce fut d'abord la naissance de musées régionaux dont la vocation était de donner un panorama de l'histoire d'une grande région française. Le propos de ces musées était à l'origine principalement illustré par du mobilier ethnographique. Il fallut attendre la multiplication des fouilles et l'étude comparative des collections anciennes pour élaborer de nouvelles présentations. Un nouveau type de musée, régional traitant d'une grande période, tel le Musée de la Préhistoire d'Ile-de-France, à Nemours est venu enrichir cette catégorie.

Les musées départementaux existant depuis le XIXe siècle connaissent quant à eux un renouveau particulièrement significatif autour de Paris, dans des départements nouvellement créés, en quête d'une identité propre (Musée départemental du Val d'Oise) ou en cours de constitution (Yvelines, Essonne), ou encore dans des zones géographiques jusqu'ici dépourvues de musées (Ardèche).

Les musées de sites sont ceux qui connaissent actuellement le plus grand développement dans notre pays, grâce surtout au rôle économique du tourisme. Signe caractéristique: ils ont fait l'objet en 1988 d'un important rapport qui, bien que très incomplet, donne un premier bilan des réalisations en ce domaine.

On trouve dans cette catégorie aussi bien de modestes réalisations destinées à marquer l'emplacement d'une fouille significative, que l'aménagement de sites considérables; ainsi le Musée de Cimiez à Nice (1989), celui de Carnac (1986),

Pl. 10.3 L'entrée des objets au musée n'est pas toujours simple!

site mondialement connu pour ses mégalithes, ou le très prometteur projet d'Arles. Certains ont su profiter d'un agrandissement pour exploiter des vestiges conservés in situ (Evreux) ou annexer une découverte difficilement transportable (docks romains de Marseille).

Mais ces réalisations ne doivent pas faire oublier que c'est dans ce domaine que les occasions manquées furent les plus dramatiques. Depuis le second bâtiment juif de Rouen (XIIe siècle) jusqu'au mithraeum de Bordeaux, bien des monuments découverts depuis vingt ans ont été froidement détruits.

Les musées polyvalents présentent parfois un panorama de l'archéologie régionale ou locale. Ce sont sans doute les plus nombreux, même si la multiplication des musées s'inscrivant dans les trois premières catégories en a fait chuter le nombre. S'ils connaissent une évolution plus lente, bon nombre ont au minimum procédé à un toilettage de leurs collections archéologiques devenues ainsi un outil pédagogique non négligeable pour la collectivité.

Un peu en marge de cette catégorie, il convient de signaler des musées très spécialisés (céramique, verre, métallurgie...) faisant appel à l'archéologie pour illustrer la technologie de fabrication des collections présentées, tel le Musée de la Céramique de Rouen.

Cette nouvelle répartition ne s'est pas opérée suivant une programmation préalablement définie. Elle a été rendue possible -voire indispensable – grâce à un afflux nouveau, longtemps désordonné, de mobilier provenant de fouilles liées aux grands travaux. Ce qui explique que bien souvent les modes d'acquisition définis ci-dessus n'ont été que très partiellement respectés et que pour parer au plus pressé on ait donné un statut juridique à divers lieux de dépôt.

Les dépôts de fouilles

Le dépôt de fouille a été défini comme "un endroit où sont mis à l'abri des objets découverts dans une ou plusieurs fouilles afin d'être classés, inventoriés et étudiés en attendant d'être déposés dans les salles d'exposition ou les réserves d'un musée". Cette définition s'est enrichie récemment de deux nouvelles notions: les dépôts-sas et les dépôts-silos. Ces dépôts apparaissent comme des lieux d'étude ou de conservation du mobilier archéologique. A cet égard, il convient de relever que la mise en dépôt pourra être enfermée, par voie conventionnelle, dans un délai déterminé à l'issue duquel le mobilier archéologique pourra entrer dans les collections d'un musée.

Toutefois on ne doit pas oublier qu'il ne suffit pas d'énoncer que la conservation du mobilier archéologique relève de la responsabilité du conservateur régional de l'archéologie, pendant sa mise à l'abri dans un dépôt de fouilles qu'il contrôle, puis de celle du conservateur de musée, lors de son incor-

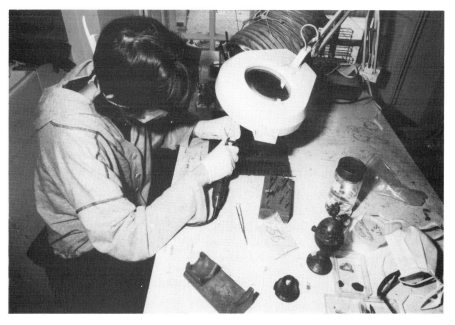

Pl. 10.4 La présence d'un laboratoire de restauration dans le musée est un gage de sécurité pour le déposant.

Pl. 10.5 Les milliers de squelettes humains trouvés chaque années dans les fouilles doivent-ils être conservés au musée?

poration aux collections du musée pour régler les problèmes juridiques que peut soulever le passage du mobilier archéologique dans un dépôt de fouille.

Une récente étude a montré que la mise en dépôt du mobilier archéologique doit aussi être appréciée au regard du droit commun. On ne peut, en effet, ignorer certains fondements juridiques au profit du pragmatisme. D'autre part, les dépôts conçus comme provisoire ont souvent tendance à durer une ou deux décennies voire à se péréniser entraînant la perte de nombreux objets par manque d'entretien ou de surveillance. Enfin ces dépôts ne sont nulle part signalés compliquant encore le travail du chercheur étranger à la région.

Le financement des acquisitions et des restaurations

Nous avons montré que le statut des objets trouvés en fouilles était loin d'être clair faute d'une doctrine correctement définie et surtout uniformément appliquée, d'une part; et de principes juridiques forts qui devraient privilégier le statut scientifique et culturel de l'objet au détriment de ses valeurs économiques et spéculatives qui prévalent actuellement, d'autre part. Aussi, bien souvent les objets sont-ils enregistrés au musée sous forme de dépôt au statut mal défini; toutefois il arrive que des lots d'objets soient acquis par un musée. Dans le cas de musées nationaux, l'Etat se rend directement acquéreur; dans celui des musées de collectivités, il subventionne l'acquéreur par le biais du Fond Régional d'Acquisition pour les Musées auquel participe à part égale le Conseil Régional. La procédure est un peu plus complexe pour les restaurations mais un gros effort a été fait au cours des dernières années. Ce qui ressort clairement c'est que la situation est très inégale et que les règles du jeu sont mal définies.

En ce qui concerne les expositions la situation est plus contrastée encore. La nécessité de montrer les objets entraîne un subventionnement temporairement très abondant des restaurations bénéfiques aux collections mais le développement des prêts a pour conséquence néfaste l'augmentation des primes d'assurances qui se répercutent lourdement sur le marché de l'art; or nous savons bien qu'en matière d'archéologie qui dit marché de l'art, dit fouilles clandestines.

Protection de la propriété scientifique et accessibilité des objets

Ce sont là deux notions qui peuvent devenir rapidement inconciliables si les règles du jeu ne sont pas clairement définies. On verra dans la convention-type reproduite en annexe que l'ensemble du paragraphe 6 est consacré à ce thème mais il ne s'agit pour l'instant que de recommandations parcimonieusement appliquées par les intéressés. En fait les problèmes sont nombreux et il n'existe pas de solution unique. On ne peut par exemple imposer un délai de publication identique à toutes les fouilles. Certaines opérations d'une durée exceptionnelle impliquent un traitement spécial mais trop de fouilles ne sont jamais publiées, d'où la nécessité de règles, même si elle doivent supporter de nombreuses exceptions. On ne saurait en effet admettre que les résultats d'une fouille échappe à la communauté scientifique pendant des décennies sous prétexte de propriété scientifique. En aucun cas les conservateurs ne doivent se rendre complice de tels agissements. La règle implicite de cinq ans renouvelables une fois en cas de fouille de grande ampleur ou demandant des analyses post-terrain très longues paraît être raisonnable.

A cet égard le rapport de fouilles, document intermédiaire, peut constituer un mode d'information pour peu que son contenu soit défini et son usage correctement réglementé.

Se pose aussi le problème des reproductions photographiques qui intéresse à la fois la propriété scientifique et la propriété artistique et commerciale; une réglementation existe mais la multiplication des moyens de reproductions de documents les rendent chaque jour plus difficiles à appliquer.

Enfin dans le choix des restaurations à effectuer sur un objet, il est important que le débat s'instaure entre le conservateur et le restaurateur, sans oublier l'archéologue qui doit pouvoir, dans certains cas apporter des données déterminantes sur les moyens à mettre en oeuvre. Cela implique que les différents points évoqués ci-dessus aient été traités en bonne harmonie afin que les différents intervenants puissent suivre l'ensemble de la chaîne des opérations depuis la sortie de terre de l'objet jusqu'à sa présentation finale en passant par toutes les phases de son exploitation scientifique.

Conclusion

L'acquisition des objets archéologiques par les musées relève d'un grand nombre de paramètres dont nous avons tenté d'évoquer les principaux. Certains reviennent lancinant depuis que l'archéologie existe, d'autres plus conjoncturels évoluent au gré des avancées de la discipline. Les moyens de les concilier diffèrent d'un pays à l'autre de la Communauté en fonction des traditions de la discipline et du cadre juridique. Cette grande diversité des législations est certes, un bon thème de colloque, elle enrichit l'historiographie de notre discipline de quelques bons titres chaque année mais je crains qu'elle ne pose de plus en plus de problèmes.

C'est pourquoi une mise en place progressive d'un code déontologique sur la protection et la propriété scientifique mais aussi d'un régime d'exportation uniforme des biens culturels doit être notre priorité.

Bibliographie

Delmas, A. 1988. Les mises en valeur de sites archéologiques en France. Ministère de la Culture et de la Communication. Département des études et de la prospective. Paris.

Marin, J.-Y. 1987. "Le statut juridique de l'objet archéologique". *Tribune libre – Musées et Collections publiques de France*, n° 176, n°3.

Marin, J.-Y. 1989. "Le statut juridique de l'objet archéologique (suite). *Tribune libre – Musées et collections publiques de France*, Supplément au Bulletin n° 183/193, déc.

Marin, J.-Y. 1990. "Commission archéologique. Bilan

1989". *Musées et collections publiques de France*, Supplément au Bulletin n°184/185.

Négri, V. 1990. "Objet archéologique, objet de droit". *Musées et collections publiques de France*, n° 186–189.

Négri, V. 1991. "Les fouilles archéologiques: chronique d'une législation". *Actualité législative Dalloz*, 15è cahier.

Négri, V. (sous la direction de) 1993. "L'organisation territoriale de l'archéologie en Europe". *Actes de rencontres européennes de l'archéologie, Montpellier 22–23–24 mai 1991. A paraître aux Editions du CNFPT.*

Négri, V. 1992. "Les aléas juridiques des dépôts de fouilles". *Musées et collections publiques de France*, n° 195, n° 2.

Négri, V. (Textes réunis et présentés par) 1992. Protection pénale du patrimoine archéologique. Actes du colloque de Lyon, 6 et 7 décembre 1989, édité par l'Hermès, Lyon.

Poinsot, P. 1967. "Musées et dépôts de fouilles" – *Bulletin des musées et collections publiques*, n° 101.

Untermaier, J. 1986. "La qualification des biens culturels en droit français" dans Droit du patrimoine culturel immobilier, sous la direction d'Yves Jegouzo, éd. *Economica.*

Séminaire de reflexion juridique: Rapports de fouilles, documents publics ou non? organisé par la Direction de l'Administration Générale et la Direction du Patrimoine le 15 novembre 1990. Publication du Ministère de la Culture. 1990.

ANNEX 1

Proposition de document-type de convention, entre l'Etat français et une Collectivité Territoriale propriétaire du musée où sera déposé l'ensemble de la part de l'Etat à l'issue d'une fouille archéologique.

Preambule

[Relater les circonstances et le lieu de la découverte, indiquer le n° et la date de la (ou des) décision(s) d'autorisation de fouille, le titulaire de cette (ou de ces) autorisation(s) et le responsable scientifique de la fouille.]

CECI EXPOSE, IL EST CONVENU CE QUI SUIT:

Article 1
OBJET DE LA CONVENTION

La présente convention a pour objet de définir, pour la part qui revient à l'Etat, les conditions de dépôt du mobilier découvert à ....
..............., à l'issue des fouilles exécutées, à partir du .... jusqu'au
....

Article 2
PROPRIETE DES COLLECTIONS

Selon les dispositions de la loi du 27 septembre 1941 portant réglementation des fouilles archéologiques, validée par l'ordonnace n° 45–2092 du 13 septembre 1945 qui régit ces fouilles, la propriété des découvertes de caractère mobilier provenant des fouilles désignées à l'article premier est partagées entre l'Etat et ...., propriétaire(s) du (ou des) terrain(s) au moment des fouilles.

Article 3
DEPOT DES COLLECTIONS

3–1. L'Etat s'engage à mettre l'ensemble du mobilier en dépôt dans les collections: de la commune de..., du département de ....
pour la part de propriété qui le concerne.

3–2. De la même façon, la commune de ....
...., le département de
................................., accepte ce dépôt qui ne deviendra effectif qu'après que: la commune de ...., le département de .... ait obtenu la ces-

sion à son profit de la part des objets appartenant au (x) propriétaire (s) du (ou des) terrain (s) désigné (s) à l'article 2.

3–3. Le lieu unique de dépôt est le musée de
....

3–4. Ce dépôt intervient à la fin de la réalisation de l'inventaire du mobilier entreposé à titre temporaire dans un dépôt de fouille contrôlé par l'Etat. Il fait l'objet d'un arrêté ministériel.

Article 4
FORME DU DEPOT
4–1. Les objets déposés au musée sont inscrits sur une liste d'inventaire établie par le conservateur régional de l'Archéologie Cette liste est rédigée en deux exemplaires, signés par le conservateur du musée dépositaire et vaut prise en charge des objets déposés. Un exemplaire sera conservé par le Directeur des Antiquités le second par le Conservateur du Musée dépositaire. Il figure au registre de dépôt du musée.

4–2. Le dépôt des objets est accompagné du dépôt d'un double de la documentation (photos, plans de fouilles...). La duplication de cette documentation sera prise en charge par le musée dépositaire.

Article 5
MESURES DE CONSERVATION:
STABILISATION/RESTAURATION
5–1. Le musée dépositaire prend toutes mesures utiles de conservation et de préservation des objets déposés.

5–2. La commune de ....
............................., le département de ....
...., s'engage à faire son affaire, avec l'aide de l'Etat (Ministère de la Communication) de la maîtrise d'ouvrage des restaurations qui seront faites. Les mesures de restauration sont effectuées à l'initiative et sous la responsabilité du conservateur du musée, en accord avec la Direction des Musées de France et l Directeur régional des Affaires Culturelles.

5–3. La classification en réserve et la présentation des objets au public sont effectuées sous la responsabilité du conservateur du musée.

5–4. Les objets non présentés au public sont conservés dans les magasins du musée; leur consultation est possible dans une salle ouverte aux mêmes conditions que les autres collections du musée.

5–5. Le conservateur du musée dépositaire informera sans délai le Directeur Régional des Affaires Culturelles de tout risque de détérioration des collections déposées.

Article 6
PROPRIETE SCIENTIFIQUE
6–1. Aucune étude concernant le mobilier ou la documentation ne sera entreprise dans un délai de cinq ans à partir de la date officielle de la mise en dépôt fixée par la signature de la présente convention, sans que le responsable scientifique de la fouille n'en ait donné expressément son accord écrit. Sauf décision contraire prise par le Ministre de la Culture sur avis conforme du Conseil Supérieur de la Recherche Archéologique et, jusqu'à expiration de ce délai, seul ce responsable scientifique est habilité à publier ou à faire publier les résultats émanant de la fouille concernée, sous le contrôle du conservateur régional de l'Archéologie.

6–2. La photographie ou la reproduction du mobilier déposé ne seront pas autorisées pendant ce délai, sauf accord du responsable scientifique de la fouille.

6–3. Une seule prolongation de ce délai, qui ne pourra excéder 5 ans, pourra être demandée par le responsable scientifique de la fouille dans le seul cas où les moyens matériels et financiers définis par le responsable scientifique de la fouille en accord avec le Directeur Régional des Affaires Culturelles n'auraient pu être obtenus dans leur intégralité et dans les délais prévus.

6–4. Le conservateur du musée sera tenu informé sur sa demande, de l'état d'avancement de l'étude de ce mobilier.

Article 7
PRET DE COLLECTIONS
7–1. Le prêt des objets définis à l'article 2 sera soumis à l'accord du Ministre de la Culture (Direction Régionale des Affaires Culturelles).

7–2. Les dispositions des articles 5 et 6 sont applicables à l'occasion de ce prêt.

Article 8
ANALYSES ET ETUDES
COMPLEMENTAIRES
8–1. Le conservateur régional de l'Archéologie peut, en concertation avec le responsable de la fouille et le conservateur du musée, proposer des analyses ou des études complémentaires.

Article 9
RETRAIT DES COLLECTIONS
Seul le non respect des dispositions énoncées précédemment peut entraîner un retrait des objets déposés par l'Etat.

Article 10
FORMALITES: ENREGISTREMENT
La présente convention n'est pas soumise au droit de timbre, ni à la formalité de l'enregistrement. Dans le cas où l'enregistrement serait requis par l'une des parties, les droits de timbre et d'enregistrement seraient à sa charge.

11. The New Archaeological Museum at Neuchâtel, Switzerland

Bruce Dunning

Introduction

The programme for the new archaeological museum has caused considerable interest and publicity because of the role and the significance of archaeology in the history of the Swiss canton of Neuchâtel. The existing archaeological museum, with its provisional arrangement, houses a number of valuable collections, most of them finds from the three important prehistoric sites of Neuchâtel (Cortaillod, Auvernier and La Tène) but also including objects from other lakeside areas, caves and the camps of hunter-gatherers, Roman villas and cemeteries of various periods on the slopes of the Jura Mountains. In recent decades the constant programme of excavations has increased tenfold the archaeological finds from the area, and, as a consequence, created the need for a new archaeological museum. As its site, the choice fell on an area of outstanding archaeological significance which includes the archaeological sites in the Hauterive-Champréveyres region and the beauty of the lakeside.

The new site has been created by the filling of the lake with earth during the construction of the new N5 motorway. The architectural competition called for the creation of a museum with reception and exhibition areas (for permanent collections and for special exhibitions), office space, storage rooms and workshops. Along with the museum, the programme also prescribed the construction of a research centre for "proto-historical" archaeological research (concentrating on the Bronze and Iron Ages) into which would be incorporated the Department of Prehistoric

Archaeology run by the local university, with its library and office space.

As a result, the brief demanded the combination of three elements:

- the construction of a memorable building on an outstanding site;
- the creation of a contemporary architectural complex of high quality, combining both museum and research centre;
- improvement of the display of the archaeological collections, into which the significant archaeological finds from the locality would be incorporated.

Archaeology and architecture are two similar activities which interweave in their search for successive superpositions of one on the other; in other words that which is architectural in the archaeological object and archaeological in the architectural.

"Architectural excavations": theoretical considerations

Archaeological objects fill museums, where visitors come to contemplate them. Because of their archaeological status, their value is guaranteed. The pieces are inevitably ancient and authentic. The architectural object seems to enjoy a special immunity. Its first quality: its architectural status is apparently assigned *sine qua non*. The object is then endowed with sub-designations, which, in turn, reconfirm its classification as architecture.

Herein lies, in certain terms, the problematics set before us: what can be the aims and ambitions of the architect or the archaeologist creating an archaeological museum, knowing that their mere production is automatically authenticated?:

"In the end, X wishes his buildings to be culturally accepted even before they are built; historically received even before they have experienced a life of their own. Because he expects his architecture to translate directly into culture, it remains ultimately deprived of the very power true architecture exercises in the making of culture, rather than its mere representation" (Kurt Forster, on a famous architect).

Generally, the archaeologist himself does not esteem the value of the archaeological object in itself, as exhibited in the museums. For him the question of context, the archaeological site itself, holds much more interest. It is there that his real work and passion start. Paradoxically, his work destroys the site: he excavates it, measures, extracts, uproots, and excavates again. The more he excavates, the more he destroys. This consumption of the site allows the archaeologist to practice. From the contextual situation of the uncovered objects, studied, dissected and examined, he paints a picture, proclaims hypotheses on past cultures: their fabrications, their use patterns, their economy, and, ultimately, their beliefs and religions.

Regarding these reconstitutions, certain archaeologists have confided that, being put together by themselves, they are in fact imprints of their own way of thinking and beliefs, and that they are consequently falsified from the start. Could it be that, the archaeologist's work be weakened by such a statement?

Kwang-chin Chang is more emphatic regarding this subject: He states that in archaeology, "to claim any knowledge other than the object itself is to assume knowledge of patterns in (present) culture and history and to apply these patterns to the past", so that "archaeology as a whole is analogy." If archaeology is analogy, then all meanings external to those which are directly linked to our own understanding of the present-day society are, *a priori*, excluded from the hypotheses. How can we understand an object that would have no present-day equivalent? That which somewhere between the past and the present would be lost or forgotten is thus necessarily irretrievable. Can any part of the archaeologist's work escape this assumption?

For him, "what is obvious, is the evolution of the objects". The evolution of objects allows the creation of typologies (a contemporary concept which allows us to view a series of objects as an evolution, etc.). These typologies allow us then to categorize down to the smallest fragment of an object. An object is thus deemed archaeologically complete when it allows its reconstrucion according to typological criteria. Since the archaeological object is essentially fragmentary, this means that its given meaning always depends upon a context that is at least as large as the object itself, and that it is always speculative. Moreover, one must bring to one's attention that the very notion of typology conceals the possibility of the other, of the unknown. To attribute a meaning to something under the pretext that it may belong to a object which, under certain circumstances, resembles a known condition, is in itself an act of reduction.

Let us come back to the archaeologist's main method, excavation. Discovery allows us, in principle, to form a hypothesis. We are at this point obliged to come to the conclusion that, in principle, excavation as an archaeological means inscribes within the same hypothesis its own imminent invalidation, and thus prevents, on the whole, its truth.

While history is written page by page, book by book, the archaeologist is forced to read the book backwards, by starting at the end. He digs towards the past and although new discoveries are, at best, verifications of existing hypotheses, they are more often their invalidation. Consequently, future discoveries constitute a considerable threat to the validity of archaeological interpretations. The possibility of a contradiction cannot leave the presumed truth intact. This very possibility inscribes itself within the structure of truth! Because of this fact, truth, although it is always undoubtedly imminent, can never be fully attained.

The result of this is that the archaeologist constructs fictions, and one must realize this in order to arouse an awareness of the true meaning of

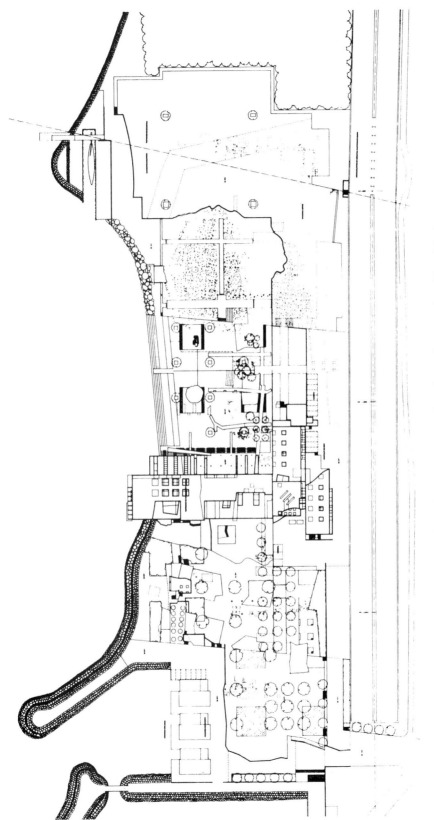

Fig. 11.1 Site plan: the new archaeological museum at Neuchâtel.

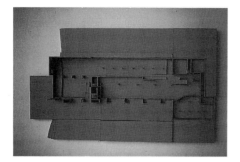

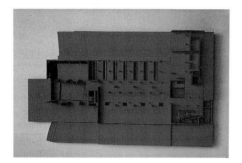

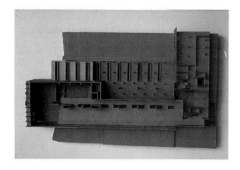

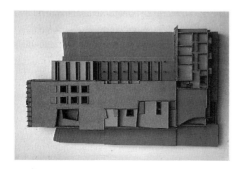

Fig. 11.2 Museum exhibition space.

archaeology. Can one dispute the fact that this meaning is and always will be marked by a rift? That is a rift between an archaeologist's deontology and his fatal inability to know the truth, or a rift created by the fundamental problem of the object's ontological continuation.

Let us come back to the archaeological object. I have said before that the object automatically attributes itself a value owing to its authenticity. So what can be said about the growing number of facsimiles, copies and imitations displayed in museums? To claim that they are real, or to show only originals would be diverting the visitor's attention from the archaeologist's work and emphasizing the value of the object itself. What would be said about genuine non-archaeological objects and how should one deal with reconstitutions, which we now know go beyond absolute truth. In other words, can one deliberately and conscientiously mislead the observer, like architects do, for instance, when they claim that all objects born out of their hands are architectural.

The architect refers to himself, and as a good archaeologist does, to prior acquisitions and knowledge in order to justify his product. These include typology, laws of composition or personal criteria such as aesthetic, metaphoric or spatial references.

Let us go back to a ficticious moment in an archaeological past: the First House. Contrary to the First Work of Art which we cannot imagine differently than representative of an existing external situation, this first architecture could but resemble itself, its own configuration. It could not even resemble the function that it was to fullfil since this function had not yet appeared by then as a possibility of form. And because of this, it is also wholly authentic. Never would the Second House see itself forced to represent, in a certain way, the First one. An archetypal condition was thus originally promised to all architectural objects. As the years passed, representation was imposed upon it, under the sole probable pretext that representation allows the establishment of an architectural discipline. But is it conceivable to describe or to generate, by the use of laws born of repetitive conditions, that which is destined to be authentic? Should one not look for architecturality on the fringe of that which is repeated? Is the automatic assumption of authenticity well-founded, or is architecture yet another victim of a reductive act that we could call typification?

Looking at the architectural product, the idea of typology refers a project to one or several previous productions; the idea of metaphor, ties it to a form that is external to the architectural domain. Both ideas have become inevitable and keep the architectural object from acquiring its due archetypal condition. Can we now say that typology is only matter for that which is non-architectural? Metaphor, by definition, deals only with foreign fields. Henceforth, metaphor can be used only when it severs its ties with the the definitive object (even though it would then become a translation and thus no longer a metaphor). Consequently, the architect becomes compelled to search for the proper meaning of the object itself despite his given means and across his acquired knowledge: in other words through a net of fictions.

What can archaeological and architectural truth be if their only foundation in the present is a fiction? Knowledge is used by the archaeologist to justify his creation. Is this really different? Can the principle of

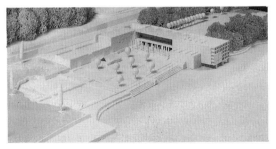

Fig. 11.3 Competition model: view of the archaeological garden.

reconstitution be anything but creative? Is it possible to rediscover the unknown or to classify the creation beforehand? How does one incarnate an enigma? Is there a fundamental difference between an archaeological object and an architectural one, upon first contact, before its naming as one or the other, when notions of genuine and fake, original and copy are still suspended? Can justification lead to creation, and can the classification be the foundation for understanding? The unknown past and the future creation seem inevitably to have to escape from reiteration-iteration. This is a *de-facto* impossibility given that the archaeologist, like the architect, is necessarily impregnated with his own culture. Thus the rift cannot be disregarded. But one must not at all infer the failure of the archaeologist or the death of architecture. The meaning of the rift will not be pejorative! Here, one must be concerned with the question of that which, by this rift, is promised to be architectural within the archaeological object and archaeological within the architectural one. In other words, are the architect and the archaeologist constrained to work, at least partly, the wrong way round? Architecture and archaeology: are they not deontologically and ontologically identical if we disregard the direction of time; that is to say, considering these objects today, now at this very moment?

The project for the new archaeological museum in Neuchâtel attempts to expose this question, by dissipating the limits between architecture and archaeology. Is the architectural object truly the one that is orthogonal, composite, whole, understandable and accessible?

Is the archaeological object the one that is amorphous, fragmentary, incomplete and enigmatic? Can the apparent distance between architecture and archaeology, manifested by the showcase-museum remain intact?

12.   Museum Archaeology in Poland: An Outline

Wojciech Brzeziński

Poland – God's playground according to Norman Davies (1979) – is a country situated in Central Europe between Germany in the west and the Ukraine, Belarus and Lithuania in the east. In the south, Poland has a common border with Czechoslovakia. In the north Poland reaches the Baltic Sea and adjoins the Kaliningrad enclave which belongs to Russia. The population of 38 million inhabits a territory of *c.* 312000 square km.

The shape of the country is a result of the Second World War. As a consequence of the Yalta agreement Poland lost 40% of her territory in the east to the Soviet Union, being compensated in the west by gaining former German areas (Fig. 12.1). These facts have particular relevance for museum archaeology in Poland because in our museums one can find collections excavated by Polish archaeologists in the territories of what are today Lithuania, Belarus and the Ukraine. On the other hand, some old German collections also survive in our stores.

Poland has a centralized state administration which is the undoubted heritage of communism. The territory of the country was divided into 49 provinces, without any connection to the old historic regions, and directly controlled by the central government. The system of local government has being introduced quite recently. This introduction is necessary to understand properly the scheme and activities of museum archaeology which is closely correlated for the time being with the state administration system.

The origins of museum archaeology in Poland can be dated to the second half of the 18th century when under the influence of the Enlightenment the first archaeological collections were established. They belonged to the last king of Poland, Stanisław August Poniatowski, and to the first Polish antiquarian, Stanisław Kostka Potocki. At the end of the 18th century Poland lost her sovereignty and was partitioned between the Austrian Empire, Russia and the Kingdom of Prussia. Obviously, this had a negative influence on the development of Polish archaeology and her museums. The first public archaeological museums were organized in the 1850's. There were the collections of the Cracow Scientific Society, the Archaeological Museum in Wilno (closed by the Russian authorities after the January uprising in 1864) and the Museum of the Polish and Slavic Antiquities in Poznań founded in 1857 (Gąssowski 1970). At the end of the 19th century Erazm Majewski set up an archaeological museum in Warsaw (Wrońska 1983–1987). The archaeological collections were also exhibited in the Museum of Industry and Commerce. The assemblages from both museums are now in the State Archaeological Museum (SAM) in Warsaw.

In independent Poland (1918–1939) there were four archaeological museums: two in Warsaw, one in Poznań and one in Cracow. Archaeological materials were also stored in museums in Wilno, Lwów and Katowice. All these museums struggled with financial, personnel and housing problems. I need only to say that the SAM, founded in 1923 as the Poland's central archaeological museum, did not have its own premises during whole this period (Antoniewicz 1933, Rajewski 1968).

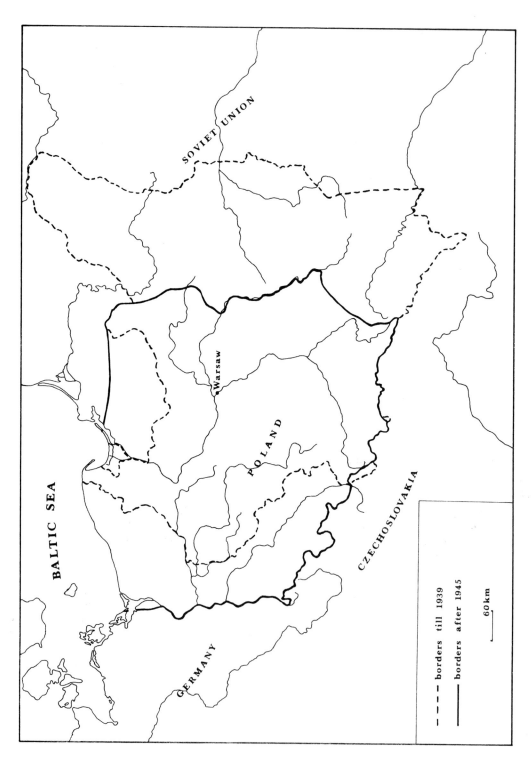

Fig. 12.1 Changes in Poland's borders after the Second World War.

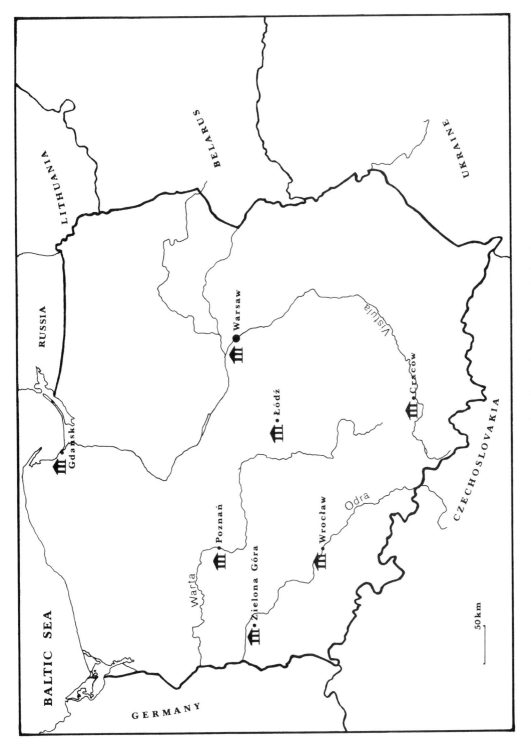

Fig. 12.2 Archaeological museums in Poland.

Fig. 12.3 State Archaeological Museum in Warsaw. (Photo T. Biniewski)

Fig. 12.4 Iron Age lake village at Biskupin. (Photo T. Biniewski)

The Second World War caused terrible damage to Poland's archaeological museums. They were plundered by the occupiers and many objects and documentation were damaged, lost, or dispersed abroad. After the War changes to the socio-economic system (the introduction of so-called real socialism) as well as moving the whole country 200 km to the west (Fig. 12.1) totally changed the situation for museum archaeology. A new, centralized organization was introduced for museums in the mid -1950s. It consisted of the three levels: 1, specialist archaeological museums; 2, archaeological departments in the multi-departmental provincial museums; 3, archaeological departments or collections in the local museums.

As the State Archaeological Museum in Warsaw possessed the richest archaeological collections and the largest number of qualified personnel it was, by common consent, officially recognized as the principal institution for museum archaeology. The museum was designed to act as consulting institution for other museums.

The above mentioned three-level system survived generally to the present day but there are exceptions (Jaskanis 1983–1987, 144). Now there are seven archaeological museums in the following towns: Warsaw, Łódź, Cracow, Wrocław, Poznań, Zielona Góra and Gdańsk (Fig. 12.2). The next group consists of 38 archaeological departments in the provincial museums. Independent of this three-level system are the multi-departmental museums, such as the Malbork Castle Museum, the Museum of Salt Mines at Wieliczka or the Royal Castle in Warsaw. In the third group there are several dozen local museums with archaeological departments or collections. In addition there are a few museums devoted to particular problems of archaeology: Museum of the Ancient Mazovian Iron Smelting at Milanówek near Warsaw or the Museum of the Piast Dynasty at Gniezno (Jaskanis 1986, 99).

The most significant institution in Poland's museum archaeology is the State Archaeological Museum in Warsaw which has been in existence for almost 70 years (Fig. 12.3). From the organizational point of view it is divided into departments dedicated to the chronological periods from the Paleolithic to the Middle Ages. There is also a spe-cial department concerned with archaeology of the Balts. The Museum has at its disposal a large conservation laboratory, the Department of the Physical Anthropology, a library etc. The Museum manages two outside branches. One of them is the Biskupin Department which is engaged in wide ranging studies of the famous Iron Age lake village (Fig. 12.4) and manages the archaeological park which is open to the public. The other one is the Storage and Study Centre at Rybno near Warsaw where the bulk of our archaeological materials is kept (Fig. 12.5). In total, about 140 people are employed in the State Archaeological Museum, among them over 40 archaeologists, including 10 at doctoral level.

The following are the main research aims of the Museum: the study of the Neolithic flint mining, the early Iron-Age fortified settlements, Polish Lands in the Roman Iron Age and the archaeology of the Balts. The SAM has organized about 10 field expeditions every year from 1970 to 1989. However, austerity-measures, which have been introduced since 1989 by the government, have suspended almost entirely all our field activities funded from our budget.

The Museum is entitled legally to supervise the archaeological departments of provincial and local museums. Practical training is organized for the archaeologists of these departments as well. This is precisely because courses in archaeology at universities in Poland do not sufficiently prepare the graduates for work in museums. Instead the programmes are mostly designed to produce candidates for scientific work at universities or in the institutes of the Academy of Sciences. This is a serious defect of these studies in the light of the fact that over 60% of the graduates are usually employed in museums.

As well as the SAM there are six archaeological museums in Poland (Fig. 12.2). The oldest, which are in Poznań and Cracow, were founded in the middle of the 19th century (Radwański 1981). The Archaeological Museum in Poznań is involved in the research of the prehistory and the early middle ages of Wielkopolska region, the cradle of the Polish state in the 9th–11th centuries. The Museum also acts as a provincial conservation board for Poznań province and leads two research projects: the archaeological survey of Poland and the identification and investigation of the early medieval hill-forts in

Wielkopolska. This institution cooperates also with the SAM in preparing the structure of archaeological databases of the collections and inventories. Over 70 people are employed there including 22 archaeologists (Poll 1990).

The Archaeological Museum in Cracow has at its disposal a staff of similar size. This Museum has been researching for many years the origins of the medieval town. The Museum also takes pride in the results of the excavation of the huge iron-smelting centre of the Roman Iron Age located in the Swittokrzyskie Mountains.

The Archaeological Museum in Wrocław specializes in the archaeology of Silesia especially in the Neolithic Linear Cultures, settlements of the Lusatian Cultures, and medieval towns and castles in this region. The most significant parts of the Museum's collections are related to these themes. The archaeological staff consists of 18 persons supported by 40 other employees. The Museum also maintains two outside branches in Sobótka and in Oleśnica (Poll 1990).

The Archaeological and Ethnographic Museum in Łódź can be numbered among the specialized archaeology museums despite the fact that it is also involved in ethnology and numismatics. The archaeological section of the Museum which employs about 10 archaeologists, has participated for 45 years in excavations of the megalithic tombs of the Funnel Beaker Culture in the Kujawy region and carried out the research into the archaeological cultures of the Roman Iron Age. It is worth mentioning that over 150 excavations were arranged by the Museum in the years 1975–1989 (Poll 1990).

In northern Poland the Museum in Gdańsk is the only archaeological museum in the full sense of this word. Its activities are concentrated on the Neolithic of the eastern Pomerania, on the problems of the early Iron Age, the late Roman Iron Age and the Migration Period in this region. The Museum, which is also responsible for the conservation of archaeological sites in the Gdańsk province, has recently organized an Archaeological Unit, which is involved in rescue-excavation and cooperation with developers. It operates almost in the same way as units in many towns in Britain. The computerization of the collections is very advanced in Gdańsk. The museum employes 40 persons including 17 archaeologists (Poll 1990). The last and the newest archaeological museum is situated in Swidnica near Zielona Góra in western Poland. It was established in 1979 mainly to take care of the archaeological objects excavated in the central part of the Odra river basin. The Museum also operates as the conservation board for the Zielona Góra province (Kołodziejski 1980).

Archaeological sections exist in some multi-departmental museums, such as the Wawel Castle in Cracow, the Royal Castle in Warsaw, the National Museum in Szezecin or the Teutonic Knights' Castle at Malbork. They consist usually of one to five archaeologists involved in the research of the on-site archaeological remains or those in the immediate neighbourhood. For instance, the archaeological team of the Malbork Museum successfully excavated the fortification systems of the early medieval Prussians which date to before the Teutonic conquest.

The most common form of museum archaeology in Poland is the archaeology department in the provincial or local museum. Today, they can be found in 38 museums located in the capitals of the provinces. Over half of these departments employ only one or two archaeologists. Teams of three to five archaeologists work in about 30% of them. Very often, especially in provincial museums established after reform of the administration in 1975, the archaeological staff consists of rather young graduates without museum experience. The overwhelming majority of these departments does not have any conservation facilities. Some of the archaeological departments of older museums have a good record of excavation, publication and presentation of the prehistory of their regions (Poll 1990). It appears from the data collected by the SAM that archaeological materials are also stored in several dozen local museums which often do not have a permanent archaeologist. Summing up, it can be said that archaeological collections or objects are be found in over 150 museums in Poland.

It is noteworthy that the above-mentioned data relate exclusively to prehistoric and early medieval objects from Poland and adjacent territories. The classical antiquities from the Mediterranean world are stored mainly in the Gallery of Ancient Art of the

Fig. 12.5 Storage and Study Centre at Rybno. (Photo T. Biniewski)

National Museum in Warsaw (Michałowski 1957; Michałowski 1973).

Over 300 archaeologists and some 70 specialists from other branches are employed in Poland's museums. About 50% of them work in the specialized archaeological museums, about 40% in the provincial and local museums, the remaining 10% in other museums. It should be pointed out that museums employ about 40% of all professional archaeologists (Jaskanis 1986)

Excavations and other field activities are the main responsibilities of museum archaeology in this country. More than 300 sites were excavated every year in the 1980's by the expeditions from various institutions: universities, Academies of Sciences, conservation boards and museums. Museums, especially, played a very important role in this research. Needless to say that about 30% of the sites were investigated by the museum teams (*Informator Archeologiczny 1967–1989*).

Regarding presentation of the collections to the general public, which is one of the main functions of the museum, it should be emphasized that all ar-

chaeological museums maintain permanent displays. They are usually dedicated to the prehistory and the early Middle Ages of the regions with a wider Central European background. The weak point of almost all of these displays is the fact that they have existed for more than 10 years and they are a little out of date. A quite new permanent exhibition has opened recently in the State Archaeological Museum in Warsaw (December 1992). The best known achievement of Polish museum archaeology abroad is the exhibition "The Balts – the northern neighbours of the Slavs" presented successfully in Greece, Sweden, Finland, Germany, Austria and Italy during the years 1984–1992.

The exhibition in the archaeological centre at Biskupin, the architectural remains of the medieval castle in Cracow and the Neolithic flint mine at Krzemionki near Ostrowiec Swiętokrzyski are the most frequently visited archaeological displays in Poland. Alas, only 14 provincial museums (among 38) have permanent displays presenting archaeological objects. The geographical distribution of these museums is very significant. Inhabitants of vast ar-

Fig. 12.6 Conservation laboratory at the State Archaeological Museum in Warsaw. (Photo B. Tropiło)

Fig. 12.7 Ceramics laboratory at the State Archaeological Museum in Warsaw. (Photo B. Tropiło)

eas of in the eastern, southern and northern parts of Poland do not have access to permanent displays. This defect is not compensated by the several dozen temporary or educational exhibitions made by the museums every year. Where the public has no permanent displays of archaeological material, the social interest in archaeology diminishes immediately. This situation is aggravated by the lack of good information on the exhibitions. Museums cannot afford the rapid increase in the printing costs for catalogues, guide-books and booklets. Many archaeologists working in museums express a lack of the interest in educational and popular activities. Despite all these disadvantages the archaeological exhibitions are visited by about 1.5 million people every year (Jaskanis 1986).

One of the most important problems which faces museum archaeology in Poland is the unsatisfactory level of the conservation care for the collections. According to recent data only four archaeological museums (SAM, and the museums in Poznań, Łódź, and Cracow) have conservation laboratories in the full sense of the word (Fig. 12.6). Basic conservation procedures are applied in some other museums. The archaeological departments in the rest of the museums usually employ one or two technicians involved chiefly in the reconstruction of the pottery (Fig. 12.7). This situation is detrimental to the preservation of objects (especially those made of metal), delaying or sometimes making impossible the cataloguing of the collections and presenting exhibitions. In an attempt to improve this the SAM organizes courses for conservators and other members of provincial museums, and offers advice on the conservation of objects.

Another major issue is the cataloguing of the collections, in other words the scientific description and classification of the objects. In Poland there is no uniform system of cataloguing in the museums, and existing methods are not entirely appropriate for archaeological materials. The objects are registered according to the sites or the excavation season. Some of them are also treated as single items such as those which have been given by private persons or institutions. Because of this it is almost impossible to compare the data of one museum to that of another.

The museum archaeologists generally support the view that cataloguing should be applied first of all to the objects of special value, for example those that are well preserved, characteristic of particular values, of typological importance, from secure contexts and well documented. The state of the cataloging varies: from the lack of a catalogue in some places to a full catalogue in museums with small archaeological collections. As regards specialized archaeological museums it fluctuates between 30% in the SAM to 80% in the Archaeological Museum in Poznań (Poll 1990). The huge size of the catalogues (amounting sometimes to several tens of thousands of cards) forced us to construct an archaeological database. This issue has been discussed in Poland by museum archaeologists since the late 1980s when the first attempts took place. In the beginning the museum archaeologists with the help of the computer analysts tried to create an universal and common archaeological database applicable to all museums. After some years of such attempts made in the SAM and in the museum in Poznań chiefly, it was concluded that because of the substantial differences in the construction of the catalogues this was impossible and the idea was abandoned. It was decided to allow the museums to create their own database with minimum common structures. The Archaeological Museum in Gdańsk and the Archaeological Museum in Poznań have two of the most advanced archaeological databases. The SAM is introducing the most complex database which links sites, assemblages and objects with the archive information and photographic and drawn documentation.

The next task for archaeological museums is to acquire materials from the institutions which are not qualified to have their own storage. The magazines of the Institutes of Archaeology of seven universities and storage rooms of the Institute of Archaeology of the Academy of Science are overloaded with unpublished and often unregistered objects. They are sometimes kept in unsuitable conditions, subject to damage or disassociation. The SAM, assuming that the museums are the only proper places for keeping these materials, has established a storage centre at Rybno, near Warsaw, for antiquities from central Poland (Figs. 12.8 & 12.9). A similar role can be played by other archaeological museums for their

Fig. 12.8 Storage buildings of the State Archaeological Museum at Rybno. (Photo T. Biniewski)

Fig. 12.9 Interior of a storeroom at Rybno. (Photo T. Biniewski)

own regions. Alas, the shortage of free space in the magazines in some of the museums prevents this action.

This outline of museum archaeology in Poland is far from complete and refers to the situation in the late 1980s. In the years 1989–1991 a great political change took place in Poland. The totalitarian political system and State-run economy were abandoned in favour of multi-party democracy and the free market economy. This change was introduced during a deep economic crisis. Succeeding democratic governments have imposed severe austerity measures including budget cuts for education and culture. The museums run entirely by the State were seriously hit by these cuts in the years 1990–1992. First of all the field activities were suspended, and in some museums the number of staff was reduced. Although none have been closed yet, such a possibility must be taken into consideration. Moreover, inexperienced and weak local governments are not able to give total support to provincial and local museums. Usually, the museums are loosing out in competition with other facilities such as schools, kindergartens, and hospitals etc.

There is no doubt that museum archaeology in Poland faces the most dangerous challenge. We must change the style of our work, intensifying our educational and exhibition activities, sometimes in unconventional ways, and demonstrate our usefulness to society. Museums have to look for other sources of financial support, besides State funding, and co-operate with developers closely.

References

Antoniewicz, W. 1933. Muzea archeologiczne w Polsce. Archaeological museums in Poland. *Pamiętnik muzealny*, 2, 47–57, Kraków.

Davies, N. 1982. *God's playground. A history of Poland.* New York. Columbia University Press.

Dąbrowski, K. 1978. Muzea archeologiczne a ochrona konserwatorska. Archaeological museums and protection of archaeological sites. *Ochrona Zabytków*, 31, 230–236, Warszawa.

Gąssowski, J. 1970. *Zdziejów polskiej archeologii.* (From a history of Polish archaeology). Warszawa. Wiedza Powszechna.

Informator Archeologiczny, 1967–1989. *Informator archeologiczny.* Ośrodek Dokumentacji Zabytków.

Jaskanis, J. 1983. Uwagi o rozwoju muzealnictwa archeologicznego w 40–leciu Polski Ludowej. (Remarks on the development of archaeological museums in the 40 years of People's Poland.) *Wiadomości Archeologiczne*, 48, 139–162, Warszawa (published in 1987).

Jaskanis, J. 1986. Informacja o muzealnictwie archeologicznym w Polsce i niektórych jego aktualnych problemach. (Information on archaeological museums in Poland and some their actual problems). *Biuletyn Informacyjny ZMOZ*, 160, 99–102. Warszawa.

Kołodziejski, A. 1980. Otwarcie Muzeum Archeologicznego w Świdnicy k. Zielonej Góry. (An opening of the Archaeological Museum at Świdnica near Zielona Góra.) *Z odchłani wieków*, 46, 83–85, Warszawa.

Michałowski, K. 1957. Galeria Sztuki Starożytnej w Muzeum Narodowym w Warszawie. (Gallery of Ancient Art in the National Museum in Warsaw). *Rocznik Muzeum Narodowego w Warszawie*, 2, 101–138, Warszawa.

Michałowski, K. 1973. Stan i perspektywy rozwojowe historii, archeologii, historii kultury materialnej. (The state and development perspectives of the history, archaeology, history of material culture.) In *II Kongres Nauki Polskiej. Materiały Kongresowe*, 86–93, Warszawa.

Poll, 1990. A poll organized by the State Archaeological Museum in Warsaw among museums keeping archaeological collections, completed in 1990. Materials in the SAM, Warsaw.

Radwański K. 1981. 130 rocznica powstania Muzeum Archeologicznego w Krakowie. (130 anniversary of foundation of the Archaeological Museum in Cracow). *Materiały Archeologiczne*, 21, 7–26, Kraków.

Rajewski Z. 1968. Państwowe Muzeum Archeologiczne w latach 1923–1968. (State Archaeological Museum in the years 1923–1968). *Wiadomości Archeologiczne*, 33, 255–294, Warszawa.

Wrońska J. 1983(1987). Muzea prehistoryczne i zbiory prywatne w Warszawie (od przełomu XIX i XX wieku do 1918 r.). (Prehistoric museums and private collections in Warsaw from the turn of the XIXth century to 1918). *Wiadomości Archeologiczne*, 48, 193–210, Warszawa.

13. Archaeology in Kiev History Museum

Ljudmila Pekars'ka[1]

Kiev was founded on one of the tall hills on the right bank of the river Dnepr in the 3rd quarter of the 1st millennium AD. It was mentioned for the first time in 854 in the manuscript "Povest' Vremennykh Let" written by the monk Nestor at the Kievo-Pecherski monastery. But archaeological finds from the most ancient, central part of the city date from an earlier period, the 6th–7th centuries. According to the manuscript, Kiev was founded by three brothers, Kyi, Shchek and Khoriv with their sister, Lybid', and it took its name from the eldest brother. Even today the old names have survived in the three Kiev hills Starokievskaya, Khorevitsa, Shchekovitsa, and in the city river Lybid'.

Ancient chroniclers called it the beauty of the world and compared its glory with that of Constantinople. Kiev was a political and religious centre, and, from the 9th century, the capital of the eastern Slav state known as Kiev Rus' (Tolochko 1983, and 1991, pp. 5–12). At the height of its power this state controlled a huge territory from Lake Ladoga in the north to the Black Sea in the south, and from the Carpathian mountains in the west to the Upper Volga river in the east. In 992 prince Vladimir introduced a new state religion, Christianity, and commemorated the event by founding the Desyatinnaya Church. This marvellous building is an example of architecture in stone, introduced from Constantinople. It marks the beginning of a new era in art for Kiev, and access to the rich culture of the Byzantine empire. The Kievan state was recognized by the Christian world, and many royal houses from the West married into that of Kiev. During the 10th–13th centuries widespread development took place in the city. Powerful fortifications were constructed which were up to 14 metres high and 25 metres wide. Within these walls, palaces and churches of stone were erected, surrounded by the building-complexes and yards of nobles, warriors, administrators, merchants and craftsmen (Kilievich 1982; Sagajdak 1982).

This period of extraordinary development was interrupted by the Mongol-Tartar invasions of 1237–1241. The southern part of Kievan territory, the present-day Ukraine, fell under the rule of the Golden Horde. It took centuries to shake off their yoke and to repair the damage they had done. Even then the weakened Ukraine was the victim of further Tartar and Turkish invasions. Since the 14th century parts of the Ukraine have been under the domination of Lithuania, then of Poland, and then of Russia. Only today is the Ukraine an independent state with its capital again in Kiev.

All stages in the history of Kiev's development are illustrated in one of the most popular of the city's museums – Kiev History Museum. Its archaeological collection is divided into two parts: one contains material from excavations in the city which took place from the late-19th to mid-20th centuries; and the other part has material found from the mid-20th century until the present. The creation of the archaeological collections has its own complicated history whose main stages are as follows. Since the beginning of the 19th century, Kiev, one of the oldest cities

---

[1] Quoted as Pekarskaya in references, where the Russion form of her name has been used.

Plate 13.1 Kiev History Museum – the Klovsky Palace, dating from the 18th century.

of eastern Europe, became a centre of active archaeo-logical investigations. As early as 1835, such significant amounts of material had been accumulated, and in such a short time, that the question arose of creating a museum of Kiev history to safeguard the objects found. The first museum of Kiev antiquities was opened in 1837 at the Imperial Kiev University of St Vladimir (Fedorova 1992, pp. 82–85). Its small museum housed valuable remains contributed from private collections and by the magistrates of Kiev. It was an institution for purely scientific purposes only, and was not open to the public. The first public city museum was opened in 1903. It contained chance finds and material from excavations made at the beginning of this century. It benefitted from the gifts of wealthy Kiev patrons and collectors such as B. Khanenko, I. Tereshchenko, T. Kibal'chich, S. Mogilevtsev, and I. Khoinovsky. Among the most important objects were silver and bronze ornaments of the 7th–8th centuries from the central area of Kiev, metal crosses and icons, female jewellery of gold and silver from the 10th–13th centuries, Byzantine and western reliefs, and 12th–13th century icons. Later on, the collections of the Kiev City Museum were divided between several museums – The State Museum of Ukrainian Art, the State Historical

Plate 13.2 Bronze pectoral crosses of Kiev type. 12th–13th century. Scale 1:1.

(a)

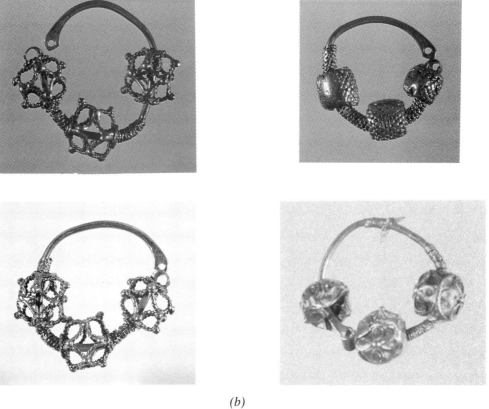

(b)

Plate 13.3 (a) Silver icon-pendant. On the obverse is the half-length frontal figure of a woman with fore-arms raised in prayer ("orans" figure); on the reverse is a snake ornament. Scale 1:1. (b) Gold earrings of Kiev type decorated with granulation and filigree. 12th century. Scale c. 4:3.

(a)

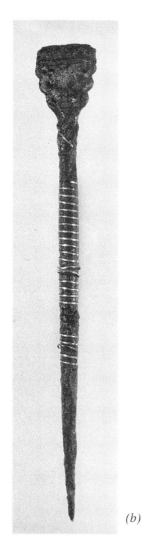

(b)

Plate 13.4 (a) Slate spindle-whorl with incised cyrillic letters and inscription "Gospodi pomozi Marii Georgios". Scale 3:2. (b) Stylus of iron with gold wire wrapped around it, for writing on a tablet. 12th century. Scale 1:1.

Museum of the Ukraine, and the Museum of Russian Art. Many museum collections in Kiev suffered severe damage during the Second World War, and material was lost or went abroad. A similar dispersal had resulted from the revolution of 1917. But most of the old museum material has been successfully identified (Pekarskaya and Putsko 1989, pp. 84–94; Pekarskaya 1989, pp. 304–7; Pekarskaya and Putsko 1991, pp. 131–8; Pekarskaya 1994, in press).

In 1978 parts of the old collection returned to the newly-opened Kiev History Museum. It is housed in the Klovsky Palace, an 18th-century building situated in an old quarter of the city that is recorded in a manuscript of the 11th century (Plate 13.1). The archaeological section of its exhibition illustrates the early and medieval history of the city. On show, for example, are chance finds dating from the 6th–7th centuries, and finds from complexes such as dwellings, workshops and graves situated in historically important parts of the city. These include, for example Starokievskaya Hora, Detinka, Khorevitsa, Kudryavets, and Podol.

The largest contribution to the Museum's archaeological collections has been made by the Ukrainian Institute of Archaeology. In 1969 it established the Kiev Expedition under the leadership of Professor P. Tolochko. Its principal aim was to explore the origins of Kiev and to document the period of its greatest achievements in the 10th–13th centuries (summarized SK 1975; ADSK 1976; AKDM 1979; NAK 1981; AIK 1985). All the material discovered previously by the expedition has been transferred to the museum, and it continues to arrive annually after the summer excavation season in which the museum is also involved. Now the collections contain some 60,000 items, a total which includes chance finds made in the city.

Three museum departments, from a total of nine, are involved in archaeological investigations. One of them, the Department of Ancient and Medieval Kiev, carries out its excavations in the central, ancient part of the city (Pekarskaya 1988, pp. 46–8). A great variety of archaeological material is found, including, for example, bronze pectoral crosses with niello inlay, ivory chess pieces, and gold and silver jewellery (Plates 13.2–13.4). In the courtyard of a stronghold built by prince Vladimir in the 10th century (the so-called Town of Vladimir), was discovered a 10th-century jeweller's workshop with stone moulds for casting earrings, buttons and bracelets (excavations by S. Kilievich). In the last 10 years, 16 lead seals have been excavated which were used to certify documents (Plate 13.5). Most are dated to the 11th–13th centuries, and had a depiction of the prince and an inscription giving his name and title. Others belonged to church dignitaries, and two 14th-century pieces belonged to a Byzantine official, the Patriarch Nil (Ivakin 1991, pp. 43–56).

Two years ago, on another site in the same complex, several dozen nielloed-silver mounts were discovered at a depth of 2 metres. The site was studied for two years by J. Borovsky, and the excavated area reached 1000 square metres in extent. Houses with ovens, the workshops of both goldsmiths and blacksmiths, and burials were found. It was from one of these, the grave of a 10th-century warrior, that the mounts came. Together there were 83 of them forming a belt-set, associated with silver buttons, bone gaming pieces, an iron shield boss, and silver horse-harness mounts. In the remains of a 13th-century dwelling, destroyed by fire, were found a group of 12th-century Byzantine icons of carved stone. They depict, for example, John the Baptist, and Christ enthroned. These are an extremely rare find in excavations because such luxury items were made in response to a commission, a circumstance which makes this find unique (Borovsky and Arkhipova 1991, pp. 119–31). Staff from Kiev History Museum also participated in these excavations (L. Pekars'ka and S. Klimovsky), and in the restoration of the metal pieces which are displayed as a complex in the museum's exhibition.

Archaeological investigations are carried out also in the areas occupied by craftsmen and merchants, as well as in the city's suburbs (I. Movchan and L. Stepanenko 1976, pp. 108–18; Movchan 1982). The most important area is called Podol, located at the foot of the Kiev hills. At the confluence of the river Pochaina with the Dnepr was a harbour area for vessels from many foreign lands. Significantly it was in this quarter, almost 50 years before the official adoption of Christianity, that the first church, dedicated to St Elijah, was active. Archaeological knowledge of the area was limited for many years because

of the density of modern buildings, and the thickness of the cultural layers which reach a depth of twelve metres in places. These factors presented great technical difficulties.

In 1971 the construction of an underground railway gave an opportunity to start excavations, undertaken by K. Gupalo and G. Ivakin. At a depth of 12 metres were found thirteen buildings. Each had a timber framework construction, and originally had two stories. Five of the buildings constituted a farm unit of the 10th century. They were built of pine with a surrounding fence of oak planks. The owner was also a wealthy merchant judging from the finds of Byzantine coins, balance weights, amphorae, gilt-bronze and ivory pieces. These last included a case for a hair brush, a knife handle, a plaque with the depiction of an owl, and a needle. This was the first time in Kiev that such structural remains had been found. Previously it had been supposed that at this period the main type of building was the mud hut. That is why in 1972 the newspapers described the site as Kiev's Pompeii. However the question arose as to how far the timber-framed buildings were typical for Podol. Every year the museum has conducted joint excavations with the Institute (Podol Expedition led by M. Sagajdak and V. Zotsenko). To date, several hundred such constructions have been found, along with timber fences, pavements, and craft workshops. An important discovery was that of a jeweller's workshop, with mounds for casting thirteen different strap ends and belt mounts (Plate 13.6). These moulds were made in the 10th century, and one of them has an Arabic inscription (Gupalo et al. 1977, p. 286; Tolochko 1978, pp. 86–90). Another workshop, for manufacturing spindle-whorls was discovered at a depth of 4.5 metres. Moulds used in casting, and spindle-material, were obtained from Ovruch, in Volyn', western Ukraine, and transported to workshops in Kiev by means of the riverine route Uzh-Pripyat'-Dnepr (Gupalo and Ivakin 1980, p. 213). The excavations showed that there was an important settlement in Podol (Gupalo 1972, p. 383; Tolochko and Gupalo 1973, pp. 339–41; Tolochko et al. 1974, pp. 352–3; Gupalo and Tolochko 1975, pp. 40–65; Tolochko et al. 1976, pp. 19–46).

Another interesting aspect of Kiev archaeology is the large number of hoards that have been found

(a)

(b)

(c)

(d)

Plate 13.5 (a) Icon of carved stone depicting Saint George. Scale 1:1. (b) Bronze icon-pendant with a depiction of the Archangel Michael. Scale c. 1:1. (c–d) Lead seals for certifying documents. 12th–13th century. Enlarged.

Plate 13.6 Moulds of Ovruch slate, for casting strap ends and belt mounts. 10th century. Scale 1:1.

in the city (summarized by Korzukhina 1954). They contain gold and silver jewellery decorated with polychrome enamel, niello, filligree, pearls, and gemstones. They range in date from the 10th to the 13th centuries. The number buried in 1240, the year of the Tatar invasion, must originally have been enormous. Their discovery has always been by accident, in laying water-pipes or drains, digging foundations, and making roads. Some, found in the 18th and early 19th centuries, are known only from police files, but most of them have been irretrievably lost to science. For example, only drawings now survive of a Kiev hoard, found in 1824, which disappeared on its way to the Imperial court (Plate 13.7). It contained silver plate, enamelled crosses, rings, earrings, and pendants (Kondakov 1896, pp. 96–105). Nothing has been heard of the material for more than 150 years, except for one piece. This is a gold medallion with the depiction of Saint Dmitry which appeared in a Düsseldorf exhibition at the end of the 19th century (Korzukhina 1954, p. 123, no. 107). Despite these losses, some 70 hoards found at various times are known. Each has its long and complicated story of passing through private collections

before its appearance in museums in Kiev, St Petersburg or Moscow. One such hoard, found in 1906, is now shared between the Metropolitan and British Museums: the gold and enamels are in New York and the silver and niello in London (Brown 1980, pp. 6–9; Korzuchina 1972, pp. 24–30). This material is one of the richest sources for the study of cultural aspects of the Kievan state. Yet the fate of much of it is unknown, while some of the most valuable pieces in the Kiev Museums lack appropriate documentation. So, at the same time as excavating in the field, the Department of Ancient and Medieval Kiev is digging in/the archives and reserve collections to reconstruct old finds. In the last few years the contents of three such hoards, previously considered to have been lost, have been re-identified (Pekarskaya 1992, pp. 83–5).

Among the numerous ancient monuments surviving in Kiev, a special place is reserved for its caves. They are found all over the area of the old city. As early as the 15th–17th centuries they aroused enormous interest, and they gave rise to legends of endless underground passages. The caves were used for praying, the burial of monks and hermits, and also

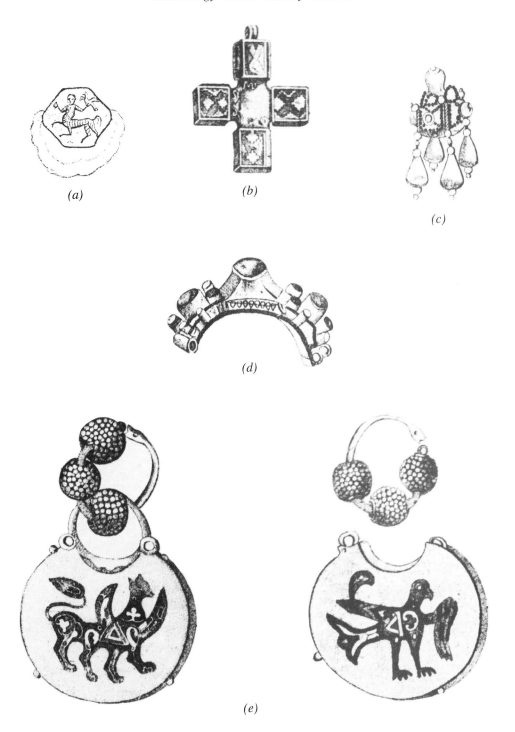

Plate 13.7 Drawings of some pieces from the hoard found in Kiev in 1824. (a) gold signet ring (b) cross-pendant (c) gold pendant (d) mount from an icon?, inlaid with jewels (e) gold earrings with granulated decoration, above, and temporal rings (kolts) of gold and enamel, below. 12th–13th century.

for economic purposes. However they were never studied in detail, and until recently archaeological investigations were only a reconnaissance. Four years ago the Department of Caves was established in the Museum (headed by E. Vorontsova). It is staffed with archaeologists, anthropologists, and geologists who study the soil structure. As a result of exploration and reconstruction works undertaken by the department, a cave monument is due to be opened to the public, the Zverinetskie caves dating to the 13th–17th centuries. Situated near the Vidubetski monastery they were dug into a hill at a depth of 14 metres. They consist of some 200 metres of galleries whose walls contain cells where monks were buried. Finds of pottery, roof-slates, gravestones, leather footwear, belts and leather crosses, which were part of the monk's vestments, were found on the floor and in the cells. Surviving inscriptions of the 13th–15th centuries, and depictions of Christian symbols, are to be seen on the walls. They have been strengthened and copied for later decoding. Now restoration of this monument is nearly complete.

One more museum department involved in archaeological excavation undertakes research into the Ugorsky Hill (led by A. Kovalenko). This site is closely connected with important events in national history, beginning in the 9th century. According to the chronicles, it was here that the Novgorod prince Oleg murdered the Kiev ruler Askold. Today the place is known as "Askold's Grave". In 1810 a church with a two-storey rotunda was built to commemorate the event. In the mid-19th century a hoard of 3,000 Arabic silver coins was found here, and a cave was discovered that had been inhabited by monks in the 12th century. Although arousing great interest in the past, this area was only poorly studied. But as the result of archival researches in Kiev and St Petersburg by the Museum, previously unknown material related to the site has become available. Our own excavations have revealed material of the 11th–17th centuries which is now displayed in the rotunda.

In conclusion, I have outlined only a few main aspects of the archaeological work undertaken by Kiev History Museum. The results can be seen in the discovery of many monuments, ranging from palaces and humbler dwellings to the remains of ma-

terial culture. Economic and financial difficulties, which the Ukraine now faces as part of the former Soviet Union, inevitably affect the quality and quantity of museum excavations. However, they do continue, even if at a smaller scale, and for the future we look forward to new discoveries about Kiev's history.

Acknowledgement

The author would like to thank Dafydd Kidd for reading and making helpful suggestions on the manuscript.

Abbreviations

ADSK *Arkheologichni Doslidzhennya Starodavn'ogo Kyeva.* Kyiv 1976.
AIK *Arkheologicheskie Issledovaniya Kieva 1978–1983gg.* Kiev 1985.
AKDM *Arkheologiya Kyeva. Doslidzhennya i Materialy.* Kiev 1979.
NAK *Novoe v Arkheologii Kieva.* Kiev 1981.
SK *Starodavnij Kyiv.* Kyiv 1975.

References

Borovsky, Ja.E. and Arkhipova, E.I. 1991. Novuie proizvedeniya melkoy kamennoy plastiki iz drevnego Kieva. *Yuzhnaya Rus' i Vizantiya.* Sbornik Nauchnuikh Trudov (k 18 kongressu vizantinistov). Kiev.
Brown, K.R. 1980. Russo-Byzantine Jewellery in The Metropolitan Museum of Art. *Apollo* vol. 111. London.
Fedorova, L.D. 1992. Pershy Muzey Kyeva. *Kyivs'ka Starovyna* no. 3. Kyiv.
Gupalo, K.N. 1972. Raskopki v Kieve na Podole. *Arkheologicheskie Otkruitiya 1971g.* Moscow.
Gupalo, K.N. and Tolochko, P.P. 1975. Davn'okyivs'kij Podil u svitli novykh arkheologichnykh doslidzhen'. *Starodavnij Kyiv.* Kyiv.
Gupalo, K.N. *et al.* 1977. Issledovaniya Kievskogo Podola. *Arkheologicheskie Otkruitiya 1976g.* Moscow.
Gupalo, K.N. and Ivakin, G.Ju. 1980. O remeslennom proizvodstve na Kievskom Podole. *Sovetskaya Arkheologiya* no. 2, Moscow 1980.
Ivakin, G.Ju. 1991. Svyazi Kieva s Vizantiey vo vtoroy

polovine 13–15 vv. *Yuzhnaya Rus'i Vizantiya.* Sbornik Nauchnuikh Trudov (k 18 Kongressu Vizantinistov). Kiev.

Kilievich, S.R. 1982. *Detinets Kieva 9–pervoy polovinui 13vv.* Kiev.

Kondakov, H. 1896. *Russkie kladui.* St Petersburg 1896.

Korzukhina, G.F. 1954. *Russkie kladui 9–13 vv.* Moscow-Leningrad.

Korzukhina, G.F. 1972. Russkie kladui v zarubezhnuikh sobraniyakh. *Kratkie Soobscheniya* vol. 129, Moscow.

Movchan, I.I. 1982. *Drevnie Vuidubichi.* Kiev.

Movchan, I.I. and Stepanenko, L.Ja. 1976. Rozkopky poselennya ta mogyl'nyka v Kytaevo. *Arkheologichni Doslidzhennya Starodavn'ogo Kyeva.* Kyiv.

Pekarskaya, L.V. 1988. Novuie arkheologicheskie otkruitiya v Kieve (po materialam raskopok 1980–kh godov). *Arkheologiya Rigi.* Riga.

Pekarskaya, L.V. 1989. Kamennaya ikonka iz Tripol'ya. Pamyatniki kul'turui. *Novuie Otkruitiya.* Moscow.

Pekarskaya, L.V. 1992. Slidamu znyklykh skarbiv. *Kyivs'ka Starovyna* no. 2. Kyiv.

Pekarskaya, L.V. 1994. Neizdannuie proizvedeniya srednevekovoy melkoy plastiki v Kieve. *Pamyatniki kul'turui. Novuie Otkruitiya.* Moscow in press.

Pekarskaya, L.V. and Putsko, V.G. 1989. Davn'orus'ki enkolpiony v Muzei istorii Kyeva. *Arkheologiya* no. 3. Kyiv.

Pekarskaya, L.V. and Putsko, V.G. 1991. Vizantiyskaya melkaya plastika iz arkheologicheskikh nakhodok na Ukraine. *Yuzhnaya Rus'i Vizantiya.* Sbornik Nauchnuikh Trudov (k 18 Kongressu Vizantinistov). Kiev.

Sagajdak, M.A. 1982. *Velikiy Gorod Jaroslava.* Kiev.

Tolochko, P.P. 1978. Nove u vyvchenni Kyeva. *Arkheologiya* vol. 26. Kyiv.

Tolochko, P.P. 1983. *Drevny Kiev.* Kiev.

Tolochko, P.P. 1991. Kiev – sopernik Konstantinopolya. *Yuzhnaya Rus' i Vizantiya.* Sbornik Nauchnuikh Trudov (k 18 Kongressu Vizantinistov). Kiev.

Tolochko, P.P. and Gupalo, K.N. 1973. Issledovaniya drevnekievskogo Podola. *Arkheologicheskie Otkruitiya 1972.* Kiev.

Tolochko, P.P. et al. 1974. Raskopki Kievskogo Podola. *Arkheologicheskie Otkruitiya 1973g.* Moscow.

Tolochko, P.P. et al. 1976. Rozkopky Kyevopodolu 1973r. *Arkheologichni Doslidzhennya Starodavn'ogo Kyeva.* Kyiv.

14. Archaeological Museums in Croatia: Past, Present and Future

Branko Kirigin

"The 15th century, time of the overall rebirth in the field of science and arts in Europe, the rebirth which was created by different circumstances and historical events, especially the fall of Constantinople into the Turkish hands and the exodus of learned men from the Greek side to the West, of which some stopped in Dalmatia, the land which was impossible not to be touched, as it was and is, from time immemorial, the bridge between the East and the West."

These are the words of Frane Bulić (1846–1934), the most outstanding name in Croatian archaeology. He wrote this in 1925 and it is the first paragraph from his detailed study "Development of Archaeological Research and Learning in Dalmatia in the Last Millennium" which he wrote when he was 80 years old (Bulić 1925, 1).

Bulić was for over 40 years director of my Museum, the Split Archaeological Museum, which was founded in 1820 and is the oldest museum in southeast Europe. Bulić became the director in 1883, but had already in 1879 started to contribute to the museum's own journal *Bullettino di archaeologia e storia dalmata* (from 1920 *Vjesnik za arkeologiju i historiju dalmatinsku*) . The journal, founded a year earlier, included a letter by T. Mommsen which speaks about the importance of the start of a new journal. Bulić edited the journal for 44 years. This oldest running archaeological journal was his *monumentum aere perennius* and in 114 years of its existence 83 volumes have been published with many supplements. Abroad, he acquired a wide reputation, especially after the successful excavations of the

early Christian church at Manastirine in Salona – the most important and impressive Early Christian cemetery *sub divo* in Europe. But as early as 1888, Bulić published the first study of early Croatian monuments found in the region of Knin. The year 1894 is especially famous for our archaeology. In that year Bulić organized the first international congress for Early Christian archaeology in Split and Solin. Its 100th anniversary will be celebrated in 1994 in Split and Poreč.

In the same year, 1894, Bulić founded the Society "BIHAĆ", with the goal to promote research in to Croatian history and its monuments (Duplančić 1982, 1059–1071; Marin *et al.* 1992, 89–93). Special credit must be given to Bulić for his research and preservation of Diocletan's Palace; and thanks to him many foreign scholars came to study the Palace and other archaeological sites in Dalmatia. Among them was Sir Arthur Evans (Fig. 14.2) (Wilkes 1976, 26–56; Kirigin 1988, 217–225). It was he who was responsible for the construction of our Museum, which was completed just at the beginning of the First World War (Fig. 14.1). Bulić became a member of many scientific institutions and societies across Europe; he was also a honorary doctor of the university of Zagreb and the honorary member of the Jugoslav Academy of Science and Arts in Zagreb, now the Croatian Academy of Science and Arts.

All this refers to Split. But in 1879 in Zagreb, the capital of Croatia, Šime Ljubić (1822–1896), a native from Stari Grad on the island of Hvar, a highly educated scholar, founded the Croatian Archae-

Fig. 14.1 The Archaeological Museum at Split between the two World Wars. (Archive of the Archaeological Museum, Split)

ological Society and the journal *Vjesnik Hrvatskog arheološkog drustva* (1879–1895) which later, in 1919, became the journal of the Archaeological Museum in Zagreb under the name of *Vjesnik Arheološkog muzeja u Zagrebu*. Before Ljubić became a member of the Academy of Science and Arts in its founding year of 1867, he was running the museum I work in, but due to political reasons he left Split and went to Vienna, and from there to Venice in whose archives he found and published material concerning the medieval history of Croatia. Coming from Venice to Zagreb he became the director of the National Museum, and one commentator wrote that "he lived in the Museum and lived for the Museum".

Ljubić was a great scholar. He was a close friend of Petar Nisiteo (1774–1866) a patrician from Stari Grad, a very learned man who had an archaeological collection at his house, with monuments from Pha-

ros on Hvar, a colony of the early 4th-century BC, founded by the Greeks from the Aegean island of Paros. He was the first Croat to be a member of the Archaeological Institute at Rome and Zentralkommision in Vienna. When Mommsen visited Nisiteo in Stari Grad while collecting inscriptions for his monumental CIL, he described him as "venerabilis vere senex". Way back in the 1830s and 1840s Nisiteo started to publish epigraphical and numismatical material from Dalmatia thus planting modern archaeology in Croatia. Nisiteo was the one who generated Ljubić's love for history and archaeology.

But luckily Ljubić had a great successor in Josip Brunšmid (1858–1929). Brunšmid came to the Archaeological department at the National Museum in Zagreb in 1893 after he received his Ph.D in Vienna on *Zur Geschischte der Griechischen Colonien in*

Dalmatien – which is even today the fundamental work on the Greek presence in Dalmatia. This was published in Vienna in 1898 under the title *Die Inscriften und Münzen der Griechischen Stäte Dalmatiens*. In the same year Brunšmid became the first professor of archaeology at the University of Zagreb – the department being in the museum where he made inventories of over 100,000 objects, publishing the journal and separate works, and making a network of volunteers in Slavonia and Lika, such as Bulić in Dalmatia.

One can freely say that Ljubić, Bulić and Brunšmid – the first trained archaeologists in Croatia – introduced modern archaeology to our country. They are not only responsible for the development of classical archaeology, but also for prehistoric and medieval archaeology. The discoveries of sites, monuments and inscriptions of Early Croatian nobles and royal families by Bulić and Lujo Marun, a Franciscan monk who founded the Museum of Croatian Archaeological Monuments in Knin in 1893, added greatly to the awakening of Croats to their long history and the right to speak and learn their own language. In 1895 the Museum in Knin founded its journal *Starohravtska prosvjeta* which continues to be published today.

Croatia in the 19th century was part of the Austrio-Hungarian empire and it was in Vienna where all of our pioneers gained their education. But the roots of the interest in the past go deeper as Bulić has clearly shown in his study which I have already mentioned above.

The first archaeological collection was formed in the early 16th century in the house of the nobleman Dominik Papalić in the heart of Diocletian's Palace in Split. From there on we have a continuous and progressive interest in exploring and preserving archaeological monuments until the foundation of the Archaeological Museum in the early 19th century when professional museum activities started (Bulić 1925, 1–151; Zaninović 1987, 1–171; Kirigin and Marin 1989, 17–23). The five archaeological museums that I am speaking of here are the leading archaeological institutions in Croatia.

The period between the two World Wars was marked first by the death of Brunšmid and then by Bulić. Both had great successors: Viktor Hoffiler

(1877–1954), who became the director of the Zagreb Museum in 1918 and Mihovil Abramić (1874–1952), who in 1926 became the director of the Split Museum. They were very active, wrote profusely, contributed to many international conferences, and had many friends abroad. In honour of their forerunners Bulić and Brunšmid, they edited two monumental volumes with papers written by the greatest archaeologists of the time (Abramić and Hoffiler 1924; Hoffiler 1928). And thanks to them the collections in Zagreb and Split did not suffer during the Second World War.

In 1943 when the Germans were attacking Dalmatia the intellectuals of Dalmatia gathered on the island of Hvar for a conference which launched an appeal to protect the cultural heritage; and in 1944 the First Congress of intellectuals of Croatia held in Topusko made similar initiatives, which on 25th of February 1945, were accepted by the National Committee of Liberation of Yugoslavia and passed as a law on protection of the cultural heritage (Zaninović 1987, 22).

During the Second World War Istria and part of Dalmatia were in Italian possession, and when Pula was under Anglo-American rule at the end of the War, all of the archaeological material, except heavy stone monunments, were taken away by the occupying troops and transported to Italy. Finally from 1947 the remaining items became part of the Archaeological Museum of Istria whose keepers have expanded their collection through excavations all over the peninsula and from the sea around it. In 1961 much of the material taken to Italy was brought back after long negotiations. For this we have to thank our Istrian colleagues, mainly the late Boris Bačić, Stefan Mlakar, Branko Marušić, Josip Mladin, Ante Šonje and Vesna Jurkić-Girardi, who is now Croatian Minister for Culture and Education. In 1970 they started to publish the journal of the museum *Histria archaeologica*, and in 1973 they opened to the public the newly renovated Museum with new displays (Jurkić *et al.* 1978). A year later a permanent archaeological display was opened on the nearby Briuni Islands with exhibits from the prehistoric and Classical periods found during excavations on these islands (Zaninović 1987, 33–35). Now the Museum is run by a very active young generation; and luckily

Fig. 14.2 Don Frane Bulić and Sir Arthur Evans in front of The Temple of the Diocletian's Palace, 1932 (Archive of the Society "Bihać" at the Archaeological Museum, Split).

Istria did not suffer destruction in the recent aggression against Croatia.

The Museum in Zadar (founded in 1830), situated until 1979 in the Church of St Donat, was very active during the rebuilding of the town after World War Two and also in North Dalmatia which is traditionally the territory of the Museum: formerly the territory of the Iron Age tribe of the Liburni. It was Mate Suić who ran the Museum after the War; and he deserves special credit for the development of archaeology in this region. The Museum grew rapidly, started to publish its own journal, *Diadora*, and in 1976 moved into a building in the heart of modern Zadar opposite St Donat's Church (Batović 1982). The library of the Museum has over 24,000 books and journals and *Diadora* is exchanged with over 400 journals in Croatia and abroad. The Museum stores over 140,000 objects. There are now six archaeologists working there and one in the collection at Nin. They have made many excavations and exhibitions, and organized the international "Neothermal Dalmatia Project" with colleagues from England.

The development of archaeology in Zagreb is also very significant as it enjoys the greatest concentration of archaeologists (49 employed). After the Second World War the Archaeological Museum moved from inadequate space in the Academy of Science and Arts into a new building in the centre of the town. This made it possible to display the rich Egyptian, prehistoric, ancient and medieval artefacts and, especially the famous numismatical collection. Recently in the back yard of the Museum a modern Lapidarium was opened to the public. The Museum has some 400,000 objects, a library with over 33,000 books and journals, publishes its own journal and has an exchange with over 300 institutions. In the last 10 years colleagues here have made 29 exhibitions, which have travelled in many parts of Croatia and in France, Germany, Austria, Spain, Russia, Italy and other republics of the ex-Yugoslavia. The Zagreb

Museum has 10 archaeologists and most of their excavation activity is connected with northern and central Croatia where they collaborate with local and regional museums.

And now I return to Split from where I started. The Museum of Croatian Archaeological Monuments which, during the Second World War, was moved from Knin to Sinj thanks to Stjepan Gunjača, and thus saved from the very probable devastation by the occupying forces; after the war it was moved to Split. To the existing holdings the early Croatian collection of the former Society of "Bihać" was added, which was a valuable enlargement. A new spacious and modern museum was opened to the public in 1978 (Jelovina *et al.* 1979). Recently the Museum has been directed by Zlatko Gunjača, who came from the Town Museum of Šibenik where the archaeological department is very active, and which has the best archaeological display in Croatia.

And at the end of this survey I will say something about the Archaeological Museum where I work and where I was director between 1982 and 1987 (Kirigin 1990, 327–352). After the Second World War the Museum had a regional role covering the area from Šibenik to Dubrovnik and from Sinj to the north and the central Dalmatian islands to the south. For the revival of the Museum the person most responsible was Duje Rendić-Miočevič, the first director of the Museum after the War. He was succeeded by Branimir Gabričević who was director for 12 years. He was also the co-director of an American-Croatian team excavating at Salona between 1969 and 1971. He later became professor of classical archaeology at Zadar. In his time the Museum was released of its responsibility for Diocletian's Palace which went to the newly founded Urban Institute of Split and Split's Institute for the Protection of Cultural Monuments whose first director was Gabričević. In the time when Mladen Nikolaci was director the Museum celebrated its 150 anniversary. A new display was made for the occasion (Rapanić *et al.* 1973) and the first international Symposium, *Disputationes Salonitanae*, was held in 1970 (Rapanić ed. 1975). Nikolanci introduced hydroarchaeology to our Adriatic coast which was later continued by Nenad Cambi and Željko Rapanić, both late directors of our Museum. Afterwards Nikolaci Željko Rapanić became

the director and in 1978 "*Disputationes Salonitanae* 2*" was organized on the occasion of the 100 anniversary of our journal, marked also with a small exhibition (Marin and Anzulović 1979). Although the employment in the museum grew there was no way to continue the work in Salona as in the times of Bulić, also as the site was threatened by intensive building activity.

In 1983 the museum managed to open at Vis its archaeological collection dedicated to the Greek colony of Issa (Kirigin 1983) but did not manage to continue excavations and survey, only sporadically.

In 1984 the Museum marked the 50th anniversary of the death of Frane Bulić with a symposium dedicated to his life and work ("*Disputationes Salonitanae 3: Bulić – 50 godina nakon smrti*" published in 1986 in the 79th volume of our journal) on which occasion an exhibition with the same title was organised in the Museum (Marin ed. 1984) That year in his *Tusculum* in Salona, next to the site which made him world-famous and where he is buried, we opened a small "Bulić's Memorial Room", and in the Museum in Split a new hall was opened named "Bulić's Hall" where lectures can be given and small exhibitions mounted.

1986 was also significant for the development of other museum activities. After several unsuccessful projects in Salona, a new one was initiated which engaged all the relevant institutions from the republics level to the local authorities. Finally the Salona Project started to be financed continuously, and 13 new persons were employed.

My successor, the present director Emilio Marin, is also very active. Now he is engaged in organizing the early Christian Congress in 1994, and in 1993 he made a major initiative: the conference and an exhibition on Early Croatian Solin – the most celebrated site of our early history (Marin *et al.* 1992). The Museum also runs two projects: one on early Christian Salona with French colleagues which started in 1982, and one with an English-Canadian-Slovenian team on Hvar, the "Hvar Project – the Archaeology of a Mediterranean Landscape" which started in 1987. Seven archaeologists now work in the Museum which has over 200,000 objects, and after Athens and Rome the largest epigraphical collection. The library (Fig. 14.3) has over 45,000 books and

Fig. 14.3 The Library of the Archaeological Museum, Split (Archive of the Archaeological Museum, Split).

journals and has over 360 exchanges of publications.

I will now turn to the future, which does not seem to be at all favourable. Although one has witnessed a constant development of museums in Croatia, the financing of systematic excavations and survey was never promoted by the government of the former Communist regime. There was no continuous and systematic fieldwork on any site or region in Croatia during the post-War period. Mostly rescue excavations were done or simple trenches which portrayed the field archaeology in Croatia as under-developed in contrast to other countries. The relatively low activity in the field contrasts markedly with the great amount of devastation especially on the coast where tourist industry has grown uncontrollably. Split has suffered the most uncontrolled imigration and expansion of cement and oil industries, along with the building of houses, roads and railways.

In Croatia (56,538 sq. km with a population of over 4,500,000) at present, apart from the five archaeological museums, there are seven public archaeological collections (Bol, Hvar, Nin, Sinj, Vela Luka, Vid and Vis), three departments at regional museums (Osijek, Dubrovnik and Sibenik) and 31 departments in local museums. Before the recent war in ex-Yugoslavia started there were 156 archaeologists employed in Croatia, in 90 institutions. After the Second World War many new regional and local museums were founded and now more than 100 archaeologists work in them. This is a significant growth, but still half of the regional authorities in Croatia have no museums and no archaeologists (Kirigin and Milosević 1991, 74–47). Although one can say that this is a significant growth and that the museums have good and modern displays, the visitor levels are very low. This is mainly because of the

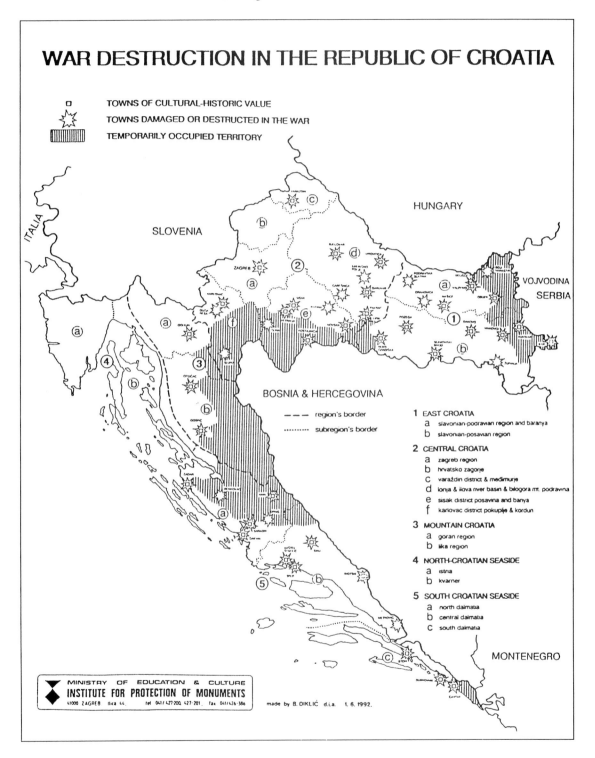

Fig. 14.4 War destruction in the republic of Croatia.

education system of the former Communist regime, especially in the 1970s, when the system allowed for no history or heritage programmes. When one looks at the school books for elementary and high schools of the period, only a few pages were dedicated to prehistory or classical and medieval history. This has been a complete catastrophy for at least 15 generations of school children in the former Yugoslavia.

Finally in Croatia what field archaeology exists is badly organized. There is a distinct lack of coordination, a fact reflected in the low employment figures: there is only one museum that employs 10 archaeologists. Specialists are lacking too. Also funds for archaeological fieldwork are inadequate and badly distributed. There are no sites of priority, be it for rescue or scientific excavations.

As a quarter of my country is under Serb occupation and has witnessed a violent and brutal devastation also of cultural monuments – most notably the towns of Vukovar, Dubrovnik and Zadar (Fig. 14.4) – it is extremely hard to start or organize museum and field work and the protection and restoration of the damaged sites and monuments.

Of the 46 museums and galleries in Coratia which have been damaged in the current war the Town Museum of Vukovar is completely destroyed and the collection taken away to Serbia; the Museum at Ilok is under Serbian occupation, and the museums at Gospić, Karlovac, Osijek, Split, Sibenik and Vinkovci have suffered shell damage. Finally, more than 200 archaeological sites that we know of, mostly in north-east Croatia, have been destroyed (Jurić ed. 1992, 7–62; Šulc 1992, 13–19).

We hope that the international community will help us after the war is over as many sites are of world heritage importance and some are protected by UNESCO.

Acknowledgements

I would like to thank kindly the directors of the Archaeological Museums of Zadar, Zagreb and Pula; Miro Jurić, Ante Rendić and Robert Matijašić, and Zlatko Gunjača, the Director of the Museum of Croatian Archaeological Monuments in Split, for their help and information which I mention in this paper.

References

Abramić, M. and Hoffiler, V. 1924. *Strena Buliciana*, Zagreb.

Batović, S. 1982. *150 godina Arheološkog muzeja u Zadru*, Zadar.

Bulić, F. 1925. Razvoj arheoloskih istrazivanja i nauka u Dalmaciji kroz zadnji milenij, Supplement to *Vjesnik za arheologiju i historiju dalmatinsku* for 1924–1925, Split.

Duplančić, A. 1982. Počeci rada društva "Bihać", *Mogućnosti*, 11–12, Split.

Gnirs, A. 1915. *Ein Führer durch die antiken Baudenkmäler und Sammlungen*, Wien.

Hoffiler, V. 1928. *Vjesnik Hrvatskog arheološkog društva* N.S. 15, Zagreb.

Jelovina, D. *et al.* 1979. *Muzej Hrvatskih arheoloških spomenika, vodič*, Split.

Jurkić, V. *et al.* 1978. *Arheološki muzej Istre*, Pula.

Jurkić, V. (ed.) 1992. *The War in Coatia: Archaeological Sites*, Zagreb.

Kirigin, B. 1983. *ΙΣΣΑ – otok Vis u helenističko doba*, Split.

Kirigin, B. 1988. Arthur Evans u Dubrovniku (1875–1882), *Arheoloska istrazivanja u Dubrovniku i dubrovackom prodrucju*, Occasional publications of the Hrvatsko arheolosko drustvo 12, Zagreb.

Kirigin, B. 1990. Rad Arheološkog muzeja od 1. 1. 1983. do 1. 1. 1988. godine, *Vjesnik za arheologiju i historiju dalmatinsku* 83, Split.

Kirigin, B. and Marin, E. 1989, *The Archaeological Guide to Central Dalmatia*, Split.

Kirigin, B. and Milosević, A. 1991. Kolege, evo gdje smo!, *Obavijesti Hrvatskog arheoloskog drustva* 23/2, Zabreb.

Marin, E. and Anzolović, N. 1979. *100 godina Vjesnika za arheologiju i historiju dalmatinsku*, Split.

Marin, E. (ed.) 1984. *Don Frane Bulić*, Split.

Marin, E. *et al.* 1992. Starohrvatski Solin, Split.

Rapanić, Z. *et al.* 1973. *Archaeological museum at Split*, Split.

Rapanić, Ž. (ed.) 1975, *Disputationes Saloniatanae* 1, Split.

Suić, M. *et al.* 1954. *Muzeji i zbirke Zadra*, Zadar.

Šulc, B. 1992. T*he Museum of Croatia in the Destruction of War, The War Apocalypse of the Cultural Heritage of Croatia*, Informatica Museologica 1/4 (1991), Zagreb.

Wilkes, J.J. 1976. Arthur Evans in the Balkans 1875–81, *Bulletin of the Archaeological Institute*, 13, London.

Zaninović, M. 1987. Antička arheologija u Hrvatskoj, *Opuscula Archaeologica* 11–12, Zagreb.

15. Artefact Research in the National Museums of Scotland

Alan Saville

My purpose in this paper (which follows closely the talk as given, with the addition of references) is to give a brief account of the origin and recent development of the Artefact Research Unit (hereafter ARU) in the National Museums of Scotland (hereafter NMS) in Edinburgh, and then to describe some of its work. As initial background, I want to stress that the ethos upon which the ARU is based and upon which it continues to operate, is that, in the context of museum archaeology, the artefact is paramount. It is primarily artefacts which are collected and curated by museums as the evidence for the material culture of the human past, and it is through the study, publication, and display of these artefacts, that museums interpret the past in the present.

While artefact research can and does take place outside museums – especially within excavation units and to a lesser extent now in universities – it cannot be complete without reference to museum collections, which provide the historical and comparative dimensions. (As for definitions, by artefact I mean any item humanly modified or created, in practice normally portable or readily moveable items, but not exclusively so, and by research I mean applied study in its widest sense, without wanting to make arbitrary divisions between types of finds work or curatorial research.) Museums themselves, particularly the national and major university and regional museums, are the obvious *loci* – as well as *foci* – for artefact research because of the depth of their collections; indeed, without active participation in research these museums are merely warehouses and shop-windows.

The archaeological collections now in the NMS have their origins in the 18th-century collection of the Society of Antiquaries of Scotland (Anderson 1989; Stevenson 1981a). This material was already voluminous by the end of the 19th century (Anon. 1892) and has continued to grow apace during the 20th century (Stevenson 1981b), inflated most recently by the past two decades or so of rescue excavation in Scotland. Fortunately, the regional and local museums throughout Scotland play an increasing role in the curation and display of new archaeological finds.

The national archaeological collection in Edinburgh is generally recognized to be one of the most comprehensive holdings of antiquities from one western European nation in a single museum (Clarke 1991). In Edinburgh this great depth of the archaeological collection is regarded unequivocally as an asset which presents a multifarious curatorial challenge, rather than in any sense as a burden.

This is not to be naive or to ignore, Nelson-like, the very real problems of coping with such extensive collections (the former ARU premises literally did have skeletons in the cupboards!). We are all only too well aware of the inadequacies which stem from limitations on museum resources – both human and material. I am not going to dwell on these problems and inadequacies, pressing though they are, in this paper; instead I want to make the point that these require novel solutions to exploit the potential of collections, to maximize their use in a dynamic sense, and simply to get as much relevant work done as possible.

One such solution in Edinburgh was the formation of the ARU in 1978. The ARU was the creation of Dr David V. Clarke, now Keeper of Archaeology in the NMS, when he was Research Assistant in the former National Museum of Antiquities of Scotland (Clarke and Wickham-Jones 1981). The immediate objectives were to foster sound and innovative artefact research by providing space, equipment, and encouragement for research workers using the collections, and also to provide the facilities for post-excavation processing and analysis of material from the Museum's own excavations, seeking to achieve a higher standard of finds work than that which then prevailed. Given the shortage of finds specialists in Scottish archaeology, the ARU was also to be a "honeypot" to attract specialists from outside.

Premises were found in Edinburgh, initially together with other outposted museum services such as photography and analytical research in Randolph Crescent (Fig. 15.1), then from 1981 onwards in the solitary splendour of an office suite in Coates Place. Imaginative accounting allowed these ARU premises to be equipped and maintained, though not – as is nearly always the problem with this kind of initiative in Britain – to have their own permanent staff. Personnel were, therefore, funded in a variety of ways: by research grants, by excavation and post-excavation budgets, particularly with funds from what was then the Historic Buildings and Monuments section of the Scottish Development Department, and by short-term Museum contracts. University postgraduate students were encouraged to work on finds at the ARU (Foxon 1991; MacSween 1990), and other workers came on an entirely voluntary basis. It has to be remembered that during much of this period there were only two or three curatorial staff in the Archaeology Department of the National Museum of Antiquities, and against this background the amount of work undertaken at the ARU during the 1980s was considerable (e.g. Clarke 1989a; Clarke and Kemp 1984; Sharples 1984; and numerous specialist finds reports).

This work included the pioneering studies of lithic raw material exploitation in Scottish prehistory by

Fig. 15.1 In the beginning: sorting sieved residues in the first ARU premises in Randolph Crescent in 1978. The recovery of artefactual and ecofactual remains by sieving was a major research theme of early work at the ARU. (Photo: NMS)

Caroline Wickham-Jones (1981; 1985; 1986), who was closely associated with the ARU during this formative period and in effect acted as its unofficial manager. These studies were followed by her excavations of a mesolithic site on the island of Rhum in the Inner Hebrides, currently the earliest known site of human occupation in Scotland. The Rhum project, funded by the Scottish Development Department from its budget for rescue archaeology, was based at the ARU, where all the post-excavation was undertaken. The final report on this project is now published (Wickham-Jones 1990), and the 130,000 lithic artefacts recovered from Rhum have been incorporated within the NMS collections.

One very significant element of the ARU's early work was an emphasis upon technology, explored by practical experiment and replication, particularly of lithic items (Clarke 1989b; Clarke 1992; McCartan 1987; Wickham-Jones 1982), but not exclusively so (Clarke and Wickham-Jones 1981; Foxon 1991; Wickham-Jones *et al.* 1986). Raw materials were collected and worked, and the lessons learnt were successfully disseminated by lectures and practical demonstrations throughout Scotland and beyond.

In 1985, under the *National Heritage (Scotland) Act*, the former National Museum of Antiquities of Scotland and the former Royal Scottish Museum were amalgamated as part of the National Museums of Scotland, both becoming known, somewhat confusingly, as the Royal Museum of Scotland. (In an attempt to resolve this confusion, as from the end of 1992, the Royal Museum of Scotland, Queen Street, is to be known as the NMS's Museum of Antiquities.)

This change in 1985 had no immediate effect on the ARU, other than a change of notepaper and signage, though as a smaller cog in a much bigger wheel, the ARU had an even harder task to gain resources, and for a time in subsequent years was operating at a somewhat low ebb. In late 1987, Dr Alison Sheridan, previously employed on a post-excavation contract in the ARU, became Assistant Keeper of the Department of Archaeology and began to press on behalf of the freelance researchers for a new operating system for the ARU. Dr Robert Anderson, then Director of the NMS, became suffi-

ciently persuaded of the merits of this small outpost of his empire to steer through the appointment of an archaeological curator with specific responsibility for the ARU, and I took up this new post of Head of the ARU in late 1989.

The opportunity also arose at about the same time to bring the ARU in from the cold in a physical sense. Since 1978 the ARU had been located in its two successive sets of separate premises in the West End of Edinburgh at some distance from the Museum collections, from its library, and from other staff, with consequent losses of efficiency, communication, and identity. One of my first tasks on appointment was to draw up plans for the fitting out of new premises for the ARU on the ground floor of York Buildings in Queen Street, an administrative base of the NMS opposite the Findlay Building, which currently houses the archaeological displays. (The space was used as storage areas at the time, but had formerly been temporary exhibition galleries, where, for example, the *Symbols of Power at the Time of Stonehenge* exhibition had been held in 1985.)

The new premises were occupied in July 1991, and provide greatly improved accommodation for an expanded range of activities. Essentially open plan, the main area has storage shelving, work-benches (Fig. 15.2), and semi-screened work-stations (Fig. 15.3). The storage shelving holds up to 1000 standard-sized boxes, containing material currently being studied, which may be from the NMS collection or may be finds in course of post-excavation, either destined for the NMS or for other museums.

A second open-plan area serves as the drawing office, the illustration of artefacts being an increasingly important aspect of the ARU's work (Fig. 15.4). Part of this same area is for visitor reception, where public enquiries can be handled and informal meetings held. Adjacent is a room for slide viewing and more formal meetings, and there are other rooms for secure storage, and a manager's office. Dirty work, such as finds-washing, wet- and dry-sieving, and practical lithic technology, takes place in the basement area of the same building.

The work in progress at the ARU on a day-to-day basis is varied, fluctuating according to which projects are active at any time. These can range from

Fig. 15.2 General view of the storage and bench area in the new ARU premises in 1992. (Photo: NMS)

Fig. 15.3 One of the work-stations adjacent to the storage and bench area in the new ARU premises in 1992. Curator Trevor Cowie working on post-excavation projects funded by Historic Scotland. (Photo: NMS)

Fig. 15.4 Illustrators Marion O'Neil and Alan Braby in the new ARU premises in 1992. (Photo: NMS)

the purely internal, arising from the NMS's own needs, to wholly external projects, sometimes undertaken on a semi-commercial basis. This is best explained by describing some recent work.

The ARU is currently undertaking a major backlog post-excavation project on behalf of Historic Scotland. This involves all the normal post-excavation tasks plus the compilation of the site report on behalf of the original excavators. This in a sense is standard archaeological unit fare, the difference and attraction as far as we are concerned being the number and quality of the finds from this particular site. The funding from Historic Scotland allows us to recruit freelance staff to work under the aegis of the ARU on this project.

Income generation is involved here, and it has to be admitted that the potential for revenue earning helps to make the ARU attractive to the NMS administrators. Income generation is clearly important for a variety of reasons, not least of which is political expediency. However, although the work of the ARU helps to give the Archaeology Department a higher

income through-put than other departments in the NMS, we also, in the absence of core staff in the ARU, spend much more on paying casual and freelance personnel; so any profit, in financial terms, is actually very modest. I would not in any case seek to justify the ARU's activities on the basis of financial gain, but prefer to assess the profit in terms of output of good finds work achieved. The outside income allows us to undertake important finds work to a high standard which otherwise might not be accomplished; and I am well aware of the potential danger of undertaking a lot of routine finds work just for the sake of increasing the profit on the balance sheet.

Nevertheless, we remain flexible and intend to keep experimenting with ways of getting finds work done. We have, for example, undertaken one project using a bench-fee approach, whereby a freelance specialist paid us for accommodation and facilities while undertaking research on a collection of steatite artefacts and waste material from the excavation of a Viking steatite quarry on Shetland; the obvious attraction for the specialist being that he did not have to find space to store nearly a tonne of rock in his flat! The material from this site will be curated by Lerwick Museum in Shetland, not by the NMS.

A smaller project, ultimately funded again by Historic Scotland, but actually undertaken for Aberdeen Art Gallery and Museums, which will curate the finds, involved specialist analysis of metallurgical debris from a medieval site. In this case we recruited a temporary technician to work under the supervision of a curator with expertise in this field (Fig. 15.5). This is the kind of work we would like to increase, not in this instance because the assemblage itself was necessarily of any great interest, but because it has a training element, which spreads much-needed artefactual and post-excavation skills within Scotland. One of our long-term objectives is a widening of the pool of artefact specialists and technicians available in Scotland.

The short supply of such skills in Scotland at the moment is emphasized by another current project. We are in the post-excavation phase of a NMS-sponsored excavation on a neolithic site at Loch Olabhat on North Uist in the Outer Hebrides (Armit 1991). The excavation of this site has produced a large and crucially important pottery assemblage of some 20,000 sherds, including a very high proportion of decorated sherds and reconstructable profiles. It was impossible to allocate the study of this assemblage to one of the departmental curators because of the amount of time needed, nor could we find anyone else within Scotland with the appropriate expertise who was available at the time to undertake the work. We thus turned to the Essex County Council Archaeological Unit in south-east England, and have come to an arrangement whereby their prehistoric pottery specialist, Nigel Brown, comes to Edinburgh to work in the ARU on this assemblage on a regular basis (Fig. 15.6), the cost being spread across three financial years. This work is proceeding well and will feed in to new archaeological displays and, in academic terms, will permit a timely re-evaluation of the neolithic pottery of the Western Isles. There is also an educational spin-off, since we have arranged for undergraduate students to visit this project in progress as part of their course on archaeological methodology.

This same project is a convenient point to mention the ARU's access to scientific expertise and analytical techniques and equipment through the NMS Analytical Research Section, headed by Dr Jim Tate, since pottery from the Loch Olabhat site is being used in a programme of research on residue analysis using gas chromatography (Nemcek and Quye 1991). Other facilities available include scanning electron microscopy, atomic absorption spectroscopy, and x-ray fluorescence analysis. Similarly, the ARU does not undertake its own conservation, but works closely with NMS antiquities conservators housed in laboratories within the same building.

The kind of artefact work which is normally undertaken in the ARU on a day-to-day basis can be described as processing: typological and characterizational studies, with a certain amount of functional analysis, geared to post-excavation reporting or museum documentation; but there are no implicit restrictions on types of approach, other than that there must always be direct reference to the objects themselves. Microwear studies were part of the original range of work covered at the ARU (Hope 1981a; 1981b), but are not currently being pursued, in part because of financial constraints, since microwear analysis is extremely expensive both in terms of equipment and labour.

Emphasis in the ARU's artefact work is placed upon the precision and clarity of identification, quantification, and descriptive analysis. This is particularly important when it comes to Treasure Trove work, in which the ARU and Department play a major and increasing role, especially now that the Department of Archaeology provides the Secretariat for the Treasure Trove Advisory Panel. Here it needs to be explained that in Scotland all archaeological finds are potentially the property of the Crown, and that the legislation known by shorthand as "Treasure Trove" applies to items of any kind, not just those of gold and silver as in England and Wales (Sheridan 1989).

Thus an important recent Treasure Trove assemblage consisted of a hoard of five flint axeheads and 170 associated flint flakes from near Campbeltown in south-west Scotland (Saville and Sheridan 1990). Work on this hoard, which is undoubtedly an Irish import, has involved comparative research at the

*Fig. 15.5 Curator Dr Mike Spearman guiding Irene Cullen in the specialist iden-
tification of metallurgical debris. (Photo: NMS)*

*Fig. 15.6 Pottery processing: Nigel Brown and the author with some of the Loch
Olabhat neolithic pottery. (Photo: NMS)*

Ulster Museum; the collection of raw material from the Antrim coast; replication studies in the ARU's knapping room; and video recording (Fig. 15.7).

Related to Treasure Trove is the work done as a result of discoveries notified to the Receivers of Wreck. A very recent case has involved fieldwork in association with the Archaeological Diving Unit and the Scottish Institute of Maritime Studies at St Andrews University, to recover and hold in stable conditions material from a newly designated historic wreck of mid-17th-century date off the coast of the Isle of Mull, in the Inner Hebrides.

The ARU is also actively involved in fieldwork of its own, within the framework of research to look at raw material procurement and exploitation in prehistoric Scotland. A first phase of this project, studying the location where raw material was obtained for the manufacture of stone axeheads and cushion maceheads of so-called Group XXIV rock, near Killin in Perthshire, has been completed and will shortly be published (Edmonds *et al.* forthcoming).

A second phase of this project is now in progress to study a flint extraction site at Den of Boddam, near Peterhead in north-east Scotland, where it is clear that digging took place on a massive scale to exploit the abundant flint cobbles available from an enigmatic, probably pre-Pleistocene deposit, which is Scotland's only major inland source of flint (Saville and Bridgland 1992). Funding for this project comes mainly from the NMS, which devotes a segment of its purchase grant to fieldwork, but the work at Den of Boddam has also benefited from generous outside sponsorship, particularly from Grampian Regional Council.

The facilities provided by the ARU are also of course regularly used by curators from the Archaeology Department for their own museum work or for projects of various kinds in which they are involved (Fig. 15.3). Since 1990, much of the Department's energy has been directed towards the creation of completely new permanent displays for a new National Museum (Anderson 1990). Building of the new museum – known at the moment as the "Museum of Scotland Project" – will begin in Chambers Street in Edinburgh in 1993, with completion and opening planned for 1998. This will entirely replace the existing museum in Queen Street, and there is

concurrently another major project in train to create a new research and storage centre at Granton in north-west Edinburgh to house the bulk of the NMS reserve collections, including the archaeological material, which at present is split between several locations. So these are very exciting times in Edinburgh, and there will no doubt be much publicity given to these developments over the next few years.

The new permanent displays being planned for archaeology by Dr David V. Clarke will be very different. Suffice it to say here that these new displays obviously involve fresh curatorial research on the collections, and that much of this is taking place in the ARU. As an example, the National collections for Scotland are extremely rich in artefacts made of bone and, particularly in the case of assemblages from the Northern and Western Isles, in artefacts made of cetacean bone, and to a lesser extent deer antler. In most previous displays these items have simply been described as a bone spindle-whorl or an antler comb, or whatever, without any reference either to the species or part of the skeleton represented, or how they were made, thus ignoring whole categories of data relevant to economy and technology. We are now attempting to make positive identifications for all the bone artefacts we intend to display, and to that end we have a bone specialist, Ywonne Hallén, working in the ARU on a temporary contract from the NMS (Fig. 15.8). This work is not restricted to identification, but seeks to develop the studies of bone technology and utilization previously undertaken at the ARU by Dr Andrew Foxon (1991; and in Clark *et al.* 1985).

There is a sense in which the work of the ARU I have described is the kind of work you might expect any national museum to undertake as a matter of course. That it does not always happen that way is precisely what we wish to avoid in Edinburgh. By using a separate name and maintaining a slightly separate identity, even though the ARU is firmly part of the Archaeology Department, we seek to maintain a high profile for artefact studies both within our own wider institution (Fig. 15.9) and also within Scottish archaeology and beyond.

We aim to promote artefact studies in the widest possible sense as an inalienable factor in museum curation and thus challenge current tendencies to

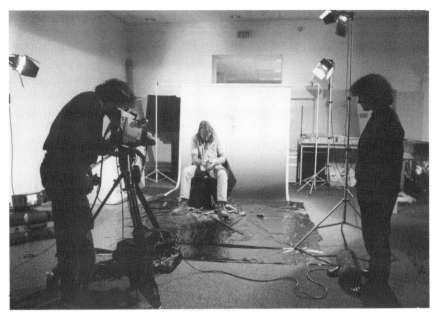

Fig. 15.7 Experimental replication of flint implements being recorded on video in the ARU by Great Scot Pictures. The knapper is Phil Harding of Wessex Archaeology. (Photo: NMS)

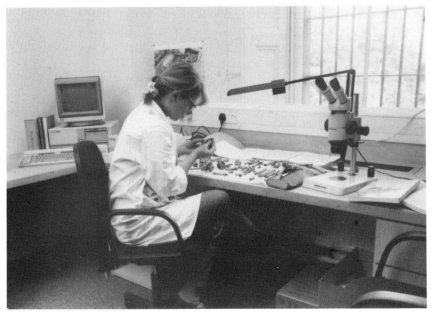

Fig. 15.8 Faunal remains analysis: bone specialist Ywonne Hallén. (Photo: NMS)

sideline them or entirely to divorce collections management from artefact research. As I maintained earlier, in the museum context artefacts are of paramount importance, and we must beware the situation of being swamped by paper or by computers or by committees or by administrators to such an extent that the artefacts themselves move into the background.

Artefacts are our direct responsibility to interpret and display and we gain by regular contact with them and frequent discussion about them. One of the incidental, but nevertheless very tangible advantages of having the ARU on the spot in Queen Street is that there are always new and interesting objects available to show visiting colleagues, scholars, students, museum specialists, Trustees, etc. This ability to show work in progress with reference to the actual artefacts is very important – even professionals are impressed by being able to see and sometimes handle objects! I can illustrate this with reference to two objects which have recently created great interest while in the ARU, one a new find and the other a very old one.

The new discovery is a Treasure Trove item, a long bow of yew found eroding from peat in Dumfriesshire, which has been radiocarbon-dated to 5040±100 uncal BP (OxA-3540) and is thus the earliest bow known from Britain (Sheridan 1992a and 1992b). The old find is a bog butter container from Glen Gell, Morvern, in Argyll, which was purchased by the Museum in 1879. It was first published in 1882, and has now been re-published by an outside researcher (Earwood 1991), who required new illustrations to be prepared in the ARU. The bog butter inside this container has recently been radiocarbon-dated to 1802±35 uncal BP (UB-3185), so the container is an early first millennium AD object, far older than was previously thought.

The approach taken in Edinburgh with the ARU is a local solution in response to local circumstances. The same configuration would not necessarily be applicable anywhere else, and similar work is undoubtedly achieved in other archaeological museums by completely different routes; the important thing is that the work is done. In an audience of museum archaeologists I am preaching to the con-

feature

Boffins move out of the backroom

Artefact Research Unit at York Buildings, Queen Street, Edinburgh (NMS)

Fig. 15.9 The heading from an article in the NMS's bimonthly magazine, recording the opening of the new ARU premises in 1991. The title for the feature was added by the magazine editor, not by the author! (Photo: NMS)

verted, but we should be aware that some of our academic colleagues are less persuaded of the value of research on artefacts. The current preference of some archaeologists working outside museums for a more mystical, more avowedly intuitive contact with the past (e.g. Shanks 1992), could be misinterpreted and promoted by those politicians and administrators who seek ever-cheaper options for our activities; it thus represents a trend which should be countered by championing the positive achievements of artefact research in museums whenever the opportunity arises.

Without venturing any further into the current debate on curatorial roles and identities, which Professor Biddle and Dr Longworth will be considering elsewhere in this volume, I will finish by expressing the hope that the work of the ARU in Edinburgh can continue to contribute towards preserving the study of finds, as a key element of both traditional and progressive archaeological scholarship within museums.

Acknowledgements

I am grateful to Dr David Clarke, Mr Trevor Cowie, Ms Annette Carruthers, and Dr Alison Sheridan for their helpful comments on draft versions of this text; any infelicities remain the responsibility of the author. All the photographs accompanying this article are reproduced by courtesy of the Trustees of the National Museums of Scotland.

Although the Artefact Research Unit is not open to the general public, visits by archaeologists, finds workers, museum professionals, and other interested individuals or groups are welcome and encouraged.

References

Anderson, R.G.W. 1989. Museums in the making: the origins and development of the national collections. In J. Calder (ed.), *The Wealth of a Nation in the National Museums of Scotland*, 1–17. Edinburgh: National Museums of Scotland.

Anderson, R.G.W. (ed.) 1990. *A New Museum for Scotland*. Edinburgh: National Museums of Scotland.

Anon. 1892. *Catalogue of the National Museum of Antiquities of Scotland*. Edinburgh: Society of Antiquaries of Scotland.

Armit, I. 1991. Loch Olabhat. *Current Archaeology* 127, 284–287.

Clarke, A. 1989a. Corse Law, Carnwath, Lanarkshire: a lithic scatter. *Proc Soc Antiq Scotland* 119, 43–54.

Clarke, A. 1989b. The Skaill knife as a butchering tool. *Lithics* 10, 16–27.

Clarke, A. 1992. Artefacts of coarse stone from Neolithic Orkney. In N. Sharples and A. Sheridan (eds), *Vessels for the ancestors: essays on the Neolithic of Britain and Ireland in honour of Audrey Henshall*, 244–258. Edinburgh: Edinburgh University Press.

Clarke, D.V. 1991. Managing output rather than input? The implications of computerising the National Museums of Scotland's archaeological information. In W.S. Hanson and E.A. Slater (eds), *Scottish archaeology: new perceptions*, 218–228. Aberdeen: Aberdeen University Press.

Clarke, D.V. and Kemp, M.M.B. 1984. A hoard of late Bronze Age gold objects from Heights of Brae, Ross and Cromarty District, Highland Region. *Proc Soc Antiq Scotland* 114, 189–198.

Clarke, D.V., Cowie, T.G., and Foxon, A. 1985. *Symbols of power at the time of Stonehenge*. Edinburgh: National Museum of Antiquities of Scotland.

Clarke, D.V. and Wickham-Jones, C.R. 1981. The Artifact Research Unit of the National Museum of Antiquities of Scotland. *Bulletin of Experimental Archaeology* 2, 14–17.

Earwood, C. 1991. Two early historic bog butter containers. *Proc Soc Antiq Scotland* 121, 231–240.

Edmonds, M., Sheridan, A., and Tipping, R. forthcoming. Survey and excavation at Creag na Caillich, Killin, Perthshire. *Proc Soc Antiq Scotland* 122.

Foxon, A.D. 1991. *Bone, antler, tooth, and horn technology and utilisation in prehistoric Scotland*. Unpublished PhD thesis, University of Glasgow.

Hope, R. 1981a. Aspects of microwear analysis of stone tools. In J. Kenworthy (ed.), *Early technology in north Britain*, 25–35. Edinburgh: Edinburgh University Press (= *Scottish Archaeological Forum* 11).

Hope, R. 1981b. The low-power microwear analysis of the flaked stone pieces. In Sharples, 45–47.

MacSween, A. 1990. *The Neolithic and Late Iron Age pottery from Pool, Sanday, Orkney*. Unpublished PhD thesis, Bradford University.

McCartan, S. 1987. Flint alternatives workshop: a report on the seminar held at the Artifact Research Unit, 2–3 April 1987. *Lithics* 8, 13–14.

Nemcek, N. and Quye, A. 1991. *Chromatographic analysis of organic residues from Scottish neolithic pottery*. Edinburgh: National Museums of Scotland (circulated report).

Saville, A. and Bridgland, D. 1992. Exploratory work at Den of Boddam, a flint extraction site on the Buchan Gravels near Peterhead, north-east Scotland. *Quaternary Newsletter* 66, 4–13.

Saville, A. and Sheridan, A. 1990. The Campbeltown flint hoard. *Past* 9, 4–5.

Shanks, M. 1992. *Experiencing the past: on the character of archaeology.* London: Routledge.

Sharples, N.M. 1981. The excavation of a chambered cairn, the Ord North, at Lairg, Sutherland by J.X.W.P. Corcoran. *Proc Soc Antiq Scotland* 111, 21–62.

Sharples, N.M. 1984. Excavations at Pierowall Quarry, Westray, Orkney. *Proc Soc Antiq Scotland* 114, 75–125.

Sheridan, A. 1989. What's mine is Her Majesty's: the law in Scotland. In E. Southworth (ed.), *What's mine is yours! – museum collecting policies,* 35–40. Liverpool: Society of Museum Archaeologists (= *The Museum Archaeologist* 16).

Sheridan, A. 1992a. A longbow from Rotten Bottom, Dumfriesshire, Scotland. *NewsWARP* 12, 13–15.

Sheridan, A. 1992b. The Rotten Bottom longbow. *Past* 14, 6.

Stevenson, R.B.K. 1981a. The Museum, its beginnings and its development. Part I: to 1858: the Society's own Museum. In A.S. Bell (ed.), *The Scottish antiquarian tradition,* 31–85. Edinburgh: John Donald.

Stevenson, R.B.K. 1981b. The Museum, its beginnings and its development. Part II: the National Museum to 1954. In A.S. Bell (ed.), *The Scottish antiquarian tradition,* 142–211. Edinburgh: John Donald.

Wickham-Jones, C.R. 1981. Flaked stone technology in northern Britain. In J. Kenworthy (ed.), *Early technology in north Britain,* 36–42. Edinburgh: Edinburgh University Press (= *Scottish Archaeological Forum* 11).

Wickham-Jones, C.R. 1982. Second international work seminar in lithic technology, Lejre, Denmark, 1981. *Scottish Archaeological Review* 1(2), 121–126.

Wickham-Jones, C.R. 1985. Stone. In D.V. Clarke, T.G. Cowie, and A. Foxon, *Symbols of power at the time of Stonehenge,* 164–175. Edinburgh: National Museum of Antiquities of Scotland.

Wickham-Jones, C.R. 1986. The procurement and use of stone for flaked tools in prehistoric Scotland. *Proc Soc Antiq Scotland* 116, 1–10.

Wickham-Jones, C.R. 1990. *Rhum, mesolithic and later sites at Kinloch, excavations 1984–86.* Edinburgh: Society of Antiquaries of Scotland (= Monograph Series 7).

Wickham-Jones, C.R., Clarke, P.A., and Barlow, A. 1986. A project in experimental archaeology: Avasjö 1982. *Review of Scottish Culture* 2, 97–104.

16.   Can We Expect Museums to Cope? Curatorship and the Archaeological Explosion

Martin Biddle

I write as both a producer and a consumer: as one who produces archaeological material by excavation and as one who expects to be able to carry out research on collections already in museums. Like libraries and archives, museums are places where we can legitimately expect the preservation of the achievements of human kind in the longest term. Although, as speakers have stressed, there has to be a balance between the roles of preservation and presentation, preservation in the longest term must be, above all else, the duty of the museum.

The public in general do not understand this role. We all know the criticisms: 'locked away in the museum's dusty basement'; 'never on show'; or, as one trustee put it to me once, 'You've got 400 African spears. You only need one'. This attitude is curious, because on the whole *big* libraries, and even *big* archives, are seen as good. The growth in Local Record Offices resulting in part at least from the Family History explosion is a case in point. Clearly, museums need to stress their 'library-like', 'archive-like' role.

Sadly, of course, 'the public' means all lay people, so that trustees, boards of managers, donors, and central and local government officers can all be equally unsympathetic to the fundamental responsibility of the museum to ensure preservation of the material achievements of humanity in the longest term – and I do mean the longest term. We must be thinking in terms of hundreds, indeed thousands of years.

Museum archaeology

For my present purpose, I shall divide museum archaeology into the two areas of excavation and curation.

In my view, museum archaeologists must have had proper experience of fieldwork and excavation in all its stages, from prospection and field survey, fieldwalking and excavation, through to publication, as part of their professional experience and training. If they do not have this, they cannot take part intelligently in the necessary discussions with archaeological colleagues on the deposition and selection of material, and still expect to be taken seriously.

Museums do not *have* to take part in active fieldwork to provide their staff with this experience. On the other hand there are many successful examples of museums which excavate. This is good and should be encouraged, but it is not necessary to insist that all archaeological museums should be excavating museums. These days we have a 'mixed economy' in our field, and it is probably here to stay, so that we now see work of all kinds, whether on, below, or above the ground, from survey to recording buildings, from field walking to excavation, carried out by museums, by units, and by contractors, and sometimes by all three in the same area. The situation probably has to be accepted, although it is fraught with problems, the greatest of which is quality control. This is not the place to go into a quagmire we all recognise, but an academic might perhaps be allowed to reflect on the virtual absence of an academic input from the universities, and on the assumption, ignoring all experience to the contrary from the United States, where the situation is far more developed than in Britain, that contract archaeology based on competitive tendering consistently delivers intellectually sound results. For our present purpose, the only requirement is that all excavators must be professional and collegial in their relationships with their museum colleagues and vice-versa, and that both sides must know enough about each other's assumptions, objectives and needs, about each other's agenda, to engage in mutually comprehensible dialogue.

Museums and archaeological storage

If we turn from museums as field-working bodies, to museums as curators of the product of archaeological activity, we need to examine three principal themes: the longest term, economies of scale, and selection.

It is worth stressing again, if only because it is always an unspoken and undefined assumption, that if a museum is not a safe store, and a safe store in the longest term, it is nothing. This above all else we have a right to assume and expect.

Let us deal next with economies of scale, with large-scale storage. Many of the problems discussed in this conference are the problems we deal with every day: bulk, quantity, shelf run, cubic metres. The problem is like one's own bookshelves: if there is no room for one more book in the right place, you shove it on top, or put it in a pile, or face re-ordering the whole lot. We all face constant problems with archaeological storage, problems of space, environmental suitability, availability. We have all experienced the sub-standard accommodation which is so often all that can be found or made available for archaeological material, the unsuitable conditions in which all too many seem to think it appropriate to keep (for how long?) expensively garnered archaeological materials of future, but inevitably unknown, potential.

We make this problem for ourselves. We think there is a problem, but only because we do not face it properly. The solution lies in the adoption of large-scale, purpose-built stores. These should

1. use the latest technology for bulk storage;
2. be under museum control. There is no point at all in having separate 'archaeological' stores under the control of non-museum archaeologists. Why waste all the accumulated experience of museum professionals in handling such problems? Unless, that is, museums refuse to face the problem of archaeological storage and decline to take any but the exhibitable, or potentially exhibitable, objects. Sad as it may be, there have been stirrings of such a view, unacceptable to any archaeologist concerned with the integrity of the archaeological product;
3. be properly staffed by store technicians, professionally trained as museum archaeological store keepers. It is nonsense to expect museum professionals to run stores, put things away, take them out, maintain stock control records, reallocate space. This is skilled technician's work, and in industry it always is. Museums are in some places beginning to work on an industrial scale and all must face up to the advantages it brings.

Let me give you an example of what I mean, the Oxford University Press distribution warehouse at Corby, Northamptonshire.[1] Here books arrive palletised from binders worldwide, at a rate of approximately 500 pallets a week. After checking the titles against delivery notes for quantity, quality, etc., and allocation of bulk store location by computer, they are fed by hand truck into the designated bulk store aisle (Fig. 16.1). In the aisle, the stock is located into racking by a narrow aisle crane according to a computer generated document. Each location has two alphabetical check digits which the driver marks on the document to verify the correct position: 16,500 pallet spaces are available, located on 11 levels, in 12 aisles, served by two cranes (Fig. 16.2). The cranes can transfer at the end of each aisle into the next required aisle. They make approximately 400 crane movements a day. When an order has to be filled, the required stock is picked from bulk via the computer system, ejected by conveyor from the bulk store, and passed through picking sections on the automated conveyor system to the packing department (Fig. 16.3).

You may tell me that museums cannot work on this scale. I say they must. Obviously this means grouping and sharing bulk storage facilities, and that means regionalisation. I recognise the problem, but rural or redevelopment sites offer the space, the labour force, and low rents per square foot.

Such a system does not mean that 'immediate stores' for material requiring frequent access and 'special stores' for material requiring special conditions cannot be maintained in museums, even if here too there may be gains from the efficiency of using the same large-scale storage facilities whenever possible. The obvious parallel is between open-shelf and on-site access in a library and book-stores off-site. Librarians may not like such stores, but it often simply impossible to combine bulk storage with immediate access in city-centre locations.

To summarise: an important part of the solution to the problem of archaeological storage is in specially designed bulk stores, maintained by trained technical staff, taking advantage of economies of site and scale and making the best use of modern technology.

Selection for permanent preservation (and thus also for disposal) is another part of this solution. There must be some degree of selection, but selection must be done by the excavating archaeologist working in the closest co-operation with archaeologically experienced museum staff. This is a collegial affair, where both parties have to understand fully and be sympathetic to each other's problems. That is why I expressed the view at the start of this talk that museum archaeological professionals must have a thorough grounding in fieldwork at all its stages. The corollary is that field archaeologists should be taught museum theory and practice, something which figures, I suspect, all too little in current university courses.

My own experience suggests that there may be real problems in the selection process. Of all the museums which hold finds from sites I have excavated only two (both represented at the conference) would be or have been competent to make the selection themselves on academic and archaeological grounds. Selection of archaeological materials has absolutely nothing to do with the question of display potential, a point perhaps worth emphasising at

a moment when arguments in favour of display potential as the important criterion have begun to be heard in certain quarters. It cannot be too strongly emphasised that decisions on selection have to be taken on archaeological and not on curatorial grounds.

Politics and finance

But how is all this to be paid for? As we all know, there are three possible sources: private, public, and the polluter.

Private finance is not a very likely source on any significant, long-term basis for museum stores. There are a few notable exceptions, such as the Ark in St Mary's Church, York, run by the York Archaeological Trust, but even here it is the Yorkshire Museum and not the Ark that is the final repository. My own experience suggests that storage comes very far down the list of attractive subjects for a donor.

Public finance, whether from local or central government, may not look very likely at the present moment, but ideas change, sometimes surprisingly fast. Bad times are the times to plan, to work out what is needed, to begin to make the case that must be urged year in, year out, and which must not be dulled by repetition, until a new climate is achieved. I am aware that this is difficult when survival may seem all that can be hoped for, but the voices of those who call for archaeological materials to be put in the middle of a field and ploughed back in (a fairly frequent refrain from a tiny minority of councillors in a certain cathedral city I know quite well) are in fact always unrepresentative, however gloomy things may sometimes seem.

Then there is the polluter. English Heritage have led the way in trying to build an element of financial responsibility for long-term storage into the requirements to be placed on the developer of an archaeological site in the event that excavation must take place. This is a very dangerous proposition. Developers cannot understand why, if they give the finds, having paid to dig them up, they must then pay for their reception and long-term preservation and storage. It is no good saying that they must do this, for people can only be pushed so far. The 'green movement in archaeology' is in great danger of destroy-

16.1

16.3

16.2

Figs. 16.1–16.3. Oxford University Press ware-house at Corby, Northamptonshire. 1, Books arrive palletised from binders worldwide, at a rate of ap-proximately 500 pallets a week. After checking against delivery notes for quantity, quality, etc., and allocation of bulk store location by computer, they are fed by hand truck, as here, into the designated bulk store aisle. 2, The stock is located into racking by a narrow aisle crane according to a computer generated document: 16,500 pallet spaces are avail-able, located on 11 levels, in 12 aisles, served by two cranes. The cranes can transfer at the end of each aisle into the next required aisle. They make approximately 400 crane movements a day. 3, Re-quired stock is picked from bulk via the computer system, ejected by conveyor from the bulk store, and passed through picking sections via the automated conveyor system, as here, to the packing department.

ing the goose that lays the golden egg by insisting on the so-called 'normal presumption in favour of preservation', all the implications of which have to be funded by the developer. There is a desperate need to inform the developer why these costs are being placed upon him, and to persuade him that, however unpalatable, they are reasonable and serve important ends. It is not good enough simply (and all too often over-zealously) to demand. There is already a backlash in this country and the example of Duisburg set out so clearly at this conference shows we are not alone (see Krause this volume).

As always, the problem is finance. However dif-ficult of achievement, it is almost certainly the re-sponsibility of local and central government to share the capital expenditure, and of local government to provide the running costs. Archives have to face this problem now with the impending round of local government reorganisation. Museums will have to face it too, if they are to cope, as certainly they must be expected to do, with the challenge of providing long-term accommodation for the products of man-kind's past achievements, archaeologically recov-ered.

Notes

1. I am grateful to Mr N.R. Killip, Director of Distribu-tion Services, OUP, Corby, and to his Secretary, Mrs Rachel Fielder, for kindly loaning me the slides which illustrated the conference paper, and for generously providing the prints used for Figs. 16.1–3, and giving permission for them to be published.

List of Contributors

JAN M. BAART
Stedelijk Beheer Amsterdam
Nieuwe Prinsengracht 19
1018 EE Amsterdam
The Netherlands

PROFESSOR MARTIN BIDDLE
Hertford College
University of Oxford
Oxford OX2 7PY
U.K.

INGMAR BILLBERG
Malmö Museer
Box 406
20124 Malmö
Sweden

DR WOJCIECH BRZEZINSKI
Panstwowe Muzeum Archeologiczne
Ul. Dluga 51-Arsenal
00-950 Warsaw
Poland

MARK DAVIES
Colchester Museums
14 Ryegate Road
Colchester
Essex CO1 1YG

BRUCE DUNNING
Dunning & Versteegh Architectes EP FL
Productions, Investigations and Architectures
Rue Jean Jarquet
1201 Geneva
Switzerland

DR DAVID GAIMSTER
Medieval and Later Antiquities
British Museum
London WC1B 3DG
U.K.

BRANKO KIRIGIN
Arheoloski Musej
Zrinsko-Frankopanska 25
58000 Split
Croatia

DR GÜNTER KRAUSE
Kultur-und Stadthistorisches Museum
Johannes-Corputius Platz 1
4100 Duisburg 1
Germany

HANS LIDÉN
Statens Historiska Museum
Box 5405
114 84 Stockholm
Sweden

DR IAN LONGWORTH
Prehistoric and Romano-British Antiquities
British Museum
London WC1B 3DG
U.K.

JEAN-YVES MARIN
Musée de Normandie
Logis des Gouverneurs
Chateau
1400 Caen
France

DR LJUDMILA PEKARS'KA
Muzei istorii kyeva
Vul. P. Orlyka, 8
252024 Kiev-24
Ukraine

ALAN SAVILLE
Artefact Research Unit
Department of Archaeology
National Museums of Scotland
Queen Street
Edinburgh EH2 1JD
U.K.

Dr Henrik Thrane
Fyns Oldtid-Hollufgård
(Fyns Stiftsmuseum)
Hestehaven 201
5200 Odense So
Denmark

Professor Francis Van Noten
Koninklijke Musea voor Kunst en Geschiednis
Jubelpark, 10
1040 Brussels
Belgium

Dr G. Jan Verwers
Rijksmuseum van Oudheden
Rapenburg 28
2301 EC Leiden
The Netherlands

Jeremy Warren
Museums and Galleries Commission
16 Queen Anne's Gate
London SW1H 9AA
U.K.